READINGS

OF THE

Platform Sūtra

EDITED BY

Morten Schlütter
&
Stephen F. Teiser

COLUMBIA UNIVERSITY PRESS

New York

COLUMBIA UNIVERSITY PRESS

Publishers Since 1893

New York   Chichester, West Sussex

cup.columbia.edu

Copyright © 2012 Columbia University Press

All rights reserved

Library of Congress Cataloging-in-Publication Data

Huineng, 638-713.

[Liuzu da shi fa bao tan jing. English. Selections.]

Readings of the Platform sutra / edited by Morten Schlütter and
Stephen F. Teiser.

p.   cm. — (Columbia readings of buddhist literature)

Includes bibliographical references and index.

ISBN 978-0-231-15820-6 (cloth : alk. paper) — ISBN 978-0-231-15821-3
(pbk.) — ISBN 978-0-231-50055-5 (electronic)

1. Zen Buddhism—Early works to 1800. I. Schlütter, Morten. II. Teiser,
Stephen F. III. Title.

BQ9299.H854L6213   2000

294.3'85—dc23

2011020758

Columbia University Press books are printed on permanent
and durable acid-free paper.

This book was printed on paper with recycled content.

Printed in the United States of America

c 10 9 8 7 6 5 4 3 2 1

p 10 9 8 7 6 5 4 3

READINGS

OF THE

Platform Sūtra

COLUMBIA READINGS OF BUDDHIST LITERATURE

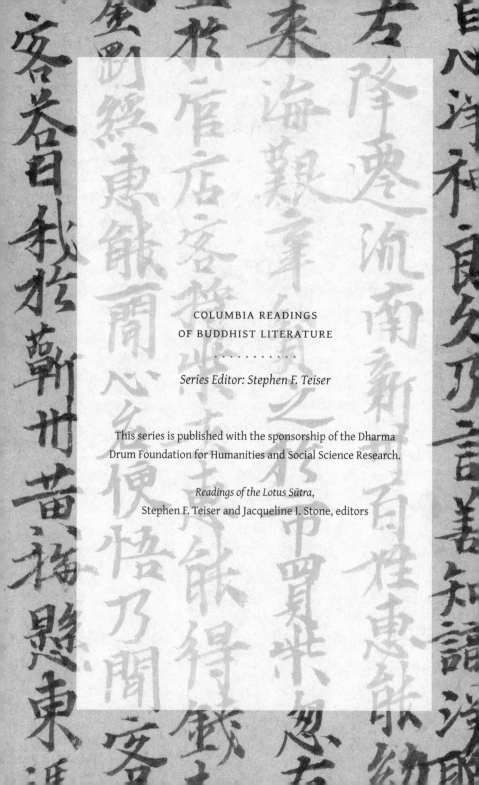

COLUMBIA READINGS
OF BUDDHIST LITERATURE

· · · · · · · · · ·

Series Editor: Stephen F. Teiser

This series is published with the sponsorship of the Dharma
Drum Foundation for Humanities and Social Science Research.

Readings of the Lotus Sūtra,
Stephen F. Teiser and Jacqueline I. Stone, editors

CONTENTS

. . . .

PREFACE

. . . .

MORTEN SCHLÜTTER AND STEPHEN F. TEISER

The *Platform Sūtra of the Sixth Patriarch* is a central text of Zen (in China known as "Chan"), a school of Buddhism based on the powerful claim that enlightenment can only be attained through a flash of direct, intuitive understanding. The scripture tells the compelling story of an underdog figure named Huineng, portrayed as an illiterate "barbarian." The Fifth Patriarch of the Chan school recognizes Huineng's penetrating insight and secretly designates him the Sixth Patriarch. In his sermons in the *Platform Sūtra*, Huineng challenges traditional ideas about meditation and enlightenment and seems to debunk all attempts to lay a foundation for religious practice.

The earliest surviving version of the *Platform Sūtra*, the focus of the present book, was written in China in the eighth century, a formative period for Chan Buddhism. With its radical approach to Buddhist practice and its claims for the hitherto unknown Huineng as the Sixth Patriarch, the *Platform Sūtra* was initially a provocative document. But eventually Huineng's status and teachings became universally accepted, and the *Platform Sūtra* was accorded canonical status. The text also proved seminal in other parts of East Asia, where it became extremely important for both monks and laypeople in Korean Sŏn and later, to a lesser degree, in Japanese Zen. To this day, for readers in Asia and the West, the *Platform Sūtra* offers a profound and intriguing statement about enlightenment, meditation, and spiritual cultivation.

Like the other volumes in this series, Columbia Readings of Buddhist Literature, this book is intended to open up the original text to new readers, to spark engagement with the text, and to advance scholarship in the field. The editors asked established experts in the study of Buddhism to write fresh essays for the project. The introduction (chapter 1) is the best place to begin, since it offers background about Buddhism, Chinese religion, and the origin and later history of *The Platform Sūtra*. Chapters 2 and 3 discuss the main figure in the text and the early Chan movement, respectively. Subsequent chapters focus on key ideas and practices propounded in the text: sudden enlightenment (chapter 4), transmission (chapter 5), and ordination (chapter 6). Chapter 7 steps back from the text to analyze the way its ideas are related to seminal concepts in early Chinese philosophy.

For our primary text we have chosen one of the earliest handwritten copies of the *Platform Sūtra*, probably dating from around 780, discovered in a hidden chamber in the cave-temples of northwest China (near the town of Dunhuang in Gansu Province) early in the twentieth century and now kept in the British Library. We have used the translation of this manuscript by Philip B. Yampolsky as our standard reference; when diverging from it, authors provide their own translation but also refer to Yampolsky's, with page or section numbers listed in parentheses. (Yampolsky's translation was first published by Columbia University Press in 1967, and a second paperback edition with the same pagination was published in 2012.) An annotated section of the bibliography in this volume lists other English translations of *The Platform Sūtra*.

In writing words and book titles in Asian languages, we give the Chinese without special notation, while Sanskrit and Japanese are marked "Skt." and "Ja.," respectively. A character glossary lists the Chinese, Korean, or Japanese characters for terms, figures, and places mentioned in romanization in the text and endnotes; the bibliography provides characters for titles of texts and authors.

We are grateful to many people for their support in putting together this book. We are, of course, especially indebted to the authors who contributed to the volume. After fulfilling their original assignments with enthusiasm, they all responded gracefully and expeditiously to our editorial interventions and suggestions for revision. They have been more than patient, and we appreciate their commitment to making a book that is, we hope, accessible to nonspecialists, useful in the classroom, and of interest to scholars of Buddhism. The anonymous readers of the original proposal and, later, the manuscript provided helpful advice about how to make the book stronger and better organized. Wendy Lochner, senior executive editor at Columbia University Press, has been an unflagging source of support and wisdom. We also wish to register our thanks to the other staff at Columbia University Press, including Christine Mortlock, assistant editor; Leslie Kriesel, copyeditor and production editor; and to Mary Mortensen, who compiled the index.

The Dharma Drum Foundation generously supported our work on this volume, and we are grateful to its founder, the late Venerable Sheng Yen (1931–2009), and its chief executive officers, Tseng Chichun and recently Lee Shen-yi, for their continuing help with this project.

Our families have sustained us over the four years we have been editing and writing this book, and as always we are grateful for their patience and support.

READINGS

OF THE

Platform Sūtra

1

INTRODUCTION

. . . .

The *Platform Sūtra*, Buddhism, and Chinese Religion

MORTEN SCHLÜTTER

The *Platform Sūtra* is a formative scripture of the Chan school (known in Japan as Zen) and one of the most popular texts ever produced in Chinese Buddhism. It has been widely read in East Asia for twelve centuries by both monastics and laypeople, and in recent decades it has also become well known in Europe and the English-speaking world in translation.[1] Through its dissemination in the modern world, the *Platform Sūtra* has become increasingly important as a statement of Chan/Zen in the West as well as in East Asia, where a renewed interest in Buddhism has resulted in many new adaptations and studies of the text and its main protagonist, Huineng (638–713), the legendary Sixth Patriarch of Chan.

The present volume focuses on the earliest surviving version of the *Platform Sūtra*, a manuscript discovered near the oasis town of Dunhuang in northwestern China, which probably dates to around 780, although it may have been preceded by earlier editions now lost.[2] The Dunhuang version of the *Platform Sūtra* is a remarkable text; rich and multifaceted, it is unlike any earlier Chinese Buddhist work. It begins with the dramatic story of the illiterate sage Huineng and his difficult path to becoming the Sixth Patriarch of Chan, then presents an engaging and provocative sermon by Huineng in a realistic setting (not unlike the sermons of the Buddha in many sūtras), goes on to a lively account of Huineng's first encounters with several disciples, and ends with his protracted deathbed instructions to his disciples. The text must be understood in part as polemical, written when the Chan tradition was still being formed and there was much contention over issues like who the real the Sixth Patriarch was, what constituted orthodox Chan teaching, and how to codify the controversial, newly minted Chan lineage going back to the historical Buddha. The *Platform Sūtra* is also a testament to the vitality of the early Chan tradition and its general appeal. It pairs the powerful message of the inherent buddha nature that all people possess with the direct statement that laypeople as well as monastics can practice Huineng's teaching. Huineng himself is understood to have become a monk only after having received the transmission as the Sixth Patriarch. The *Platform Sūtra* also introduced a number of innovative doctrinal formulations and gave a new twist to already established ideas. Furthermore, it included a special ritual for bestowing precepts on both monastics and laypeople, as noted in an addendum to the already cumbersome title of the Dunhuang version, which runs in full, "*The Sūtra of the Perfection of Wisdom of the Supreme Vehicle of the Sudden Teaching of the Southern Tradition: The Platform Sūtra Taught by the Great Master Huineng, the Sixth Patriarch, at the Dafan Monastery in Shaozhou*, in one scroll, including the bestowal of the formless precepts; recorded by the Disciple Fahai, Spreader of the Dharma."[3] The powerful ritual of bestowing "formless precepts" no doubt added much to the early appeal of the text. As Paul Groner's chapter in this book demonstrates, taking vows or precepts was central to Chinese Buddhist practice for both laypeople and monastics.

The *Platform Sūtra*'s unusual style, innovative format, radical interpretation of doctrine, and persuasive representation of the Chan lineage, together with its empowering precept ritual, must have had a profound impact on its audience. It is not surprising that a few decades after the appearance of the text Huineng was implicitly declared the Sixth Patriarch of Chan by an imperial commission,[4] and the teachings represented in the *Platform Sūtra* became the foundation for further developments in Chan Buddhism. All later Chan practitioners trace their lineage back to Huineng. The *Platform Sūtra* itself, which alone among all texts concerning Chinese Buddhist historical figures is called a sūtra (sacred Buddhist scripture), became a veritable monument to him. The Dunhuang *Platform Sūtra* thus both points back to the contentious period of early Chan, when ideas about patriarchy and doctrine were still being battled over, and forward to the mature Chan school, in which basic issues of orthodoxy and lineage were no longer in question.

Chan Buddhism continued to develop in China from the eighth to twelfth centuries, when it reached its mature form, and it has persisted as a major form of Chinese Buddhism to the present day. Chan was also transmitted to Korea, where it became known as Sŏn, and to Japan, where it became known as Zen; in both countries it has had a lasting impact on the cultural and religious landscape. Chan/Zen Buddhism continues to be a force in contemporary East Asia. There is much popular interest in the school's ideas and practices, and modern philosophers continue to draw on Chan/Zen in articulating new modes of thought. In the West, Japanese Zen in particular has become extremely well known. Through the work of intercultural figures like D. T. Suzuki (1870–1966) and other, sometimes idiosyncratic interpreters, Zen has exercised considerable influence on modern culture and spirituality.

BUDDHISM IN CHINA

Buddhism began in India, probably in the fifth century B.C.E. It was founded by Siddhārtha Gautama, commonly known as the Buddha Śākyamuni (or simply "the Buddha"), who told of a great awakening that had enabled him to see cosmic reality unmediated and directly. The Buddha's teaching appears to have been mainly directed to the monastic order of monks and nuns that he established, but he also included laypeople in various ways, especially as donors to and supporters of the monastics. He taught a path of insight and meditational experience leading to *nirvāṇa,* ultimate liberation from the cycle of birth, death, and rebirth that all living beings have gone through from beginningless time. The Buddha also emphasized the importance of morality and the accumulation of merit (or good *karma*) that could in the short term lead to a good rebirth in the human realm or the realm of the gods.

In the centuries following the death of the Buddha, Buddhism continued to develop and spread over the Indian subcontinent. In the span of several hundred years, schisms within the order had created about twenty different schools, each with their own, albeit similar, canons. Around the first century B.C.E. a movement that called itself Mahāyāna (Great Vehicle) arose and eventually produced a multitude of new scriptures, understood to be the direct teachings of the Buddha. Drawing on a number of ideas that may already have had a long history, Mahāyāna greatly expanded the Buddhist universe. It introduced a host of buddhas and bodhisattvas (enlightened beings who forego nirvāṇa until everyone is saved), formulated a teaching of the ultimate emptiness of all things, and established the goal of full buddhahood for all sentient beings. In Mahāyāna, the Buddha Śākyamuni was seen as a cosmic being who was enlightened eons ago, but who let himself be born on Earth to help all sentient beings to enlightenment. Many early Mahāyāna sūtras include severe criticism of the adherents of the already established schools of Buddhism, disparagingly referred to as "Hīnayāna" (Small Vehicle).[5]

Sometime in the first century C.E. Buddhism entered China, probably originally introduced by non-Chinese immigrants, some of whom must have brought Buddhist monastics with them.[6] It seems at first to have mainly interested members of the imperial court of the Han dynasty (206 B.C.E.–220 C.E.) and the upper classes. However, in the long period of disunity that followed the Han dynasty, Buddhism became increasingly important to the general populace, especially in north China, where ruling families of non-Han Chinese origin were comfortable with it as a foreign religion (that is, one originating outside of China). The establishment of the short-lived Sui dynasty (581–618) reunited the Chinese empire, and the first Sui ruler astutely used Buddhism as a unifying and legitimizing ideology. Buddhism continued to flourish under the subsequent Tang dynasty (618–907), when several new Buddhist schools appeared— among them Chan. By the Tang, Buddhism had become a powerful economic, political, and spiritual force in Chinese society, and with some ups and downs it maintained this position through the subsequent dynasties and until the present day.

Buddhism in India and later, it seems, in Central Asia had produced a very large body of texts. Over the centuries, much of this corpus was translated into Chinese. This was a crucial development that eventually made a wide range of Buddhist sūtras, monastic codes, commentaries, histories, and treatises available to educated Chinese. It is safe to assume that the readership of this literature was not just elite monastics but included many members of the educated secular elite. Chinese Buddhists soon also began to produce their own writings. Some of these were in the guise of translated sūtras and other canonical texts (such pretend translations are often referred to as "apocrypha"), but most were bona fide histories, philosophical treatises, collections of sermons, and different kinds of essays. The many translated scriptures also led some Chinese Buddhists to pursue the question of how to harmonize the vast range of teachings found in the Buddhist scriptures that sometimes seemed to contradict each other. As a result, Buddhist philosophers proposed hierarchies for organizing the scriptures and different strategies for interpreting them.

When Buddhism first became known in China, the ethical teachings of Confucianism were already the foundational ideology of the state, a precedent that made itself felt throughout Chinese history. Confucianism derives from the teachings of Confucius (Ch.: Kongzi, 551–479 B.C.E.), who emphasized filial piety, the mutual obligations between ruler and subject, righteousness and morality, and the importance of ritual propriety.[7] The educated elite, which supplied the administrators of the empire, was steeped in Confucian ideology. For most of Chinese history, to be educated meant to have studied the Confucian classics, so much so that we have come to refer to the literati as "Confucians," although this term was not used in China. Buddhism was early on accused by Confucians of being unfilial because it invited young men to become monks and leave their families, to lead a celibate life that could cut off the family lineage, and to vow allegiance to a group (the Buddhist saṅgha) outside the family. Buddhists countered that nothing would generate greater merit for parents than letting their sons become monks. They reasoned that by entering the monastery, a son was performing the ultimate filial act; allowing a daughter to become a nun was generally thought to create less, but still significant, merit. Supporters of Buddhism were eager to display evidence of their support of the family as a social institution. Several sūtras were translated in which the Buddha expounds on the debt children owe their parents and prescribes rituals that can help parents in the afterlife. Chinese Buddhists also produced their own apocryphal sūtras on filial piety purported to be translations from the Sanskrit.[8]

Native Daoist teachings also wielded strong religious and ethical influence in China. The central concept in Daoism, the Dao (the Way), is understood to be the ultimate creative and life-giving force in the universe. Two famous Daoist works were widely read by members of the educated elite: the *Daode jing* (*Classic of the Way and Its Power*), attributed to the mostly mythical figure Laozi (fifth century B.C.E.?), and the *Zhuangzi*, by the philosopher Zhuang Zhou (fourth century B.C.E.).[9] The *Classic of the Way and Its Power* describes the Dao as a mystical and unknowable force behind all that exists. The *Zhuangzi* is a playful text that questions the nature of reality, emphasizes the relativity of everything, and celebrates the constant transformations of the Dao. However, Daoism is also a highly organized religion that first took shape around the time Buddhism was introduced to China. In the Daoist religion of the late Han dynasty, Laozi was at once the highest god and the personification of the Dao, who commanded a host of other deities in ruling the heavens. The ultimate soteriological goal of Daoism is transcendence (gaining immortality), or at least longevity, attained by dissolving oneself mystically in the Dao or merging one's identity with the gods who embody it. Daoist priests also were religious specialists who possessed secret texts and magic formulas that enabled them to invoke the gods on behalf of their clients—individuals or families who frequented Daoist temples or sometimes whole villages that called upon the priests for divine assistance. In this way, Daoism was sometimes a direct competitor to Buddhism, and there were many disputes between religious specialists belonging to the two teachings.[10]

Finally, respect and reverence for deceased ancestors have a very long history in China. It was thought that for ancestors to be comfortable in the afterlife, their descendants needed to perform periodic ritual offerings; in return the ancestors would send down their blessings. This is sometimes referred to as "Confucianism" because of its conceptual connection to filial piety and its institutionalization in ritual codes. In fact, though, it predates Confucianism and should be seen as a part of a nameless religious complex that also includes the worship of numerous local gods (different from the gods of the Daoist pantheon) and the warding off of ghosts, which were assumed to be a constant threat. This "popular religion" or "folk religion" had no written scripture and no formal priesthood, but it permeated Chinese society and in many ways still does, forming the backdrop to all other religious conceptions.[11]

As elsewhere in Asia, the most recognizable forms of Buddhism in China revolved around monasteries and their residents. Although the ancient order of nuns died out, or was never established, in the rest of Buddhist Asia, in China it has survived to the present. In the imperial past significantly fewer than half of all monasteries were nunneries, while today more women than men become monastics. In late imperial China, tens of thousands of Buddhist temples dotted the landscape, especially in the southern half of the country. Most of these were small local monasteries with relatively few monks or nuns in residence. Such monastics were typically not highly educated, but were trained in ritual and recitation and performed ceremonies for the dead and other services at the request of local people. A smaller number of monasteries were more illustrious. They were usually located in or near the national or provincial capitals or other larger cities and often received direct support from the imperial court and high-ranking members of the educated elite. The monks (and sometimes nuns) at these monasteries were usually very highly educated and well versed in both Buddhist texts and Confucian literature. In fact, most seem to have come from families belonging to the educated elite. Among these elite monastics, new Chinese interpretations of Buddhist doctrine and practice began to appear. As discussed below, Chan must be seen as one of these developments.

Buddhism always had a complex relationship with the Chinese state. While most Chinese dynasties supported Buddhism in various ways, they also tried to control and limit the number of monasteries and their residents. On the one hand, rulers sought to benefit from the merit that donations to the saṅgha and the performance of rituals by monks and nuns were thought to generate. On the other hand, Buddhists were often accused of violating Confucian societal norms, and monasteries with their nonproductive monastics were considered a drain on society, suspected of harboring criminals, tax evaders, or insurgents. At times, such views led to official suppressions of Buddhism in which clergy were defrocked and monastic property claimed by the state. However, Buddhism always revived after these episodes, and it has remained a significant presence in society throughout Chinese history. Although some textbooks still give the impression that Buddhism went into a steady decline after the Tang dynasty, recent research has shown that it was a vibrant tradition in later dynasties as well.[12] After the establishment of the People's Republic of China in 1949, Buddhism (along with other religious institutions) underwent many decades of suppression, but after the end of the Cultural Revolution (1966–76) laws and policies on religion began to change, and today it is experiencing a large-scale revival.[13]

In spite of the acceptance and support Buddhism received from the imperial state and its popularity among the general populace, China never became what could be called a Buddhist nation. The ideology of rulership was almost always cast in Confucian terms, even when individual rulers favored Buddhism and added Buddhist symbolism to their political philosophy. Other teachings developed alongside Buddhism, most notably Daoism (which also received imperial support), Confucianism, and the ubiquitous popular religion of gods, ghosts, and ancestors. It is important to remember that few Chinese have ever felt it necessary to affiliate themselves exclusively with one particular religion, and that most people would regularly participate in a variety of religious practices, such as worship of local gods, exorcism performed by Daoist priests, and Buddhist rituals for ancestors. All of these traditions mutually influenced one another, and much cross-fertilization took place, as the essay by Brook Ziporyn in this volume makes clear. In short, religious identity in premodern China was much more fluid than it traditionally has been in the West.

Even though few Chinese, aside from monks and nuns, would define themselves exclusively as "Buddhists," many people felt that Buddhism provided special access to powerful forces in the universe and often appealed to buddhas and bodhisattvas for assistance in their daily struggles. Because they possessed special ritual knowledge, Buddhist monastics frequently performed ceremonies for laypeople, especially rites to help deceased ancestors in the afterlife. Many in the educated elite found Buddhism philosophically satisfying, while those of an ascetic mindset sought in it powerful means to achieve purity and transcendence. Over the centuries, Chinese sensibilities increasingly influenced Buddhist doctrine and ritual forms. Although most Chinese were aware that the historical Buddha lived in India and that Buddhism originated there, numerous people and places in China were understood to be invested with sacred power. Some Chinese mountains were believed to be the holy residences of buddhas and bodhisattvas, and people born in China were thought to be incarnations of originally Indian figures or to be authentic transmitters of ideals that originated in India. Huineng, the Sixth Patriarch of Chan, is a prime example of such a person.

SCHOOLS OF CHINESE BUDDHISM

Buddhism attracted a number of original thinkers and dedicated practitioners, and over time, several schools or traditions developed in China.[14] However, differences between Chinese Buddhist schools did not develop into strict sectarian divisions, and sects or denominations like those known in later Japanese Buddhism or in Protestant Christianity were never established. Although distinct trends within Buddhist thought and practice did emerge in China, they were rarely understood to be mutually exclusive, and many monastics studied within several of the schools. Throughout Chinese history, anyone becoming a monastic was ordained into the wider Buddhist order, not into any particular school or tradition.

Chinese schools of Buddhism cannot be seen as direct extensions of earlier distinctions in India and Central Asia. None of the early schools of Indian Buddhism, later referred to disparagingly by the emerging Mahāyāna tradition as Hīnayāna, was transferred directly to China. Moreover, it was probably a century or more before the differences between Mahāyāna and Hīnayāna as they had developed in India became clear to Chinese interested in Buddhism, and at that time basic Mahāyāna ideas, such as the efficacy of bodhisattvas, the notion of many buddhas, and the teachings on emptiness, were already well established. Thus all of Chinese Buddhism belongs to the broad category of Mahāyāna. The Mādhyamika ("Doctrine of the Middle") and Yogācāra ("Teachers of Yoga") systems of thought that had developed earlier in India did inspire Chinese schools of Buddhism, but both informed several different traditions and thus cannot be exclusively associated with specific Chinese schools.

In the centuries after Buddhism was first introduced to China, several exegetical traditions (not considered full-fledged schools) emerged in connection with specific sūtras and treatises.[15] Only in the sixth century did these begin to develop into distinctive arrays of doctrine and religious practice. Below, we will trace the development of the major Chinese Buddhist schools of Tiantai, Faxiang, Huayan, Mijiao, Jingtu, and Chan. Still, these should not be understood as sects in the sense of exclusive sets of beliefs, and they were not organized into schools in the sense of independent institutions.

It was the monk Zhiyi (538–597) who first created a comprehensive system of Buddhist thought and practice, solidly based on translated sūtras and commentarial literature and highly innovative.[16] Zhiyi's teachings especially emphasized the emptiness doctrines of the *prajñāpāramitā* ("perfection of wisdom") sūtras, the Mādhyamika philosophy that was based on them,[17] and the tenets of the influential *Lotus Sūtra* (*Miaofa lianhua jing*),[18] as well as a range of meditation practices and repentance rituals. Zhiyi also began exploring ideas about a lineage that could be traced back to the Buddha, and this notion was further developed by his disciples. His system later came to be known as the Tiantai school, derived from the name of the mountain in Zhejiang where Zhiyi's monastery was located. Like many important figures associated with schools of Buddhism in China, Zhiyi received support directly from the imperial court (in his case, the Sui dynasty). Also, like other "founders" of Chinese Buddhist schools, he only came to be considered a founder in the generations following him.

Somewhat later, the school of Faxiang ("Characteristics of *Dharmas*," also known as Weishi or "Consciousness-only") took form, based on the translations and philosophy of the pilgrim and scholar-monk Xuanzang (600?–664), who had traveled in India and South and Central Asia for fifteen years. In India Xuanzang studied Yogācāra doctrine, and when he came back to China in 645 he translated a number of important Yogācāra texts that became the foundation for the Faxiang school. Yogācāra holds that the external world is produced by karmic consciousness and that all human experience thus can be said to be a product of the mind. Yogācāra thought is therefore much concerned with phenomenology and the structure of consciousness, as well as the experience of the true nature of the mind in meditation.[19]

Some Chinese Buddhists viewed the Faxiang school with suspicion because it taught that some people are forever incapable of achieving enlightenment. This contradicted the almost universally held Chinese belief that all sentient beings possess buddha nature. The teaching of buddha nature was based on the notion of *tathāgatagarbha* ("womb [or embryo] of the thus-come"), which was considered closely related to the Yogācāra teachings, but nevertheless held that all beings have the potential for enlightenment, or even are inherently enlightened. The doctrine of buddha nature would later become crucial to Chan thought.

The Huayan school is associated especially with the monk Fazang (643–712), who based his system of thought on the *Huayan* (Flower Garland) *Sūtra*, which teaches the interpenetration of all phenomena.[20] Fazang soon attracted the attention of Empress Wu (r. 690–705), who had usurped the Tang-dynasty throne from her son and founded her own short-lived dynasty, the Zhou. As a female ruler and usurper, Empress Wu was unacceptable to Confucian ideology, and she turned to Buddhism as a legitimating power for her reign. She therefore patronized outstanding Buddhist masters like Fazang and was no doubt crucial for the Huayan school's success. Later, Empress Wu was also a supporter of several monks from the early Chan school.

Esoteric Buddhism (Mijiao) was introduced to China in the eighth century and was transmitted secretly from teacher to initiates, constituting a higher or esoteric (secret) knowledge of publicly performed rituals.[21] Esoteric ceremonies, utilizing initiations, incantations, a complex array of deities, and the ritualized merging of practitioner and deity, exercised a great influence on Chinese Buddhist ritual in general.

Even more widespread was Pure Land Buddhism (Jingtu),[22] based on several sūtras that tell of the Buddha Amitābha (or Amitāyus), who through his immeasurable merit created a kind of paradise into which those who call upon him can be reborn. Once believers are in Amitābha's pure land, eventual enlightenment is guaranteed because the impurities that normally afflict people, such as human birth, sexual desire, greed, and hunger, do not exist there. Pure Land ideas and practice, especially the recitation of Amitābha's name, became immensely popular in all of Chinese Buddhism, including Chan (in spite of the *Platform Sūtra*'s seemingly disapproving comments in sec. 35).

EARLY CHAN AND THE *PLATFORM SŪTRA*

The Chan school perhaps deserves the designation "school" better than most others during the Tang dynasty since it did develop a distinct awareness of its own identity. However, Chan did not start as a self-conscious movement. As Henrik Sørensen details in his chapter on the early history of the school, the first transmitter of Chan in China was in retrospect considered to be the Indian monk Bodhidharma (d. ca. 530). However, the actual beginnings of Chan should probably be traced to the Chinese monk Daoxin (580–651) and his disciple Hongren (601–674), who were both active at the monastery at Huangmei (literally "Yellow Plum") on East Mountain in present-day Hubei and who cannot be linked directly to Bodhidharma.[23] Although we only know about the teachings of Daoxin and Hongren from later sources, it seems they both put great emphasis on meditation and the notion of inherent buddha nature.[24] In fact, the term "Chan" derives from the Chinese transcription of the Sanskrit term *dhyāna*, which indicates the practice and mental states of meditational absorption (originally written *channa* in Chinese and later shortened to *chan*). Hongren apparently had a large number of students over his lifetime, and it was probably among his disciples (or their disciples afterward) that the notion of a Chan lineage going back through a series of transmissions to Bodhidharma, and from him all the way back to the Buddha Śākyamuni, first appeared. This understanding of lineage became crucial to the self-definition of the Chan school. Wendi Adamek's chapter explores the philosophical implications of the much-debated claim that the Chan school transmitted that which is impossible to express in words. According to the early Chan scheme, Bodhidharma was the First Patriarch in China and Hongren was the Fifth Patriarch. There seems to have been considerable contention among Hongren's disciples, or perhaps his disciples' disciples, about who was Hongren's main heir (and so the Sixth Patriarch). The picture is complicated by the fact that another group, known as the Niutou (Oxhead) tradition, also laid claim to the lineage of Bodhidharma, not through Hongren but through his teacher, Daoxin. However, the Niutou seems to have taken a conciliatory approach to other Chan groups by accepting them all as valid, perhaps because it was never in a position to dominate.[25]

The competition among the descendants of Hongren and among their disciples was no doubt augmented by the patronage they received from the court of Empress Wu, who, as noted above, had ruled behind the scenes for years and finally took the throne in 690, founding her own dynasty. Empress Wu presented herself as a Buddhist-inspired righteous monarch and a female bodhisattva and did much to support Buddhism in visible ways. For example, Shenxiu (?606–706), who in the *Platform Sūtra* is presented as the main rival of Huineng, was in 701 received in the palace by Empress Wu with unprecedented honors.[26] However, we hear nothing of Huineng in this period from surviving sources. It was only well after Empress Wu was deposed and the Tang dynasty restored that a monk named Shenhui (684–758), who claimed to be a disciple of Huineng, appeared on the scene. From 730 onward he waged a vigorous campaign to have Huineng recognized as the Sixth Patriarch (and, it would seem, himself as the Seventh). Huineng is mentioned only once or twice before the time of Shenhui and seems to have been one of the more obscure disciples of Hongren (if, indeed, he was Hongren's disciple at all). However, Shenhui claimed that Huineng was, in fact, Hongren's only fully enlightened disciple and that only he received the position as patriarch. In this view, Shenxiu and his followers had usurped Huineng's rightful position. Shenhui successfully associated Shenxiu and Hongren's other disciples with the alleged excesses of Empress Wu. He invented the term "Northern School" (or "Northern Chan") for the Chan lineages of Shenxiu and Hongren's other disciples, while calling Huineng's Chan the "Southern School." According to Shenhui, Northern Chan distorted Hongren's teachings and taught an inferior practice of gradual enlightenment that involved purifying the mind. Shenhui claimed that only Huineng had truly understood Hongren's dharma (teaching), propounding a sudden teaching and a kind of enlightenment that emphasized the original, pure buddha mind possessed by all people. John Jorgensen's chapter further explores the different dimensions of the biography of Huineng.

This distinction between sudden and gradual enlightenment was an old one that Shenhui successfully pressed into service. In China, the debate over sudden and gradual first erupted in the work of the monk Daosheng (ca. 360–434), who argued that enlightenment must be sudden and complete and cannot be attained in stages: one is either enlightened fully or not at all. It was also Daosheng who first argued that all beings without exception have buddha nature and therefore the ability to become enlightened.[27] Later Buddhist thinkers, especially in Chan, extended this to claim that all people are already enlightened but most are unaware of it. Here sudden enlightenment becomes the abrupt realization of one's own inherent buddhahood. Although the idea of sudden enlightenment initially met with resistance, it eventually became *de rigueur* in Chinese Buddhism, and by Shenhui's time gradual enlightenment had come to be regarded as an inferior position. Peter Gregory's chapter discusses the *Platform Sūtra*'s teachings of enlightenment and explains how they were related to other key doctrines of Chan.

THE TEXT OF THE *PLATFORM SŪTRA*

Scholars do not (and may never) agree on who wrote the original *Platform Sūtra*, when it was written, or what it might have looked like in its earliest version. Much of the text in the version from Dunhuang clearly represents Shenhui's polemical claims in favor of Huineng and against Shenxiu and the Northern School. It is the specific mission of the *Platform Sūtra* to promote Huineng as Sixth Patriarch and to demonstrate that his teaching is sudden, opposed to the gradual teaching of Shenxiu that was rejected by Hongren. Within Chan as a religious tradition, the story told in the *Platform Sūtra* was accepted as true. All followers of Chan believed that Huineng spoke the words attributed to him in the text, that the actions recorded in it actually happened, and that the text had been accurately preserved. From a modern critical perspective and within the field of religious studies, however, scholars realize that we cannot accept the text's claims about itself as historically true. Modern scholarship has shown that the *Platform Sūtra* could not have been spoken by Huineng and that the story it tells—of Huineng's exchange of poems with Shenxiu, for example, and of how he received the patriarchy from Hongren—did not take shape until years after Huineng's death.

The influence of Shenhui and his disciples on the text of the Dunhuang version of the *Platform Sūtra* seems to have been considerable: the text praises Shenhui for being the only one not to cry at the death of Huineng (sec. 48) and seemingly predicts his crusade to establish Huineng as the Sixth Patriarch (sec. 49). But discrepancies between Shenhui's writings and the text of the *Platform Sūtra* have made scholars think it unlikely that Shenhui or his disciples actually wrote the *Platform Sūtra* as we now have it. Some scholars believe that Shenhui's camp was directly involved with the early creation of the text; others think other groups of Chan likely were responsible. Thus the famous Japanese scholar of Chan, Yanagida Seizan, has suggested that the *Platform Sūtra* was first written by a Niutou school member and only later modified by Shenhui's disciples and others, and a similar view has been put forward by John McRae.[28] However, toward the end of his career Yanagida suggested that other, now largely forgotten groups who traced themselves back to Huineng may have authored the *Platform Sūtra*.[29] Future research may make further progress, but no matter how the provenance of the text is decided, interpreting the earliest version as it now exists and understanding the role it played in the formative period of Chan are still important tasks. The essays in this book are dedicated to helping readers of the *Platform Sūtra* pursue these goals.

The text of the *Platform Sūtra* has a very unusual history. The earliest surviving manuscript, the Dunhuang version that is the focus of this book, was hidden for centuries in a sealed cave containing tens of thousands of manuscript books near the oasis town of Dunhuang in northwestern China (Gansu Province) on the famed Silk Road. Dunhuang was a bustling center of trade, a crossroads where different groups of people from inside and outside the Chinese empire lived together. Many of them shared a belief in the efficacy of Buddhism, and a number of Buddhist monks made their home in the area. In the late fourth century monks began to construct cave monasteries dug into the limestone cliffs near the town of Dunhuang; these became known as the Mogao Caves. This eventually became a vast complex of lavish private temples, many decorated with stunning paintings and sculptures of buddhas, bodhisattvas, and various deities. At some point, one of the carved-out chambers became a storage room for what may have been the contents of several temple libraries, and in the eleventh century the chamber was sealed up. During the Ming dynasty (1368–1644) the Silk Road fell into disuse and the Mogao cave temple complex was abandoned. In the early 1900s, the chamber with the stored documents was discovered by accident by a Daoist priest who lived at Mogao; the dry desert air had kept the documents in perfect condition. Later, British, French, and Russian expeditions persuaded the priest to part with many of the documents, which included numerous manuscripts as well as the oldest surviving dated printed book (a copy of the *Diamond Sūtra* from 868).[30] Among the documents was the *Platform Sūtra* (in at least two copies) and many other texts relating to early Chan Buddhism, such as sermons of Shenhui and texts attributed to Hongren and Bodhidharma. These texts had otherwise not survived and were unknown to the world, or, as in the case of the *Platform Sūtra*, only existed in much later versions that were significantly different. The Dunhuang texts have made it possible for scholars to gain completely new insights into the history of Chinese Buddhism, especially Chan Buddhism, and the chapters in this volume draw extensively on research on this material.

The *Platform Sūtra* found at Dunhuang stunned scholars because it is so different from the version that had been known in China prior to 1900. This later version dates to sometime after 1290 and is almost twice as long as the earlier Dunhuang version.[31] Later in the twentieth century still other versions of the *Platform Sūtra* came to light in Japan, where they had been held in monastic libraries for centuries. From examining all the different versions of the text now known, it is clear that the *Platform Sūtra* underwent significant editing a number of times through the ages.[32] Thus, as Chan developed, ideas about what Huineng could have said and taught, as well as who his main disciples were, changed, and the text was adapted to reflect that. The *Platform Sūtra* seems to have been a popular text throughout its history, but the version produced after 1290 quickly came to be seen as orthodox and others fell out of use. The study of the different versions of the *Platform Sūtra* is an important task that can tell us much about how Chan evolved over the centuries.[33] However, in this book, we focus on the development of early Chan and on the Dunhuang version of the *Platform Sūtra* that so fortuitously was preserved in its desert cave, allowing us a unique window into this period.

LATER CHAN, ZEN, AND SŎN

As noted above, the Dunhuang *Platform Sūtra* differs significantly from later versions of the text. Perhaps most importantly, the Dunhuang text does not contain any "encounter dialogue" (*jiyuan wenda*),[34] the puzzling, often shocking or bizarre dialogues between Chan masters and others that so famously characterize the sayings of the later Tang Chan masters. In fact, this kind of dialogue is not documented until almost 200 years after the compilation of the Dunhuang *Platform Sūtra*, in the 952 *Anthology from the Halls of the Patriarchs* (*Zutang ji*). Later, in the Song dynasty (960–1279), encounter dialogue became the basis for the tradition of the "public case" (*gong'an*, Ja.: *kōan*), in which Chan masters lectured on famous stories about the ancient sages of Chan. Such lectures were collected in "recorded sayings" (*yulu*, Ja.: *goroku*), which were much studied in China and later in the Japanese Zen schools and Korean traditions of Sŏn. Chan and Zen lore contains many stories of students who became enlightened upon hearing or reading stories containing encounter dialogue. Eventually some Chan masters began to assign these stories as objects of meditation to their students, and it is this use of public cases that is best known in the West.[35]

Although encounter dialogue and public cases properly speaking do not appear in the Dunhuang *Platform Sūtra*, the text contains some of the earliest surviving examples of vernacular dialogue between a Chan master and his students, who are presented in a realistic setting and not just as stylized interrogators. Some of these conversations seem to foreshadow later encounter dialogue, as when Huineng hits Shenhui in response to Shenhui's presumptuous question of whether Huineng sees or not when sitting in meditation (sec. 44), or when, in response to Shenxiu's disciple Zhicheng's admission to having been a spy, Huineng cryptically says: "'The very passions are enlightenment' is also like this" (Yampolsky, 164). It seems likely that the text of the *Platform Sūtra* was one of the inspirations for the later creation of encounter dialogue.[36] Although the *Platform Sūtra* does not contain the disruptive language of later Chan writings, it does present many of the teachings that eventually became standard, including the fundamentally pure nature of all sentient beings (inherent buddha nature), the teaching of emptiness, the centrality of lineage, and the rhetoric that downplays seated meditation.

The Dunhuang *Platform Sūtra* also differs from the later, orthodox version in its sections on Huineng's disciples and its presentation of the transmission of the text itself. In the later version, several disciples not mentioned in the Dunhuang text at all have been given long entries describing their interactions with Huineng. These disciples in retrospect came to be seen as crucial transmitters of Huineng's teachings and so had to be included, often with extensive encounter dialogue. The later version of the *Platform Sūtra* also presents Huineng's disciples as equal to him in having received the transmission going back to the Buddha, while the Dunhuang version is more focused on the disciples as the transmitters of Huineng's teaching.[37] The later version also deleted most of the references to the transmission of the *Platform Sūtra* itself. Furthermore, the ritual of "formless precepts," a crucial part of the Dunhuang text, came to be significantly downplayed in later versions.

However, the core of the *Platform Sūtra*, Huineng's dramatic autobiography and his spirited sermon that celebrates the inherent buddha nature of all, have remained essentially unchanged through its different versions, and today the text still has the power to entertain and inspire readers.

NOTES

1. The most well-known translation of the text and the one we refer to throughout this book is Philip B. Yampolsky, *The Platform Sutra of the Sixth Patriarch* (New York: Columbia University Press, 1967); a second edition retaining the original pagination was published by Columbia University Press in 2012. Normally we cite Yampolsky's section number or page number in parentheses. See also a popular but still useful translation of a slightly different version of the text in Red Pine (Bill Porter), *The Platform Sutra: The Zen Teaching of Hui-neng* (Emeryville: Shoemaker & Hoard, 2006). For the best English translation of the text in its later and longer version, see John R. McRae, *The Platform Sūtra of the Sixth Patriarch*, BDK English Tripitaka (Berkeley: Numata Center for Buddhist Translation and Research, 2000); available for free download at http://www.numata center.com/default.aspx?MPID=81. An annotated listing of translations of *The Platform Sūtra* into English is contained in the bibliography of this volume.

2. The Chinese text of the Dunhuang version is conveniently found in the back of Yampolsky, *The Platform Sutra*. The original manuscript, held at the British

Library (S. 5475), contains many miswritten characters and some missing sentences, and was amended by Yampolsky. A second early manuscript copy of the *Platform Sūtra* recently came to light in the collection of the Dunhuang County Museum (no. 77); the text of this manuscript is in much better condition. It is translated and reproduced in Red Pine, *The Platform Sutra*. Red Pine's translation uses the same section numbering as Yampolsky's translation, making it easy to compare passages.

3. This translation differs from that of Yampolsky, 125, especially in following the currently most accepted understanding of *shou* as meaning "bestow" rather than "receive."

4. According to the Chan historian Zongmi (780–841), this took place in 796. See the translation of his remarks in Jeffrey Lyle Broughton, *Zongmi on Chan*, Translations from the Asian Classics (New York: Columbia University Press, 2009), 74.

5. Today, the Theravāda school of Buddhism in South and Southeast Asia is the only surviving descendant of the twenty schools of Buddhism that the Mahāyāna referred to as Hīnayāna.

6. The best, although somewhat dated, overview of the history of Buddhism in China is found in Kenneth Ch'en, *Buddhism in China: A Historical Survey* (Princeton: Princeton University Press, 1964).

7. The main source for Confucius's thought is the *Lunyu* (*Analects*), which contains sayings attributed to Confucius and brief conversations with his disciples. Good English translations include Edward Slingerland, trans., *Confucius: Analects* (Indianapolis: Hackett, 2003); and Arthur Waley and Sarah Allan, trans., *The Analects* (New York: Knopf, 2000).

8. See the translations from the Chinese by Yifa and Peter Romaskiewicz, *Yulan Bowl Sutra and Collection of Filial Piety Sutras* (Rosemead, CA: Buddha's Light Publishers, 2008); downloadable at www.woodenfish.org/sutra/texts. See also Kenneth Ch'en, *The Chinese Transformation of Buddhism* (Princeton: Princeton University Press, 1973); Alan Cole, *Mothers and Sons in Chinese Buddhism* (Stanford: Stanford University Press, 1998); and Stephen F. Teiser, *The Ghost Festival in Medieval China* (Princeton: Princeton University Press, 1988).

9. Good English translations of both works are available, including P. J. Ivanhoe, *The Daodejing of Laozi* (New York: Seven Bridges Press, 2002); D. C. Lau, *Tao Te Ching* (New York: Penguin, 1964); Burton Watson, *Zhuangzi: Basic Writings* (New York: Columbia University Press, 2003); and Brook Ziporyn, *Zhuangzi: The Essential Writings with Selections from Traditional Commentaries* (Indianapolis: Hackett, 2009).

10. See, e.g., Livia Kohn, *Laughing at the Tao: Debates Among Buddhists and Taoists in Medieval China* (Princeton: Princeton University Press, 1995).

11. For a study of popular religion in contemporary China see Adam Y. Chau, *Miraculous Response: Doing Popular Religion in Contemporary China* (Stanford: Stanford University Press, 2006). See also the description of Chinese popular religion in Taiwan in the 1970s in David K. Jordan, *Gods, Ghosts, and Ancestors: Folk Religion in a*

Taiwanese Village, 3rd ed. (San Diego: Department of Anthropology, UCSD, 1999), http://anthro.ucsd.edu/%7Edkjordan/scriptorium/gga/ggamain.html; and the methodological discussion in Catherine Bell, "Religion and Chinese Culture: Toward an Assessment of 'Popular Religion,'" *History of Religions* 29, no. 2 (1989): 35–57.

12. See, e.g., Peter N. Gregory and Daniel Getz, eds., *Buddhism in the Sung*, Kuroda Institute, Studies in East Asian Buddhism, 13 (Honolulu: University of Hawai'i Press, 1999); Jiang Wu, *Enlightenment in Dispute: The Reinvention of Chan Buddhism in Seventeenth-Century China* (Oxford and New York: Oxford University Press, 2008); and Morten Schlütter, *How Zen Became Zen: The Dispute Over Enlightenment and the Formation of Chan Buddhism in Song-Dynasty China*, Kuroda Institute, Studies in East Asian Buddhism, 22 (Honolulu: University of Hawai'i Press, 2008).

13. See the essays on Buddhism in Yoshiko Ashiwa and David L. Wank, eds., *Making Religion, Making the State: The Politics of Religion in Modern China* (Stanford: Stanford University Press, 2009); and in Mayfair M. Yang, ed., *Chinese Religiosities: Afflictions of Modernity and State Formation* (Berkeley: University of California Press, 2008). See also Raoul Birnbaum, "Buddhist China at the Century's Turn," in *Religion in China Today*, ed. Daniel L. Overmyer (Cambridge: Cambridge University Press, 2003).

14. For convenient overviews of Chinese Buddhist traditions (with useful bibliographies) see the recent *Encyclopedia of Religion*, 2nd ed., ed. Lindsay Jones (New York: Macmillan, 2005); and *Encyclopedia of Buddhism*, ed. Robert E. Buswell (New York: Macmillan Reference USA, 2004).

15. See Stanley Weinstein, "Buddhism, Schools of: Chinese Buddhism," in *Encyclopedia of Religion*, ed. Mircea Eliade (New York: Macmillan, 1987), 2:482–87. See also the newer entry by John R. McRae, "Buddhism, Schools of: Chinese Buddhism," in *Encyclopedia of Religion*, 2nd ed., 2:1235–41.

16. For Zhiyi's thought, see Leon Hurvitz, *Chih-i (538–597): An Introduction to the Life and Ideas of a Chinese Buddhist Monk*, Mélanges chinois et bouddhiques 12 (Brussels: Institut Belge des Hautes Études Chinoises, 1962); and Paul L. Swanson, *Foundations of T'ien-T'ai Philosophy: The Flowering of the Two-Truth Theory in Chinese Buddhism*, Nanzan Studies in Religion and Culture (Berkeley: Asian Humanities Press, 1989).

17. See Richard H. Robinson, *Early Mādhyamika in India and China* (Madison: University of Wisconsin Press, 1967).

18. On the *Lotus Sūtra* and its interpreters, see Stephen F. Teiser and Jacqueline I. Stone, eds., *Readings of the Lotus Sūtra*, Columbia Readings of Buddhist Literature (New York: Columbia University Press, 2009).

19. For an explication of Yogācāra, partly informed by the Japanese tradition, see Tagawa Shun'ei, *Living Yogacara: An Introduction to Consciousness-Only Buddhism* (Somerville, MA: Wisdom, 2009).

20. See Francis. H. Cook, *Hua-yen Buddhism: The Jewel Net of Indra*, Institute for Advanced Studies of World Religions (University Park: Pennsylvania State Univer-

sity Press, 1977); and Imre Hamar, ed., *Reflecting Mirrors: Perspectives on Huayan Buddhism*, Asiatische Forschungen (Wiesbaden: Harrassowitz, 2007).

21. See Charles D. Orzech, Henrik H. Sørensen, and Richard K. Payne, eds., *Esoteric Buddhism and the Tantras in East Asia*, Handbook of Oriental Studies, Section 4: China, 24 (Leiden: E. J. Brill, 2010); and Chou I-liang, "Tantrism in China," *Harvard Journal of Asiatic Studies* 8 (1945): 241–332; reprinted in Richard Karl Payne, ed., *Tantric Buddhism in East Asia* (Somerville, MA: Wisdom, 2006), 33–60.

22. See Kenneth K. Tanaka, *The Dawn of Chinese Pure Land Buddhist Doctrine: Ching-ying Hui-yüan's Commentary on the Visualization Sutra*, SUNY Series in Buddhist Studies (Albany: State University of New York Press, 1990).

23. The dates for early Chan figures are all tentative; in this book we follow the dating suggested in John R. McRae, *Seeing Through Zen: Encounter, Transformation, and Genealogy in Chinese Chan Buddhism* (Berkeley: University of California Press, 2003), 13.

24. John R. McRae, *The Northern School and the Formation of Early Ch'an Buddhism*, Kuroda Institute, Studies in East Asian Buddhism, 3 (Honolulu: University of Hawai'i Press, 1986), 132–36.

25. On the Oxhead school see John R. McRae, "The Ox-head School of Chinese Ch'an Buddhism: From Early Ch'an to the Golden Age," in *Studies in Ch'an and Hua-yen*, Kuroda Institute, Studies in East Asian Buddhism, 1, ed. Robert M. Gimello and Peter N. Gregory (Honolulu: University of Hawai'i Press, 1983), 169–252. McRae here argues that the *Platform Sūtra* was written by a member of the Oxhead school; see the discussion of this theory below.

26. McRae, *Seeing Through Zen*, 46–48.

27. See the discussion of Daosheng in Ch'en, *Buddhism in China*, 112–20. On the sudden and gradual debate, see the essays in Peter N. Gregory, ed., *Sudden and Gradual Approaches to Enlightenment in Chinese Thought*, Kuroda Institute, Studies in East Asian Buddhism, 5 (Honolulu: University of Hawai'i Press, 1987).

28. See Yanagida Seizan, *Shoki zenshū shisho no kenkyū* (Kyoto: Hōzōkan, 1967), 136–212 and 253–77, summarized in Carl Bielefeldt and Lewis Lancaster, "T'an Ching (Platform Scripture)," *Philosophy East and West* 25, no. 2 (1975): 197–212. For John McRae's views, see his "The Ox-head School of Chinese Ch'an Buddhism" and *Seeing Through Zen*, 56–69, where this position is implied but not directly stated.

29. See Yanagida Seizan, "Goroku no rekishi: Zen bunken no seiritsu shiteki kenkyū," *Tōhō gakuhō* (Kyoto) 57 (1985): 211–663.

30. On art of the Dunhuang cave temples, see Roderick Whitfield and Anne Farrer, *Caves of the Thousand Buddhas: Chinese Art from the Silk Route* (London: British Museum, 1990). On the variety of Buddhist documents discovered in the caves, see Robert E. Buswell Jr., ed., *Chinese Buddhist Apocrypha* (Honolulu: University of Hawai'i Press, 1990); Victor H. Mair, *Tun-huang Popular Narratives* (Cambridge: Cambridge University Press, 1983); and Stephen F. Teiser, "*The Scripture on the Ten Kings*" and the Making of Purgatory in Medieval Chinese Buddhism, Kuroda Institute,

Studies in East Asian Buddhism, 9 (Honolulu: University of Hawai'i Press, 1994).

31. An excellent English translation of the whole text with all its attached materials is found in McRae, *The Platform Sūtra of the Sixth Patriarch*.

32. See Morten Schlütter, "A Study in the Genealogy of the Platform Sutra," *Studies in Central and East Asian Religions* 2 (Autumn 1989): 53–115.

33. A forthcoming book by Morten Schlütter will discuss key aspects of the development of Chan Buddhism in China as seen through the different editions of the *Platform Sūtra*.

34. A term coined by Yangida Seizan, only occasionally found in premodern Chan sources. See John R. McRae, "The Antecedents of Encounter Dialogue in Chinese Ch'an Buddhism," in *The Koan: Texts and Contexts in Zen Buddhism*, ed. Steven Heine and Dale S. Wright (New York: Oxford University Press, 2000), 47.

35. Much has been published on *gong'an/kōan* study, most of a popular nature. For a collection of academic studies see Steven Heine and Dale S. Wright, eds., *The Kōan: Texts and Contexts in Zen Buddhism* (New York: Oxford University Press, 2000).

36. On the development of encounter dialogue, see John R. McRae, "The Antecedents of Encounter Dialogue in Chinese Ch'an Buddhism," in *The Kōan*, 46–74.

37. See Morten Schlütter, "Transmission and Enlightenment in Chan Buddhism Seen Through the *Platform Sūtra* (*Liuzu tanjing*)," *Chung-Hwa Buddhist Journal* 20 (2007): 379–410.

2

THE FIGURE OF HUINENG

. . . .

JOHN JORGENSEN

The biography of Huineng offered in the *Platform Sūtra* is a compelling story of a hero who perseveres against great odds. Focusing closely on that narrative, this chapter presents the plot, traces the historical process through which it was created, discusses variations in the story, and considers related genres of writing in order to understand the *Platform Sūtra*'s long-lasting appeal.

The *Platform Sūtra* is a composite text, combining what purports to be an autobiography with sermons, interviews with students, and deathbed instructions. However, the autobiography is not actually by Huineng (638–713); rather, it should be understood as a hagiography, or biography of a saint portraying him as a hero. This pseudo-autobiography was written to give authority to the teachings in the sermon, which many people in the days the *Platform Sūtra* started to circulate may have regarded as radical, and to boost claims to an exclusive and authoritative lineage for Huineng that went all the way back to the Buddha. The first person to write about Huineng as a saint and hero in an exclusive lineage was Shenhui (684–758), and it seems likely that in composing this hagiography, one of Shenhui's heirs simply added to what Shenhui had written. As Shenhui's claims later came to be contested, various modifications were made, resulting in the *Platform Sūtra* as found at Dunhuang, the text on which this book focuses. (See the chapters by Morten Schlütter and Henrik Sørensen for other perspectives on the provenance of the text.) As very little was known about Huineng before Shenhui wrote about him, we have to ask: was the Huineng portrayed by Shenhui in the *Platform Sūtra* merely fiction and the product of propaganda, and can we know anything about him for sure? Shenhui's lineage lasted only a few generations after his death, yet his image of Huineng was adopted as truth, with a few modifications, by the surviving lineages of Chan. Why? Were the dramatic scenes from Huineng's life the reason for his lasting appeal? Do the resonances of the autobiography of Huineng with the dominant ideology of Confucianism explain the work's popularity? How did the text's claim to status as a sūtra contribute to the continuing authority of the figure of Huineng?

SUMMARY OF THE AUTOBIOGRAPHY

In the *Platform Sūtra* the figure of Huineng declares in his self-introduction that his father was an official from Fanyang (near modern Beijing) who was dismissed and sent into exile as a commoner to Xinzhou (in the hinterland of Guangdong). Fanyang was in the heartland of Chinese civilization and the seat of one of the most influential clans of the day.[1] Exile to Xinzhou would have been understood by contemporary Chinese as akin to a death sentence, as Xinzhou was at the far southern frontier of Chinese civilization, full of malaria and tribal peoples, where only exiles, adventurers, and the desperate would live.[2] In traditional China, exile was a common punishment for officials who had displeased the emperor or high-ranking court officers, and exile to the south was considered especially severe. Huineng goes on to relate that his father died when Huineng was a small child, and after leaving that district he and his mother lived in poverty in Nanhai (a district of modern Guangzhou or Canton). At the time this was the provincial capital, a thriving trade port, full of foreign sailors and corrupt officials, a tough place (as many ports are reputed to be). The story continues that Huineng made a living selling firewood in the marketplace. One day a government official bought some firewood, which Huineng carried to an official lodging house. After being paid, he heard a lodger chanting the *Diamond Sūtra*, a famous digest of the doctrine of emptiness in the *prajñāpāramitā* system of thought, which immediately produced a flash of enlightenment. Huineng then asked the lodger where he had obtained the scripture and was told that he had gotten it from the monastic assembly of the Fifth Patriarch, the monk Hongren (601–674), at Dongshan (East Mountain) in Huangmei County in Qizhou. The lodger reported that Hongren had advised clerics and laypeople alike to read the sūtra so that they would see their own natures and directly become buddhas. Hearing this, Huineng realized that this encounter was predestined and so left his mother and went to see Hongren. A contemporary reader would have understood that for a mere wood seller with no education or connections to travel such a long distance alone must have taken much courage.

The story continues with Huineng arriving at Hongren's monastery. Hongren asked where he had come from and why. Huineng replied he had come from Xinzhou and was there to venerate Hongren and to obtain the Buddhist teaching from him. But Hongren retorted that Huineng was a *gelao*, a term referring to tribal people living in the south, regarded as uncivilized barbarians. In those days, *gelao* may even have been thought cannibals, but certainly they hunted and ate meat, so how could Huineng become a buddha? True Buddhists did not eat meat and were absolutely prohibited to kill. Responding to the northern Chinese insult that he was not even worthy of being taught, Huineng used the doctrine of the universality of buddha nature. He declared that, just as buddha nature has no north or south, so too there could be no difference between Huineng and Hongren in their potential to become a buddha. Although deeply impressed with Huineng's answer, Hongren sent him to work for the monastery's assembly, which allocated him the task of treading a pestle in the shed behind the monastery. This lowly job was no doubt thought suitable for a *gelao* and publicly confirmed the class rankings in Chinese monasteries.

The literate sons of the Chinese elite who became monastics could not be demeaned by such physical chores,[3] so it was left to the sons of the lower orders to work as laborers in the monastery.

Huineng had toiled as a menial laborer for eight months when Hongren summoned all his pupils and castigated them for only seeking merit, which they were content with because their own buddha nature was obscured. Most Chinese Buddhists believed in the accumulation of merit, especially for a better rebirth, but the early Chan movement was elitist, at least in its rhetoric, stressing that the true aim was enlightenment. Hongren thus ordered his disciples to examine themselves, asserting that those with wisdom would see their original nature, i.e., their innate buddhahood. They were then to write a *gāthā*, a Buddhist verse, and present it to Hongren, who would thereby determine if one of them was enlightened and qualified to become the sole heir to the direct line of mind-to-mind transmission from the Buddha Śākyamuni and to receive Bodhidharma's robe, which symbolized the position of patriarch. Hongren said to hurry, as this was urgent—perhaps implying he would soon die and needed a successor—but the disciples went to their rooms and decided there was no need to write a verse, as their instructor Shenxiu (606?–706) was the only one capable. After all, Shenxiu was a member of the literate elite, and one modern scholar has even suggested that he was a member of the imperial clan.[4] Shenxiu, however, was concerned that he was not yet qualified and worried that if he wanted to gain the position of patriarch, then that impulse would be self-defeating. Such an intention would constitute a desire, and in Buddhism desires lead to suffering and are an obstacle to enlightenment. But Shenxiu decided he might learn something of the dharma if he presented the verse expressing his mind anonymously. So he secretly went out at night to a wall in the monastery's corridor where a scene (*bianxiang*) of the five patriarchs transmitting the robe and the dharma was to be painted and there wrote out his verse.[5] Shenxiu doubted his own ability but hoped that perhaps Hongren would judge the verse worthy, in which case he would then own up to its authorship. The verse equated the body with the *bodhi* tree (the tree of awakening, under which the Buddha was enlightened) and the mind to a clear mirror that had to be continually polished to keep the dust of perceptual contaminants from polluting it. In this sense the verse demonstrated signs of gradual practice (the act of polishing) and attachment to form (the objects of bodhi tree and mirror).

When Hongren saw the verse the next day, he paid the painter for his trouble, even though he had not painted a stroke, on the pretext of the statement in the *Diamond Sūtra* that "all of that which has form [*xiang*, as in *bianxiang*] is unreal and false" (Yampolsky, 130), an implicit criticism of Shenxiu's verse. Yet Hongren, supposedly thinking that this verse could assist some of his pupils who did not have the requisite wisdom for the sudden teaching, assembled his disciples and asked them to recite it, stating that it would prevent them from sliding into a lower state of rebirth because it encouraged the merit of continuous practice. In a somewhat contradictory fashion, he told them they could see their own natures by reflecting on it.

Next, surmising who had written the verse, Hongren summoned Shenxiu, who admitted he had written it but did not dare seek to be the patriarch. Shenxiu asked whether he had wisdom or not. Hongren replied that he had reached the threshold of true understanding but had yet to enter it, a parallel to a disciple of Confucius (551–479 B.C.E.) in the *Analects* (*Lunyu*, XI.14) who "ascended the hall but had not entered the room." He then told Shenxiu to go back to his room, think about it for some days, and come up with a new verse. Soon after, an acolyte (a trainee monk too young to be tonsured) recited the verse as he passed by Huineng. Huineng immediately discerned that the author had not seen his own nature and so asked the boy who had composed it. The acolyte told Huineng about the challenge that Hongren had issued and how Shenxiu had composed the verse in response. Huineng asked the boy to show him the verse on the wall so he could bow to it and recite it in order that he might be reborn into a pure land, a statement clearly meant to imply that the verse possessed only minimal value. When they arrived, Huineng asked another person to read the verse out loud because he himself was illiterate. As soon as Huineng heard it again, he realized the deepest truth and asked someone to write down his own responses next to Shenxiu's verse. As Peter Gregory's chapter in this volume shows, Huineng's verses skillfully deny and invert Shenxiu's verse, concluding that there is nowhere for the dust or contaminants to settle and that the buddha nature or mirror is always clean, not requiring any polishing. All that is really needed is a sudden change of mental paradigm.

Hongren immediately realized that Huineng had a complete understanding and so called on him in the middle of the night and taught him the *Diamond Sūtra*, at which point Huineng became thoroughly enlightened. Hongren then conferred the dharma on Huineng and gave him the robe, making him the Sixth Patriarch. He entreated Huineng to transmit the dharma and to enlighten people. Hongren warned Huineng that the transmission hung by a thread, since other disciples would be jealous and try to harm him. So secretly they left the monastery and Hongren led Huineng to the Jiujiang Stage, the nearest and most important ferry crossing over the Yangzi River in its central reaches. From there a road led south through Jiangxi Province across the Dayu Pass to Shaozhou. Hongren enjoined Huineng to go south and not preach the dharma for three years, as it would be too dangerous.

According to the biography in the *Platform Sūtra*, it took close to two months for Huineng to reach the Dayu Pass, implying that the poor commoner, not yet a monk, would have walked. The pass was extremely treacherous, just a track through a forest and some ravines crossed by rope bridges.[6] Huineng was not aware that several hundred men were chasing him, to kill him and take the robe, but all except one gave up when they reached the pass. This monk-disciple of Hongren, a former general with the monastic name Huishun (later called Huiming, d. 780), was a violent man, and he caught up with Huineng and threatened him. But when Huineng surrendered the robe Huishun would not accept it, saying that he only wanted the teaching. Huineng then preached to him, whereupon Huishun was immediately enlightened. Huineng sent him back north to teach, then continued over the pass and on into Guangdong Province.

THE CONTINUATION OF THE STORY BY FAHAI

The above summarizes Huineng's autobiography, after which the text continues with Huineng's sermon. That finished, the voice of the text shifts (Yampolsky, sec. 38). No longer is Huineng the speaker whose words are simply recorded in the text. Now the declared editor, Fahai, takes over as narrator, relating a series of interviews between Huineng and his disciples, including Shenhui, that serve as opportunities to expound doctrine.[7] This section is framed by a statement that for over forty years Huineng lived at Caoqi, where he taught the people of Shaozhou and Guangzhou, had several thousand pupils, and used the *Platform Sūtra* as a symbol of the transmission of his teaching. Fahai also invokes the difference between the Northern and Southern lineages of Chan, Shenxiu leading the Northern lineage, Huineng the Southern. The superiority of the Southern lineage is demonstrated immediately thereafter in an episode where a pupil of Shenxiu is shown to have changed his allegiance to Huineng (secs. 38–41). Huineng is also said to have had ten disciples who would become regional teachers (Yampolsky, 170), and after recording a sermon addressed to them, Fahai tells of Huineng's death in 713 and his farewell to his disciples. According to this, he passed away at the age of seventy-six at midnight to the accompaniment of miracles. Huineng was interred at Caoqi, and Wei Ju, the prefect who had listened to the main sermon and ordered Fahai to record it, is said to have written an inscription in his memory.

ANALYSIS

This autobiography is a form of romance, a successful quest involving a journey to distant parts; a contest, in this case through the medium of poetry; and a life-and-death struggle in which the hero triumphs because he is superior. By contrast, the continuation of the story in the narration by Fahai contains less action and serves more as a presentation of further teachings. The autobiography implies that the hero had an aristocratic background but has fallen on hard times, being orphaned and forced to make a living as an illiterate woodcutter and seller.[8] A chance encounter leads to Huineng's realization that he could become a buddha, so he sets out on his quest. He now has to prove himself and overcome his illiteracy and image as a country bumpkin or savage. However, Huineng demonstrates his understanding that all people are essentially buddhas and are the same in this respect (Yampolsky, 153), and Hongren immediately discerns Huineng's enlightenment.[9] Interestingly, the final proof is demonstrated via poetry, normally the province of the literate elite. Through the power of his verses, Huineng thus becomes the next patriarch in a lineage allegedly stretching unbroken back to the Buddha, through which the sudden teaching was transmitted over the generations from mind to mind.

Anyone reading the *Platform Sūtra* would now understand that all people, no matter how base or barbarian, have the potential to become a buddha, a position summed up by the doctrine of universal and inherent buddha nature. Moreover, the story thus far makes clear that one could achieve buddhahood as a layperson and an illiterate: it was not the exclusive domain of monastics. The text also shows that the true, eternal teaching of the Buddha was passed exclusively through the Southern Chan lineage, clearly superior to the Northern lineage, whose aristocratic leader, Shenxiu, was defeated in the verse contest by Huineng. The narrative also shows that true Buddhist leaders could reside on the periphery of China, outside of the metropolitan area where the great monasteries and clerics were located.

HISTORICAL CONTEXT

Astute contemporary readers, who may have seen this sūtra sometime between the 780s and 820s, would have been familiar with the campaign Shenhui started in 730 to champion the person of Huineng as the true Sixth Patriarch of a Chan lineage going back to the Buddha and to attack the heirs of Shenxiu, especially Puji (651–739), for claiming to be the Seventh Patriarch. Shenhui's position was that the Southern lineage, with its teaching of sudden enlightenment, was the only legitimate one, and that it passed through Huineng. Shenhui asserted that the so-called Northern lineage headed by Shenxiu and Puji taught gradual enlightenment and so was not genuine. Between 730 and the early 750s Shenhui built up a hagiography of Huineng almost identical to that found in the surviving Dunhuang version of the *Platform Sūtra*, with the exception of the verse contest. Indeed, Shenhui appears in the *Platform Sūtra* as a disciple who "always attended on the Master" and is listed as the last of the ten disciples and the only one who did not weep when Huineng announced his impending death, suggesting that his understanding was deepest (Yampolsky, 170, 174). It is likely, then, that much of the *Platform Sūtra* was built on the inventions of Shenhui, and the textual evidence suggests that the work was written soon after his death.

The problem for the historian is whether Shenhui's account of Huineng and his lineage has any historical basis. Shenhui's version of the patriarchal lineage is seemingly impossible, because only eight Indian patriarchs fill the period of over one thousand years between the Buddha and Bodhidharma (d. ca. 530).[10] Another invention seems to be the robe as a symbol of transmission. Shenhui seems to have developed his hagiography over time. The earliest documents attributed to him simply state that Huineng was the Sixth Patriarch who received the robe of transmission from Hongren, the Fifth Patriarch. Early pieces by Shenhui also claim that Shenxiu's disciple Puji sent a lackey to Shaozhou, Huineng's place of residence, and there tried to decapitate his corpse. Shenhui further alleged that another student of Puji attempted to steal the robe.[11]

Shenhui's later and more developed hagiography, which was largely adopted by the *Platform Sūtra*, moves in new directions. Here Huineng becomes the son of an official surnamed Lu sent to Xinzhou. In this version, at the age of twenty-two, Huineng goes to see

Hongren, who challenges Huineng's ability to become a buddha because he is an unkempt southerner. After this episode, also in the *Platform Sūtra*, Huineng treads the grain mill in the monastery, but eight months later Hongren secretly visits him at night and realizes he should be the next patriarch. Hongren tells him to leave for the south and escorts him to the Jiujiang crossing. Three days later Hongren tells the assembly to disperse. Some of them chase after Huineng. Only the ex-general Huiming catches up with him at Dayu Pass, but he does not want the robe, only instruction in the dharma. Huineng then goes to Caoqi, where he stays for forty years, using the *Diamond Sūtra* as a basis for his teaching. In 712 he returns to his birthplace of Xinzhou, where he dies in 713. Just before Huineng's death his pupil Fahai asks about a successor and the robe of transmission. He is told that the robe transmission has ended and is given a not-so-veiled prediction of the appearance of Shenhui as the successor. Later, Huineng's corpse is taken to Caoqi and the inscription for him by Wei Ju is erased by Northern Chan rivals.[12]

In addition to these other versions of the story about Huineng surviving in early documents attributed to Shenhui, slightly later evidence paints a different picture of Huineng. An epitaph (formal funerary inscription written on stone) for Huineng by the noted poet Wang Wei (700–759 or 761), commissioned by Shenhui, is in several ways at odds with Shenhui's account. It does not attack Northern Chan and it adds new information on a monk, Yinzong (627–713), who is said to have tonsured Huineng. Wang Wei probably wrote this around 752, and although he certainly composed the inscription under his own constraints, the differences suggest some problems in Shenhui's account. While Shenhui was a propagandist or evangelist preaching to crowds, with a certain disdain for mundane facts, Wang Wei was an artist, poet, and government official whose elder brother was a prime minister.[13] Wang used the poetic language of generalities and literary tropes, but he also had to keep in mind the sensibilities of the state bureaucrats and elite clans.

Wang Wei is more circumspect than Shenhui. Although his stele inscription was commissioned by Shenhui, Wang removed references to Puji because his mother was a devout follower of his, and Wang himself had connections with other pupils of Shenxiu. Bowing to political considerations, Wang toned down the confrontational aspects of Huineng's story. Because the state abhorred disruptive religious disputes, Wang specifically stated that Huineng was not a member of a distinguished clan. He did not provide specific dates and places of residence. Wang's poetic tropes suggest that Huineng lived with peasants in Guangdong and then went to Hongren's monastery, where he worked in the kitchen. In this epitaph Hongren knows of Huineng's enlightenment but does not announce it, giving Huineng the robe of the patriarchal transmission just before his death. Huineng then is said to have gone south again and lived among commoners for sixteen years. Finally he met master Yinzong, who was impressed by Huineng's understanding of the *Nirvāṇa Sūtra*, ordained him as a monk, and became Huineng's pupil. Yinzong was probably introduced in Wang Wei's narrative here because he had been sponsored by Wang Wei's grandfather to set up ordination platforms, perhaps like the one Huineng speaks from in the *Platform Sūtra*. Wang also says that Empress Wu (r. 690–705) and Emperor Zhongzong (r. 684, 705–710) invited Huineng to court but he declined, and they sent him gifts instead. Later Huineng died (in a place not specified) and his corpse was buried at Caoqi. Wang wrote that Shenhui met Huineng near the end of Huineng's life, when Shenhui was middle-aged. He notes that Shenhui was the best of Huineng's pupils but was not publicly appreciated.[14]

These two accounts, one in the early *Platform Sūtra* stemming from Shenhui and one by the poet Wang Wei, are probably the earliest surviving substantial sources concerning Huineng. They were later combined or mined to create other variations of Huineng's hagiography. It would appear that virtually nothing was known in north China about Huineng until Shenhui began to promote him in 730.[15]

It is unlikely, despite his claims, that Shenhui ever met Huineng or was his disciple. Shenhui was born in 684 in the north into an elite family and was schooled in the Confucian and Daoist classics. As a member of the elite, he was no doubt expected to have the standard career as an official—but instead, Shenhui became a pupil of a dharma teacher in his hometown and was ordained as a monk sometime around 704. He probably studied with Shenxiu around the year 700. Aside from Shenhui's self-serving assertions, there is no evidence that he ever met Huineng, who except for a period of time in Qizhou with Hongren (who died in 674) seems to have lived his entire life in the remote south. Shenhui lived all his life in the north, and all attempts to claim that he went to Caoqi or Guangzhou show gross chronological errors.[16] As Shenhui had little information about the actual Huineng, he had to invent a biography of him. He also created the fiction of a Northern lineage headed by Shenxiu (or more specifically, his pupil Puji) and a Southern lineage headed by Huineng, and claimed that the difference between the two hinged on gradual versus sudden understandings of enlightenment.

THE MODEL FOR THE AUTOBIOGRAPHY/ BIOGRAPHY OF HUINENG

As far as can be determined from surviving evidence, Shenhui possessed little or no reliable information on Huineng except that he was a disciple of Hongren, lived in Shaozhou, and was regarded by some Chan followers as a teacher of only regional importance.[17] It would seem that Shenhui invented the figure of Huineng, for his claims would make Shenhui the true heir of the single line of transmission from the Buddha in the Southern lineage. Shenhui needed a template for this romance and he found it, consciously or not, in the legend of Confucius as recorded in the *Historical Records* (*Shiji*) by Sima Qian (ca. 145–ca. 86 B.C.E.), also known as the "Grand Historian."[18] The *Historical Records* was the most important literary model for Chinese historians, and since Confucius had been promoted to almost godlike status as the founder of the main ideology of the state and its bureaucrats, this legend was universally known among the literate population. Sima Qian tells us that Confucius was the product of an irregular marriage between a descendent of an eminent family originally from another state and a local woman. His father died when Confucius was very young, leaving him and his mother poor. In Sima Qian's version, Confucius was barely tolerated by the elites of his native state, a minor player in the politics of the day. He held a low clerical job but was eventually dismissed even after showing great ability. He subsequently traveled around north China, making his living by teaching. According to the prototype in the *Historical Records*, Confucius's life was threatened on several occasions, but his efforts were sustained by his confidence that he was heir to the culture of the saintly rulers of the past and destined to preserve it. He used interviews and poetry in his teaching to test students, rather like Huineng did later. He had many pupils but only ten true disciples, and he died in relative obscurity.

Shenhui's borrowings from Confucian prototypes are also clear outside of his biographical fashioning of Huineng. Shenhui had been trained in Confucianism, and he was later compared to Confucius by the Buddhist scholar Zongmi (780–841), while Zanning (921–1001), the author of the *Biographies of Eminent Monks Compiled in the Song Dynasty* (*Song gaoseng zhuan*), compared him to Yan Hui, the favorite pupil of Confucius.[19] Shenhui had also adopted ideas about an ancestral lineage (*zong*) with only one heir per generation from the tradition of southern learning of Confucianism. Southern learning, which prevailed during the time of Shenhui, argued that seven ancestral temples or rooms in the imperial shrine were required in order to constitute an imperial lineage (denoted by the same term, *zong*). Lesser aristocrats, such as dukes and earls, were permitted fewer rooms, and thus fewer ancestors, in their shrines. As Shenhui would thus become the seventh patriarch or ancestor, this would create an "imperial lineage" of seven ancestors or patriarchs for Chan, at the same time constituting a parallel to the seven buddhas of antiquity—six buddhas culminating in Śākyamuni Buddha—who are mentioned in the *Lotus Sūtra* and included in the *Platform Sūtra*.[20] In Shenhui's grand construction, then, the Chan was the greatest of all possible lineages—like that of the Chinese emperor and that of the Buddha.

Shenhui introduced not only the model of the culture hero, Confucius, but also the Chinese tropes of the distinction between north and south (discussed below) to heighten tension in the biography, making Huineng the opposite of Shenxiu and his heir, Puji. Thus Shenxiu and Puji were from the north, were aristocratic associates of metropolitan rulers, and taught gradualism. Huineng was from the south, was a near barbarian from the distant frontier who associated with hillbillies and animals, and taught a sudden doctrine of enlightenment. The son of an exiled official who died when he was still young, Huineng grew up on the periphery of China. Similarly, Confucius's father was a remote descendent of exiled nobility who died when Confucius was only three, leaving him in relative poverty. Confucius was born in the state of Lu, not in the metropolitan region of the Zhou kings, and although literate, he had to work as a record keeper of herds and was once refused attendance at a banquet because he was not deemed nobility. Huineng worked as a woodcutter and was illiterate, but he was predestined to meet Hongren, who initially rejected him as a non-Chinese barbarian. In the construction of these two biographies, both Huineng and Confucius struggled to find acceptance and recognition, both barely avoided assassination and foretold the time of their death, and both had ten main disciples.

The biographical patterns noted above were simply a general template, their elements borrowed in a wide range of accounts, including the life of Hongren. Furthermore, Shenhui, the major inventor of the legend of Huineng, may have borrowed specific tropes from elsewhere, such as the hagiography of Sengyai (488?–559?) as found in the *Continued Biographies of Eminent Monks* (*Xu gaoseng zhuan*), with which Shenhui was familiar. Sengyai belonged to a hunting tribe from Sichuan, obtained the secret respect of his meditation teacher, received a robe from another teacher, and understood the sūtras despite being illiterate. But Sengyai, unlike Huineng, burned himself to death in a grand display and was not heir to an exclusive lineage.[21] At any rate, it is likely that Shenhui was influenced by a variety of traditions even while constructing a biography of Huineng indebted largely to the existing legend of Confucius.

SHENHUI AND IMPERIAL POLITICS

Shenhui employed common stereotypes of the differences between northern and southern culture. In this conception, northerners accepted joint inheritance while southerners were more individualistic or exclusive. The northern tradition of scholarship was scholastic and exhaustive, while southern scholarship was fixed on the core point. In addition, Shenhui probably drew on the ideas of Xie Lingyun (385–433), a southern aristocrat and poet who wrote: "The south is saintly and the north is stupid. . . . Because one does not stay in the north, one can leave stupidity behind and one can reach the south, thereby attaining enlightenment. . . . If by thinking of emptiness one can cleanse the mind, and by destroying existence one can disperse entanglements, then existence [is for] the stupid and emptiness [is for] the saintly."[22]

Xie's ideas may have reached Shenhui via Huang Kan (488–545), a leading writer of the southern learning school of Confucianism. Like Shenhui, Huang Kan had a suspicion of the written word and championed no-mind and the sealing (yinke, imprimatur) of the transmission.[23] Xie combined the theories of Daosheng (ca. 360–434) about sudden enlightenment and all beings having buddha nature with southern learning to claim that enlightenment admits of no stages and to champion immediate enlightenment. According to Xie, immediate enlightenment is characteristically Chinese and gradual enlightenment more Indian.[24] Hence for Xie, the doctrines of sudden enlightenment and emptiness taught by Southern Chan are more suited to the Chinese temperament than Northern Chan's doctrine of gradual enlightenment.

Ideas like this, plus historical opportunities, gave Shenhui, a consummate evangelist and politician, a propaganda advantage over his well-connected rivals—rivals this ambitious monk had, it seems, created himself by his outrageous claims. Shenhui first attacked his opponents, whom he labeled Northern Chan (or more strictly, the Northern Lineage, Beizong), for their involvement with Empress Wu, who at the time was considered by some as having sponsored a materialistic Buddhism that was court-centered, scholastic, and relic worshipping. Like some other rulers of imperial China, Empress Wu had created vast Buddhist projects such as huge statues and monumental religious halls. After her death, her son, Zhongzong, had an existing temple, Shengshan Monastery, posthumously dedicated to her.[25] These policies had been extremely expensive and were perceived by many as contributing to the corruption of the Buddhist order. Her usurpation of the throne to create her own Zhou dynasty was partly based on Buddhist ideas of the *cakravartin* (literally "wheel turner"), a great enlightened Buddhist ruler. She also disseminated prophecies about the imminent reincarnation of Maitreya as a female deity who would become the ruler of the entire world.

After the overthrow of Empress Wu's dynasty the restored Tang dynasty engineered a masculine backlash, consciously reviving Confucian patriarchal ideology, especially that of southern learning. Under Emperor Xuanzong (r. 712–756), there was also an anti-Buddhist reaction, with increasing restrictions placed on Buddhism, such as the closure of unofficial monasteries and higher qualifications required of candidates for ordination into the saṅgha.[26] Shenhui capitalized on the resentment toward Empress Wu and her associates. In many ways his propaganda attempted to forge a masculine, patriarchal lineage that denigrated materialist Buddhism, relic worship, and the monks associated with Empress Wu. His innovations even extended to ignoring the scripture earlier favored by Chan, the *Laṅkāvatāra Sūtra*, the retranslation of which Empress Wu had sponsored. Instead, Shenhui elevated the *Diamond Sūtra* and the antimaterialistic stance of its emptiness teachings. No doubt alluding to

Empress Wu's massive pagoda (or *stūpa*, a mound enshrining relics) projects, Shenhui cited the *Diamond Sūtra*, which said even the use of all the gems of the universe to build a *stūpa* higher than the heavens is not the equal of chanting the *Diamond Sūtra*.[27] In this sense he promoted the cult of the book (symbolized by the *Diamond Sūtra*) over the cult of the relic (represented by Empress Wu's pagodas). Riding on the ideas of Xie Lingyun, who cited the *Diamond Sūtra*, Shenhui vilified the practices of those associated with Empress Wu and Northern Chan followers who built lavish reliquaries for their Buddhist teachers.[28] Shenxiu had been invited by Empress Wu to court in 700 or 701, where, contrary to imperial court protocol, she kowtowed to him. Perhaps in response to this turn of events, the *Platform Sūtra* portrays Huineng winning the verse contest against Shenxiu, with Shenhui anointing Huineng, not Shenxiu, the Sixth Patriarch. Shenhui made the *Diamond Sūtra* a feature of his preaching, and in the *Platform Sūtra* Huineng claims that the *Diamond Sūtra* was responsible for his initial awakening. The *Platform Sūtra* portrays Hongren teaching the *Diamond Sūtra* to Huineng (Yampolsky, 127, 130, 133, 149, 151), and, as Peter Gregory's chapter in this volume shows, the text plays a powerful symbolic role in the *Platform Sūtra*.

Furthermore, Shenhui's emphasis on the unbroken lineage of one male patriarch per generation also resonated with the reassessment of Empress Wu's reign. Not only had she arrogantly claimed to be both a *cakravartin* ruler and an incarnation of Bodhisattva Maitreya, who in Buddhist teaching were not supposed to coexist in the same era, she also reigned while two former emperors, Ruizong and Zhongzong (both her sons), were still alive.[29] In other words, there was more than one patriarch or ruler in a single generation. Moreover, in the reevaluation of her reign, by 725 the leading Confucian ritual specialist, Zhang Yue (667–730) (ironically a supporter of Shenxiu), had used southern learning to argue for removing a woman from the imperial lineage and labeling Empress Wu's reign illegitimate. He argued for rectifying the proper dynastic succession and designating the ruling emperor, Xuanzong, the sixth emperor in the Tang. In fact, Empress Wu had usurped the ancestral shrine of the imperial Li clan, making her own ancestral temple (of the Zhou family) into the imperial seven rooms, and after her death the issue of the number of rooms was contested in court debates.[30] These intense debates over legitimacy and succession are reflected in the *Platform Sūtra*. The text calls Huineng the Sixth Patriarch and records the verses of the preceding five patriarchs in China. The *Platform Sūtra* points out that Śākyamuni was the seventh of the buddhas and predicts the advent of Shenhui (Yampolsky, 176–79), seemingly implying that Shenhui would be the Seventh Patriarch of Chan.

Historical sources show that although Shenhui achieved some success in his campaign, Northern Chan leaders such as Puji and some of his heirs remained influential. Consequently, in early 753, Shenhui was accused of fomenting disorder, and after an audience with Emperor Xuanzong, he was sentenced to several years of minor banishment. However, the outbreak of the destructive An Lushan rebellion in north China in 755 provided Shenhui another opportunity to ingratiate himself by raising money selling ordination certificates to help the court fund its military defense. He was so successful that in 758 he was invited by the new emperor, Suzong, to the court chapel, but Shenhui died soon after.[31] However, this did not mean he had won the contest he had generated over legitimacy. Many Northern Chan monks had moved south before the An Lushan rebellion and so avoided the warfare. In Luoyang, the second capital, Puji's heir, Hongzheng (d. after 755), who likewise had numerous pupils, resided in the Shengshan Monastery dedicated to Empress Wu. After having been destroyed in 762, Shengshan was rebuilt ca. 770–771 and had several Northern Chan monks as abbots up to the 830s.[32]

Thus, when the *Platform Sūtra* was written there was still a contest over the lineage, with Northern Chan making Puji the Seventh Patriarch and possibly positing Hongzheng as the Eighth. There were even court-ordered debates sometime after 785 and again in 796 over the legitimacy of the different lineages, with the two sides represented by a disciple of Shenhui, Huijian (719–792), and the Northern Chan monk Zhanran (d. 796).[33] Moreover, after the An Lushan rebellion there was a return to large-scale Buddhist patronage projects following the model of Empress Wu. Some of the claims in the *Platform Sūtra* seem to criticize these efforts directly. The text stresses that the correct lineage went via Huineng and not Shenxiu, and it reiterates Shenhui's tale of Bodhidharma telling Emperor Wu of Liang (r. 502–549) that there is no merit in the building of monasteries or statues (Yampolsky, 155–56).[34] Readers would have naturally associated the Liang emperor, known as a devout Buddhist and donor of massive Buddhist projects, with Empress Wu and her excesses, while the true Chan of Bodhidharma would have been associated with Shenhui.

SHENHUI AND LATER BUDDHIST POLITICS

In the period after the An Lushan rebellion there were several competing lineages of Chan: the Northern Chan lineage, the heirs of Shenhui, the Baotang group in Sichuan that authored the *Record of the Dharma Jewel Through the Generations* (*Lidai fabao ji*) between 774 and 780, the newly emergent Hongzhou lineage of Mazu Daoyi (709–788) in south and central China claiming descent from a pupil of Huineng, and the Niutou lineage. The first and last of these did not claim descent via Huineng. The Baotang group believed that the robe passed to Huineng, who was the true heir of Hongren, and then to Empress Wu after she invited Huineng to court but he declined. Empress Wu then allegedly passed the robe on to Zhishen (609–702) of Sichuan and it went via a suspiciously indirect route to Wuzhu, the hero of the *Record of the Dharma Jewel Through the Generations*. However, Shenhui's influence is very marked in the *Record*, for the source incorporates his entire hagiography of Huineng.[35] As in Shenhui's account, but unlike in the *Platform Sūtra*, there is no verse contest. Even the subtitle of the work has plagiarized several of Shenhui's book titles. In the second part of the *Records*, ten disciples of Hongren are listed, and they include both Huineng and Shenxiu. Later, Huineng is reintroduced with the familiar interview with Hongren and the transmission of the robe. (See the chapter by Wendi Adamek in this volume for more about the Baotang school.)

Another group, likely based in Caoqi or Shaozhou, sometime around 781 produced a separate hagiography devoted to Huineng, entitled *Biography of the Great Teacher of Caoqi* (*Caoqi dashi zhuan*), written in part to counter the claims in the *Record of the Dharma Jewel Through the Generations*. The account is meant to promote Baolin Monastery at Caoqi, where Huineng supposedly taught. For our purposes, the *Biography of the Great Teacher of Caoqi* demonstrates the important variations in the biography of Huineng and the influence of local Buddhist politics on the development of the emerging Chan tradition. The *Caoqi* biography emphasizes the role of the *Nirvāṇa Sūtra* (not the *Diamond Sūtra*), and there is no mention of a poetry contest or Shenxiu. The rest of the account is about the relationship of Baolin Monastery and its master, Huineng, with the imperial court. It also covers Huineng's death in 713, stating that his corpse was lacquered and his neck enclosed in iron leaf. It relates that in 739 an attempt was made to decapitate the corpse, the source of later disputes.[36] (The "true body" or "mummy" enshrined even today at Nanhua Monastery on the same site may be the same mummy the account mentions.) Although the *Caoqi* hagiography incorporated some of the inventions of the *Record of the Dharma Jewel Through the Generations*, its main aim was to assert that Baolin Monastery at Caoqi held the mummy of Huineng and the robe of transmission. *The Biography of the Great Teacher of Caoqi* also wrote Empress Wu and Shenxiu out of the account altogether, inventing imperial decrees to bolster Huineng's authority as the Sixth Patriarch. It has no account of earlier patriarchs, for it seems that by this time Huineng had already been accepted by many in the Chan movement as the culmination of the lineage. At this point in history, then, the vital question seems to have been not whether Huineng was the legitimate Sixth Patriarch but rather who were his legitimate heirs. However, the text of the *Caoqi* biography soon stopped circulating in China, perhaps because it was tied only to the fortunes of one specific temple, Baolin Monastery. By contrast, the story of Huineng in the *Platform Sūtra* survived because its narrative and its intentions were not tied to one place; instead, the text was portable and available to a range of different groups.

The eventual success of the *Platform Sūtra* and the triumph of one particular story about Huineng and Shenhui were also determined in part by political factors. As noted above, Shenhui had served the court of Emperor Suzong during the An Lushan rebellion by raising funds from ordination platforms, and he was honored for his loyalty by this emperor in 758. According to Xu Dai, writing in 806, Huijian (719–792), a pupil of Shenhui, was ordered sometime in the period 766–780 to build a lineage hall of the Seven Patriarchs, with Shenhui venerated as the Seventh in this "imperial" lineage. Soon after 785, Huijian was summoned to the imperial court to debate the orthodoxy of the Chan lineages. According to Zongmi, who saw himself as a spiritual descendant of Shenhui, in 796 Emperor Dezong ordered the heir-apparent, the future Shunzong (r. 805), to gather Chan monks in the capital to determine which lineage was proper and which lineages were subordinate. Zongmi tells us that Shenhui's lineage was judged to be the orthodox one, but apparently this was opposed by representatives of the lineage of Mazu Daoyi, especially by Dayi (746–818), who also defended a version of the *Platform Sūtra*. Thus a version of the *Platform Sūtra* appears to have emerged as a compromise between the lineages of Shenhui and Mazu, which began to coalesce.

Like Wang Wei before them, famous literati such as Liu Zongyuan (773–819) and Liu Yuxi (772–842) contributed to the public recognition of Huineng.[37] Both had associations with Shenhui and Mazu lineage members. In late 815 or early 816, after Ma Zong (d. 823), the military commissioner for Lingnan (Guangdong and Guangxi provinces), petitioned the emperor that Huineng be imperially granted the posthumous honorary title of Dajian (Great Mirror), Liu Zongyuan was commissioned to write a commemorative inscription for Huineng. Liu Yuxi, who had written a funerary inscription for Chengguang (717–798), a disciple of Shenhui, in 819 wrote a second stele inscription for Huineng on request from monks from Caoqi. As a result of these campaigns for state recognition, plus the merging of branches of the Shenhui lineage with that of Mazu, a compromise *Platform Sūtra* was produced.[38] Later versions of the sūtra altered, added, or deleted material on Huineng.[39]

In later periods, still other traditions concerning Huineng emerged. One of the critical responses from the Hongzhou camp of Mazu was *Biographies from the Forest of Jewels [Monastery]* (*Baolin zhuan*, which survives only in part) of ca. 795, which adopted many of the hagiographical elements about Huineng from the *Caoqi* biography and some of the doctrine and verses of transmission from the *Platform Sūtra*. Throughout later Chinese Buddhist history, the picture of Huineng presented in the *Biographies from the Forest of Jewels* and the Dunhuang version of the *Platform Sūtra* became the orthodox image of Huineng as the Sixth Patriarch. Much of this was then taken up by the officially authorized histories of Chan, such as the *Records of the Transmission of the Lamp Compiled in the Jingde Era* (*Jingde chuandeng lu*) of 1004, which is a synthesis of competing claims.

The image of Huineng as a Chinese "living Buddha" (in the words of the government official quoted in the *Platform Sūtra*, Yampolsky, 162) survives in the modern Chinese consciousness and was even incorporated into popular lay religion. Today Huineng remains a controversial figure. Some Communist Party members see him as a reactionary, while others believe he made Buddhism truly Chinese, accessible to everybody, even claiming that he belonged to a non-Han minority ethnic group. Huineng is also the protagonist of *Snow in August* (*Bayuexue*), a play by the Nobel laureate Gao Xingjian, who portrays him as a mystic who defies the establishment.

THE APPEAL OF HUINENG

Why has Huineng proven to be such an appealing figure for so many centuries? There are surely many possible answers. One clear factor is the resemblance of his biography to the traditional account of the life of Confucius, who has remained perennially popular in Chinese culture. Even today a commentary on Confucius's *Analects* is the most popular book in China.[40] Another reason is the romantic image of Huineng. Almost every hagiography of him contains dramatic flourishes such as the poetry contest, the secret transmission of the robe, and a chase scene in which rivals threaten the life of the hero, who then goes into a period of hiding. Unlike most Buddhist literature under the rubric of sūtra, this genre was more akin to popular literature, a mixture of spiritual guide and gripping entertainment, showcasing a poor, young, illiterate commoner triumphing over a polished aristocratic monk in a battle of words that tests their true spirituality.

A more historically specific reason for the enduring popularity of the image of Huineng has to do with the success of Mazu's Hongzhou branch of Chan, as noted above. Claiming descent from Huineng, Hongzhou Chan in the late ninth century moved beyond its original base in Jiangxi and spread over most of China, gaining influence in the courts of Dezong (r. 780–805), Shunzong (r. 805), and Xianzong (r. 806–821). The more ecumenical attitude of Hongzhou Chan, combined with the increased importance of regional governors and officials with whom it had cultivated relations, led to its success inside China and even in Silla Korea. As Mazu gained recognition and support in important circles, so too did the figure of Huineng. Just as Mazu was receiving honors from the emperor and high officials in 815 or 816, so too was Huineng granted the honorific name of Dajian. Furthermore, Liu Zongyuan's famous stele inscription commemorating that act of grace compared Huineng's teachings to those of Confucius, an association that runs throughout the many versions of the Huineng legend. Huineng's actions in the *Platform Sūtra* were also akin to the verbal jousts of master and disciple in the Hongzhou tradition. Thus the image of Huineng was spread along with the dominance of Hongzhou Chan.[41]

Huineng's biography was also appealing as a particular variation on the genre worked by the *Platform Sūtra*. Sūtras normally began with the authoritative words marking the circumstances of their transmission, "Thus I have heard, when the Buddha was in . . ." This opening indicates that the words of the text were related by Ānanda or another disciple of the Buddha who heard him preach the sermon in a specific time and place. By using the word "sūtra" in its title, the authors of the *Platform Sūtra* seem to be claiming that Huineng was a living buddha. At the same time, no reader would confuse Huineng with the historical Buddha, and the gap between the two figures— though overcome in the claims of Chan transmission—could not be easily denied. Perhaps this explains why the later Chan tradition turned to the particularities of the Chan lineage and the importance of noncanonical transmission to justify itself. In phrases that became standard in the Song dynasty, Chan was not identified with the traditional sūtras but rather with "a separate transmission outside of the teachings" and "nonreliance on the written word."

Autobiographies had become an important component of Chan tradition during the centuries of the Tang dynasty, and this genre seems also to have influenced the development of the story in the *Platform Sūtra*. These were not so much full, independent representations of a life but rather introductions to (or explanations of) a work using public or exemplary facts.[42] Huineng's self-introduction to the *Platform Sūtra*, which avoids using the first-person pronoun, explains his accession to the position of the Sixth Patriarch and how he came to Shaozhou and preached the sermon. Thus, Huineng's self-introduction corresponds to the genre of autobiography, conjoined to the sūtra that follows.

Another likely generic model for the biography in the *Platform Sūtra* would have been the kind of Buddhist canonical story in which the Buddha narrates his previous lives leading up to his birth as Śākyamuni and his achieving enlightenment, usually called *jātaka* (birth story) in Sanskrit. In these accounts the Buddha stands in a lecture hall and uses the third-person voice to relate his past lives. These texts begin with the standard "Thus I have heard . . ." and include an implied witness or auditor who then relates what the Buddha said. In the *Platform Sūtra* this hearer would be Fahai, relating the words of the Chinese Buddha, Huineng, whose biography is told to form the frame for the sermon that is the main portion of the sūtra. Careful readers may wonder how the final sections of the *Platform Sūtra*, which describe the compilation of the text and stipulate who is qualified to transmit it, conform to the genre. In the Chinese understanding of the category, the ending of the *Platform Sūtra* was perfectly consistent with other sūtras. Beginning in the fourth century at the latest, Chinese commentators typically divided sūtras into three portions: a preface (*xufen*), the main teachings of the sūtra or sermon itself (*zhengzong fen*), and the section on dissemination (*liutong fen*). Following this organization, the autobiographical introduction corresponds to the first section, the sermon to the main teachings, and the discussion of the text's transmission to the third section.

Thus, even while the image of Huineng was increasingly cast in the model of witty interactions in the literature known as "recorded sayings" (*yulu*; Ja.: *goroku*; Kor.: *ŏnok*) of a Chan master, it also partook of Chinese forms of autobiography, the model of Confucius's biography, and Buddhist *jātakas* and sūtras. Unlike the Indian figures of the Buddha and Bodhidharma, princes and renunciants who practiced austerities or begged for food, Huineng was a commoner who (at least initially) labored for a living and overcame great obstacles. These factors undoubtedly contributed to the enduring popularity of Huineng's biography as contained in the *Platform Sūtra*.

NOTES

1. For the aristocratic clan system, see David G. Johnson, *The Medieval Chinese Oligarchy* (Boulder: Westview Press, 1977); and Patricia Buckley Ebrey, *The Aristocratic Families of Early Imperial China: A Case Study of the Po-ling Ts'ui Family* (Cambridge: Cambridge University Press, 1978).
2. For contemporary views of the south, see Edward H. Schafer, *The Vermilion Bird: T'ang Images of the South* (Berkeley: University of California Press, 1967).
3. On this ranking and education, see Erik Zürcher, "Buddhism and Education in T'ang Times," in *Neo-Confucian Education: The Formative Stage*, ed. Wm. Theodore

de Bary and John W. Chaffee (Berkeley: University of California Press, 1989), 19–56. To be officially ordained, a candidate for the monkhood was required to pass an examination testing his memory of set amounts of Buddhist scripture.

4. John McRae, *The Northern School and the Formation of Early Ch'an Buddhism*, Kuroda Institute, Studies in East Asian Buddhism, 3 (Honolulu: University of Hawai'i Press, 1986), 46–56.

5. For *bianxiang*, see Victor H. Mair, *Painting and Performance: Chinese Picture Recitation and Its Indian Genesis* (Honolulu: University of Hawai'i Press, 1988).

6. See P. A. Herbert, *Under the Brilliant Emperor: Imperial Authority in T'ang China as Seen in the Writings of Chang Chiu-ling* (Canberra: Australian National University Press, 1978), 54–55, for a description by a contemporary from Shaozhou.

7. Fahai is unlikely to have been a pupil of Huineng and was probably invented by Shenhui. The compilation of the source text for the Dunhuang *Platform Sūtra* was probably later attributed to Fahai, but who made this attribution is unclear.

8. An early manuscript attributed to Shenhui (684–758) reports that Huineng's father was a member of the aristocratic Lu clan of Fanyang. See *Nanyang Heshang wenda zazhengyi* (*Reverend Nanyang's Miscellaneous Soliciting of the Meanings via Dialogue*), in Yang Zengwen, *Shenhui Heshang chanhua lu* (Beijing: Zhonghua shuju, 1996), 109. The hagiography of Huineng by Shenhui is translated from this text in John Jorgensen, *Inventing Hui-neng, the Sixth Patriarch: Hagiography and Biography in Early Ch'an*, Sinica Leidensia, 68 (Leiden: Brill, 2005), 133–37. Reverend Nanyang is Shenhui.

9. The *Platform Sūtra* writes, "His enlightenment will be no different from your own" (Yampolsky, 133n45), and "If you are able to awaken another's mind, he/you will be no different from me" (Yampolsky, 133). The justification can be found in the *Lotus Sūtra*: "only a Buddha can understand a Buddha"; cf. Leon Hurvitz, trans., *Scripture of the Lotus Blossom of the Fine Dharma: Translated from the Chinese of Kumārajīva* (New York: Columbia University Press, 1976), 22–23.

10. See the different lists of patriarchs in Yampolsky, 8–9.

11. *Putidamo Nanzong ding shifei lun* (*Discussion on Settling the Correct and Incorrect Southern Lineage of Bodhidharma*), in Yang Zengwen, *Shenhui*, 27–33.

12. Yang Zengwen, *Shenhui*, 109–11. Note that nearly identical characters are used for Wei Ju in the Dunhuang *Platform Sūtra*, and there is some variation in the various Dunhuang copies. The surname is the same, and only the radical for the personal name differs. The characters are Ju and Qu, easily confused in handwriting.

13. For a brief introduction to Wang Wei, see G. W. Robinson, *Poems of Wang Wei* (Harmondsworth: Penguin, 1973).

14. Text translated in Jorgensen, *Inventing Hui-neng*, 145–51, using notes in Ding Fubao, *Liuzu tanjing zhujie* (n.p.: Ruicheng shuju yinhang, 1922), 1–18; and Yanagida Seizan, *Shoki zenshū shisho no kenkyū* (Kyoto: Hōzōkan, 1967), 539–58.

15. For other early sources, see translation and discussion of *Lengqie shizi ji* (*Records of Masters and Disciples [in the Transmission] of the Laṅkāvatāra*), written by Jingjue between 713 and 716, in Bernard Faure, *Le bouddhisme Ch'an en mal d'histoire: Ge-*

nèse d'une tradition religieuse dans la Chine des T'ang, Publications de l'École Française d'Extrême-Orient, 158 (Paris: École Française d'Extrême-Orient, 1989), 87–182; Bernard Faure, *The Will to Orthodoxy: A Critical Genealogy of Northern Chan Buddhism* (Stanford: Stanford University Press, 1997); and *Chuan fabao ji* (*Annals of the Transmission of the Dharma Treasure*), ca. 713, translated in McRae, *The Northern School*, 255–69.

16. For studies of Shenhui, see John R. McRae, "Shenhui as Evangelist: Re-envisioning the Identity of a Chinese Buddhist Monk," *Journal of Chinese Religions* 30 (2002): 123–48; Jacques Gernet, "Biographie du Maître Chen-hoeui du Ho-tsö (668–760): Contribution à l'histoire de l'école du Dhyāna," *Journal Asiatique* 239 (1951): 29–68; and Jorgensen, *Inventing Hui-neng*, 62–68.

17. Noted in the *Records of Men and Methods [in the Transmission] of the Laṅkāvatāra* (*Lengqie ren fa zhi*), compiled by Xuanze; now lost but quoted in the *Records of Masters and Disciples [in the Transmission] of the Laṅkāvatāra* (*Lengqie shizi ji*), compiled by Xuanze's disciple Jingjue. See the appendix to Henrik Sørensen's chapter in this book.

18. For the biography of Confucius in the *Historical Records*, see Michael Nylan and Thomas Wilson, *Lives of Confucius: Civilization's Greatest Sage Through the Ages* (New York: Doubleday, 2010), 12–28. For the cult of Confucius during the Tang dynasty, see ibid., 101–64; and David McMullen, *State and Scholars in T'ang China* (Cambridge: Cambridge University Press, 1988), chapter 2.

19. Jorgensen, *Inventing Hui-neng*, 169.

20. On the affinities with the southern learning of Confucianism, see John Jorgensen, "The 'Imperial Lineage' of Ch'an Buddhism: The Role of Confucian Ritual and Ancestor Worship in Ch'an's Search for Legitimation in the mid-T'ang Dynasty," *Papers in Far Eastern History* 35 (1987): 89–133. On the seven buddhas, see Yampolsky, 179; Hurvitz, *Lotus Blossom*, 158.

21. See James A. Benn, "Written in Flames: Self-Immolation in Sixth-Century Sichuan," *T'oung Pao* 92 (2006): 410–65.

22. *Bianzonglun*, by Xie Lingyun, in *Guang hongming ji*, Daoxuan (596–667), T no. 2103, 52:225c11, 226c13–15. On Xie Lingyun, see J. D. Frodsham, *The Murmuring Stream: The Life and Works of the Chinese Nature Poet Hsieh Ling-yün (385–433), Duke of K'ang-lo*, 2 vols. (Kuala Lumpur: University of Malaya Press, 1967).

23. For Huang Kan's thought, see John Makeham, *Transmitters and Creators: Chinese Commentators and Commentaries on the "Analects"* (Cambridge, MA: Harvard University Press, 2003), Part II, 79–167.

24. Jorgensen, *Inventing Hui-neng*, 469–72.

25. Chen Jinhua, "The Statues and Monks of Shengshan Monastery: Money and Maitreyan Buddhism in Tang China," *Asia Major*, third series, 19, parts 1–2 (2006): 111–60, esp. 117–37.

26. See Stanley Weinstein, *Buddhism Under the T'ang* (Cambridge: Cambridge University Press, 1987), 51–54.

27. Jorgensen, *Inventing Hui-neng*, 54.

28. Jorgensen, *Inventing Hui-neng*, 331–32.

29. For Empress Wu and her claims, see Antonino Forte, *Political Propaganda and Ideology in China at the End of the Seventh Century* (Napoli: Istituto Universitario Orientale, 1976); and R.W.L. Guisso, *Wu Tse-t'ien and the Politics of Legitimation in T'ang China*, Western Washington University, Program in East Asian Studies, Occasional Papers, 11 (Bellingham: Western Washington University, Program in East Asian Studies, 1978).

30. Details in Jorgensen, "'Imperial' Lineage," esp. 104–14.

31. Jorgensen, *Inventing Hui-neng*, 66–68, 461–62.

32. Chen, "Shengshan Monastery," 139–45; Jorgensen, "'Imperial' Lineage," 93–95.

33. Chen, "Shengshan Monastery," 139–41; Jorgensen, "'Imperial' Lineage," 120–21.

34. See also Shenhui's *Putidamo Nanzong ding shifei lun*, recorded by Dugu Pei, cited in Jorgensen, *Inventing Hui-neng*, 117, 131.

35. Wendi L. Adamek, *The Mystique of Transmission: On an Early Chan History and Its Contexts* (New York: Columbia University Press, 2007), 321–23.

36. Yampolsky, 70–76; for a translation see Jorgensen, *Inventing Hui-neng*, 677–705; for the mummy and its theft, Jorgensen, *Inventing Hui-neng*, 190–355. For later uses of this account, see John Jorgensen, "Ssanggye-sa and Local Buddhist History: Propaganda and Relics in a Struggle for Survival, 1850s–1930s," *Seoul Journal of Korean Studies* 21, no. 1 (2008): 87–127.

37. Jo-shui Chen, *Liu Tsung-yüan and Intellectual Change in T'ang China, 773–819* (Cambridge: Cambridge University Press, 1992).

38. For Zongmi's opposition to this compromise, see Peter N. Gregory, *Tsung-mi and the Sinification of Buddhism* (Honolulu: University of Hawai'i Press, 2002), 236–44. On the different versions of the *Platform Sūtra* at this time, see Morten Schlütter, "Transmission and Enlightenment in Chan Buddhism Seen Through the *Platform Sūtra* (*Liuzu tanjing*)," *Chung-Hwa Buddhist Journal* 20 (2007): 388; and Jorgensen, *Inventing Hui-neng*, 595–640.

39. John Jorgensen, "The *Platform Sūtra* and the Corpus of Shenhui: Recent Critical Text Editions and Studies," *Revue Bibliographique de Sinologie* (2002): 399–438, esp. 413–16, based on In'gyŏng, *Mongsan Tŏg'i wa Koryŏ hugi Sŏnsasang yŏn'gu* (Seoul: Pur'il, 2000), 95–171.

40. The popularity of the *Lunyu* is noted by Jonathan Spence in the first of his Reith Lectures for 2008, "Chinese Vistas." Transcript and podcast are available at http://www.bbc.co.uk/radio4/reith2008/index.shtml.

41. For discussion and reevaluations of Hongzhou Chan, see Jinhua Jia, *The Hongzhou School of Chan Buddhism in Eighth- Through Tenth-Century Chan* (Albany: State University of New York Press, 2006); and Mario Poceski, *Ordinary Mind as the Way: The Hongzhou School and the Growth of Chan Buddhism* (New York: Oxford University Press, 2007).

42. See Pei-Yi Wu, *The Confucian's Progress: Autobiographical Writings in Traditional China* (Princeton: Princeton University Press, 1990).

3

THE HISTORY AND PRACTICE
OF EARLY CHAN

. . . .

HENRIK H. SØRENSEN

T raditional Chinese accounts of the history of Chan Buddhism depict it as originating with the historical founder
of Buddhism, Śākyamuni, whose truth of enlightenment
was passed down through a succession of Indian patriarchs until it
reached the famed Bodhidharma (d. ca. 530), the First Patriarch, who
traveled to China, where the lineage continued until it reached the
Sixth Patriarch, Huineng (638–713). In other words, the history of
Chan Buddhism was perceived as the unfolding of a monolithic tradition grounded in, and essentially identical with, the message of liberation taught by the Buddha. This claim was conveyed as part of a
twofold strategy, one diachronic and one synchronic.[1] The diachronic
track takes the form of a formal lineage history (actually lineage histories), in which the original message of enlightenment is transmitted via an unbroken line of patriarchs (*zushi*) extending back to the
Buddha himself. These patriarchs were considered holy persons,
but living in the historical continuum and succeeding each other as
pearls on a string. The main idea behind this notion was to provide
authenticity and orthodoxy to the Chan tradition, and as John Jorgensen demonstrates in his chapter in this volume, it was modeled on
the ancestral genealogies known from traditional Chinese society.[2]

The other mode, the synchronic, consists of a repeated affirmation of the universal—and in a sense static—state of enlightenment

first attained by the Buddha and handed down through the lineage of the Chan patriarchs in the same way the flame of one lamp is used to light the next (*chuandeng*, transmission of the lamp). The idea was that the original enlightenment of the Buddha was (and still is) preserved in identical form in all the successive masters of the tradition. The reaffirmation of enlightenment is effectuated though a series of doctrinal truths concerning the inherent nature of enlightenment in all sentient beings, variously expressed as the buddha mind (*foxin*), the one mind (*yixin*), the original mind (*benxin*), buddha nature (*foxing*), and so on.[3] Although the underlying concept of the absolute truth of inherent buddha nature has remained virtually static in the history of the Chan tradition since its obscure beginnings, the doctrines and terminology with which it was expressed changed greatly over the course of the centuries.

The conception of the patriarchs of early Chan was expressed in a lineage that from the beginning was codified as going from Bodhidharma to Huike (485–555? or after 574) to Sengcan (d. 606) to Daoxin (580–651) to Hongren (601–674).[4] This lineage is first found in a funerary stele inscription for Faru (638–689), who is presented as succeeding Hongren.[5] Right from the start, the main issue was who was the primary heir to Hongren, that is, who was the real Sixth Patriarch. This controversy was battled over in a series of lineage histories or genealogies, the earliest of which date from the beginning of the eighth century. They include the *Annals of the Transmission of the Dharma Treasure* (*Chuan fabao ji*)[6] by Du Fei (early seventh century); the *Records of Men and Methods [in the Transmission] of the Laṅkāvatāra* (*Lengqie ren fa zhi*),[7] compiled by Xuanze (d. ca. 725); and the *Records of Masters and Disciples [in the Transmission] of the Laṅkāvatāra* (*Lengqie shiji ji*),[8] compiled by Xuanze's disciple Jingjue (683–ca. 750) around 713–716. Each of these histories promoted a slightly different version of the Chan lineage, especially as it took shape after Hongren. The *Platform Sūtra* itself, with its radical claim that the otherwise almost unknown Huineng was the real Sixth Patriarch, should be understood in the context of these histories. The eventual success of the *Platform Sūtra* and its version of the lineage meant that the other histories all disappeared, and we know about them now only because they were preserved in the hidden cave library found at Dunhuang in the last century.

The Chan notion of a lineage of patriarchal succession has been a powerful and enduring construct. Lying at the heart of Chan self-identity, it served both spiritual and practical aims. The authority of individual Chan masters and the right to establish a given teaching as orthodoxy were of major importance to the medieval Chan lineages. In fact, the continuous struggles over lineage and orthodoxy that took place throughout the eighth and ninth centuries shaped the Chan tradition in late medieval China and beyond.

The practice of meditation, in particular seated meditation (zuochan), seems to have been a defining characteristic of Chan Buddhism from early on.[9] The earliest material on Chan, exemplified in the writings associated with the so-called East Mountain tradition (which Shenhui [684–758] later referred to as Northern Chan), describes meditation as a practice in which the adept calms and focuses his mind, attaining a mental state devoid of thoughts (linian).[10] This process is further described as anxin (calming the mind), kanxin (beholding the mind), guanjing (contemplating purity), and shouxin (maintaining one-pointedness).[11] Shenhui later criticized these practices, claiming they were gradual in nature and based on a dualistic understanding. As the following chapters of this book make clear, a major line of argument in the Platform Sūtra attacks practices such as these. According to the Platform Sūtra, although Northern Chan may have understood that enlightenment is an instantaneous and direct awakening to the buddha nature inherent in all people, it wrongly thought this could be attained through a gradual process.

A SCHOLARLY PERSPECTIVE ON THE HISTORY OF EARLY CHAN BUDDHISM

Although several theories exist about the formation of the early Chan school, scholars today generally agree that the traditional Chan perception of an unbroken patriarchal lineage from Śākyamuni to a series of Chinese patriarchs is the product of pious imagination and sectarian assertions. In other words, the early Chan lineage cannot be understood to have any historical reality prior to the ex post facto efforts of its creators.

Proposing a Chan lineage can be seen as a desire on the part of developing Chan communities to assert themselves in their struggle for religious and worldly recognition. These lineages can be compared to similar assertions in other early traditions of Chinese Buddhism, especially the Tiantai and Three Treatise (Sanlun) schools, although these never claimed an unbroken lineage going all the way back to the historical Buddha.[12] The lineage claims of early Chan reflected a search for identity and legitimacy and a need to stand out from other forms of Buddhist sectarianism. The creation of a spiritual ancestry going back to the founder of the religion was a viable way of securing both spiritual authority and distinctive identity. Seen from this perspective, the Chan tradition simply copied a good idea that was working for other Buddhist denominations. Also, it must not be forgotten that both the Tiantai and the Three Treatise schools were at least partly traditions of meditation, and therefore potential competitors with Chan for secular support. This fact can hardly have been overlooked by the founders of the early Chan communities, who may have felt pressured to come up with a sectarian history similar to those of their closest competitors. Therefore, strengthening a history and defining an identity through the formulation of a patriarchal lineage were of primary importance to the institutional process of early Chan.

But of even greater concern to the individual Chan lineages was a need to distinguish themselves from other competing Chan lines, even collateral ones descending from the same spiritual ancestor. Therefore, during the late seventh and early eighth centuries Chan monks from various lineages increasingly defined themselves as belonging to a tradition that was distinct from, better than, and more true than their competitors. The issues at stake were of the highest import, for with acceptance and public recognition came political, economic, and in some cases even imperial support.[13]

Despite the constructed and artificial nature of the patriarchal lineages, many scholars have come to realize that, together with doctrinal material that has survived, they provide meaningful data on the history of early Chan. Hence by applying a combination of discourse analysis and textual criticism to the records of these lineages, it is possible to distill a relatively large amount of historical data to help us understand the way early Chan Buddhism developed in China.

MEDITATION AND THE FORMATION OF EARLY CHAN

Before turning to the rise of Chan Buddhism as a sectarian phenomenon, let us first review what we know about the practice of meditation in Chinese Buddhism prior to that. The term *chan* is a short form of the word *channa*, which means "meditation" and is a Chinese rendering of the Sanskrit word *dhyāna*. In traditional Mahāyāna Buddhism, *dhyāna* is used as a general term denoting a wide range of Buddhist contemplative practices, including meditative concentration and insight (Skt.: *śamatha-vipaśyanā*), visualization (*guan*), Buddha invocation/recollection (Skt.: *buddhānusmṛti*), and reflective contemplation (*guanxin shi*), in which the practitioner focuses the stream of his thinking on a particular doctrinal theme such as causality, impermanence, impurity, or emptiness. It may also involve the contemplation of a specific object, such as a decomposing corpse. Hence, references to a Buddhist monk engaged in meditation in principle could indicate any of the above types of practices.

During the early period of Chinese Buddhism (first to fourth centuries C.E.), the main sources on Buddhist meditation and contemplation were several canonical sūtras and treatises of Indian origin with instructions on the practice of various forms of meditation (*dhyāna*). Many of these texts belonged to the so-called Hīnayāna traditions and focused on breath control and mind purification. Later, the great translator Kumārajīva (344–409 or 413) produced a number of meditation treatises that became extremely influential in Chinese Buddhism. Even though these works reflect Indian Buddhist practices, there are indications that Kumārajīva may have modified their contents in accordance with his own understanding of Mahāyāna Buddhist practice. A prominent exponent of meditation during this phase of Chinese Buddhism was Huiyuan (344–416) of Mount Lu, who was greatly inspired by Kumārajīva's translations.[14]

Together this material gives evidence of a slow but persistent development from what we might call Hīnayāna-style meditation (*dhyāna* carried out on the basis of a dualistic, pietistic, exclusivist view of reality), through Hīnayāna-style meditation based on Mahāyāna doctrines, ending with Mahāyāna-style meditation based on Mahāyāna doctrines.[15] This progression reflects a changing understanding in China of Buddhist practice and its goal, both of which were increasingly influenced by key Mahāyāna philosophical concepts such as universal emptiness, mind only, and nondualism. These changes are more concerned with spiritual attitude and ideas of the path (Skt.: *mārga*) than with technical aspects. Meditation continued to be practiced primarily seated cross-legged with the hands resting in the lap.

Generally speaking, Chinese Buddhist meditation during the period in which the early patriarchs of the Chan tradition are supposed to have lived, roughly 450 to 650, does not appear to have been exclusive to a special class of monks but was part of the common program of Buddhist training followed by all monastic communities. Of course there were monks who specialized in one or more of these aspects of Buddhist training, but the vast majority would have engaged in a combination of scriptural study and the practice of some form of meditation as outlined above. This is indicated by the biographies of the monks in the section on *dhyāna* practitioners found in Daoxuan's (596–667) *Continued Biographies of Eminent Monks* (*Xu gaoseng zhuan*, hereafter *Continued Biographies*).[16]

BODHIDHARMA AND HIS LINEAGE

At one point during the late Northern Wei dynasty (386–534) a meditation master from India by the name of Bodhidharma arrived in Luoyang. The earliest source to mention him is the *Record of the Saṃghārama [Monasteries] of Luoyang*, which portrays him stereotypically as a foreign pilgrim-monk without providing any real information about his teaching or background.[17] Bodhidharma next appears a century later, in Daoxuan's *Continued Biographies*. Daoxuan's work is an important source for understanding the early history of the Chan tradition because it was written before a self-conscious Chan lineage took shape. From this source a picture emerges of Bodhidharma as a master of *dhyāna* who taught a Mahāyāna-oriented style of meditation. Daoxuan mentions that Bodhidharma taught "calming the mind by doing wall contemplation," a kind of meditation that, at least on the surface, would seem like a rather traditional practice of meditative concentration.[18] We know little directly about Bodhidharma's meditation practice. Only one of the works attributed to him, *The Treatise on the Two Entrances and Four Practices* (*Erru sixing lun*), is considered authentic. Although it does touch upon the issue of meditation, it is largely a doctrinal tract with an eccentric formulation of the idea of nondualism.[19]

Daoxuan appears to have had some reservations about Bodhidharma's teachings. In a section discussing different approaches to meditation, Daoxuan calls Bodhidharma's style "abstruse and complex." He notes that Bodhidharma's teaching was based on the teaching of emptiness propounded in the *prajñāpāramitā* (perfection of wisdom) tradition, and suggests that Bodhidharma took these teachings to an overly idealistic extreme when he states that Bodhidharma only wanted to "negate and discard." Daoxuan also claims that Bodhidharma rejected the principles of karmic retribution (sin and merit) and that he chose to abstain from words, and he rebukes Bodhidharma's followers for their failure to uphold the prescriptions of the *vinaya* (the Buddhist monastic rules).[20] In general, then, it seems that Daoxuan felt that Bodhidharma's approach implied the rejection of the traditional concepts of path and goal, viewing them as dualistic and gradual. Although such an approach is based on the teachings of the perfection of wisdom, nevertheless from the perspective of monastic training it was understood by many to be problematic, even dangerous, as it could result in the rejection of traditional Buddhist practice and monastic discipline. Daoxuan appears to have thought that many of Bodhidharma's successors came close to rejecting tradition this way; he attacks them as superficial and immature, unable to grasp Bodhidharma's teachings.

From Daoxuan we know the names of a number of monks who are said to have trained under Bodhidharma, or at least to have been exposed to his teachings. They include his immediate disciples Huike (who emerged as the Second Patriarch of Chan in China), possibly Sengfu (first half of sixth century), and some of their followers.[21] Daoxuan was writing more than one hundred years after the time of Bodhidharma and his immediate disciples, so it is difficult to judge how accurately he described their teachings. The negative review of their practice of meditation may also have been influenced by sectarian struggles in Daoxuan's own day. In any event, most of the early sources appear to indicate that the adherents of Bodhidharma's tradition of *dhyāna* expounded a radical understanding of the perfection of wisdom that emphasized emptiness and the overcoming of dualism. This, of course, fits well with later Chan notions of sudden enlightenment.[22]

Another clue about Bodhidharma is contained in Daoxuan's linking him with the *Laṅkāvatāra Sūtra*. Daoxuan claims that Bodhidharma transmitted the scripture to his disciple, Huike, and that Huike passed down the tradition to his students as well.[23] However, other early sources are silent about this connection, so we have no basis for asserting that Bodhidharma preached the text. Later sources, by contrast, claim that the sūtra was fundamental for Bodhidharma and the East Mountain Chan tradition—despite the fact that the sūtra and its ideas about consciousness seem never to have been particularly influential in East Mountain Chan doctrine.[24] The reason for this later claim is not hard to fathom. The *Laṅkāvatāra* was especially important in Chinese Buddhism during the sixth century, and the Second Patriarch, Huike, was considered an exponent of the scripture. Hence, it is likely that the later Chan tradition connected the text to Bodhidharma to further solidify the lineage.

According to Daoxuan's biographical account, Bodhidharma and his followers constituted only one among several different traditions of *dhyāna* in north China during the sixth century. Another group, which formed under Sengchou (sixth century), was concerned with mental purification in what would seem to be a more gradualist manner. Daoxuan clearly favors this tradition, perhaps because it conformed more closely to orthodox Indian Buddhist practices. It is not improbable that the tension between the followers of Bodhidharma and their seemingly radical style of meditation and Sengchou's more traditional *dhyāna* practice could have been the origin of the later debate over sudden versus gradual enlightenment. In any case, as noted above, we should not lose sight of the fact that most of the information contained in Daoxuan's biography was compiled during the middle of the seventh century, a full century after many of the events it describes.

DAOXIN, HONGREN, AND THE RISE OF THE EAST MOUNTAIN TRADITION

Although the link between Bodhidharma and Huike may well have been historical, this does not hold true for the link between Huike and his obscure disciple Sengcan, whom the later Chan histories uniformly claim as the Third Patriarch. There are no reliable or contemporary sources on which to establish this connection, and it would appear to be a fairly late fabrication. Only with Daoxin,[25] the alleged Fourth Patriarch of Chan, roughly contemporary with the historian Daoxuan, can we begin to give some historical credit to the development of sectarian Chan.

Daoxuan's biography is the earliest surviving source about Daoxin, and it places him as head of a group of monks at East Mountain in Huangmei. Daoxuan relates that on his deathbed, Daoxin is asked about the future of his teachings. He answers that he has already given a number of transmissions but mentions no names. At other places in the biography, however, Hongren is mentioned twice while other disciples of Daoxin are not.[26] Given that Daoxuan was a contemporary of Daoxin, we are justified in accepting Daoxuan's data at more or less face value. Although we have no clear idea about the content of Daoxin's teachings, he and Hongren were probably related as master and disciple. Interestingly, in the *Annals of the Transmission of the Dharma Treasure,* Daoxin is said to have only grudgingly appointed Hongren as his successor.[27]

In any case, it seems clear that Hongren took over from Daoxin and continued to develop the growing community at Huangmei. The sole surviving text attributed to Hongren is the *Treatise on the Essentials of Mind Cultivation (Xiuxin yao lun),* although it is not certain that the current version was authored by him.[28] The text offers a clear philosophy and guide to meditation. It also uses the metaphor of the dusty mirror, which would later appear in Shenxiu's poem in the celebrated verse competition in the *Platform Sūtra.* Although Hongren's numerical designation as fifth in the series of patriarchs was probably created posthumously, nevertheless it is with him that we begin to see the outlines of the first Chan Buddhist community in the institutional sense. We may consider him the real founder of Chan Buddhism in the sense that he formulated a distinct type of meditation practice and doctrine and was probably one of the first *dhyāna* masters who established an entire community around a uniform type of practice.

HONGREN'S DISCIPLES: THE COLLATERAL BRANCHES OF NORTHERN CHAN

According to the *Records of Men and Methods [in the Transmission] of the Laṅkāvatāra,* Hongren had ten major disciples, all of whom are said to have transmitted his teaching of Chan.[29] Of these, Shenxiu (606?–706), Faru, Lao'an/Hui'an (588?–708), and Xuanze (d.u.) were evidently the most prominent and influential—or at least, that is how they are portrayed by the authors of the early Chan sectarian histories and other contemporary sources. Huineng, who would become so famous later as the Sixth Patriarch in the so-called Southern Chan tradition, and around whom the *Platform Sūtra* revolves, is also mentioned in the *Records of Men and Methods* among these ten disciples. However, all that is said about him is that he lived in Shaozhou and was a teacher of only local significance. From the perspective of the authors of this work, Huineng—although recognized as a disciple of Hongren—was a marginal figure. (The changing understanding of Huineng during this period is discussed at greater length in John Jorgensen's chapter in this volume.)

As far as the history of the transmission lineage of early Chan goes, it is obvious that as early as the end of the seventh century a process had begun in which various monks, in particular those who claimed to be disciples of Hongren (or perhaps their disciples again), had begun to position themselves as heirs in a Chan lineage. This had already started before Shenxiu passed away but accelerated greatly after his death, resulting in the creation of at least four contending branches of what came to be called Northern Chan.[30] Each seems to have put forward its own candidate as the Sixth Patriarch.

Shenxiu, the most important of the contenders, figures preeminently among the disciples of Hongren. He was a prolific writer who authored a number of Chan works, including the *Treatise on the Contemplation of the Mind* (*Guanxin lun*) and the *Treatise on Complete Brightness* (*Yuanming lun*). The latter features a presentation of meditation in stages. Shenxiu produced many distinguished disciples, and it is neither surprising nor coincidental that he stands out as the greatest among the masters of Northern Chan. He enjoyed almost unprecedented favor from the imperial court, especially from Empress Wu (r. 690–705), and had numerous followers among the elite.[31]

Faru is noteworthy for being associated with the earliest expression of a transmission lineage in Chan Buddhist history, as detailed in his funerary stele inscription.[32] The inscription wants us to believe that Faru was the primary of Hongren's disciples, although it does not necessarily imply that he was the only successor. In any case, it is an important document in the sectarian struggles that took place after the demise of Hongren. Faru or his followers may have been the first to formulate the transmission lineage going from Hongren back to Bodhidharma and ultimately to the Buddha.

Lao'an (also known as Hui'an) also seems to have been promoted as the main heir to Hongren by his disciples.[33] He was successful in the capital and at the court and came to be venerated for his old age. However, contemporary sources on him are meager, and the biographies contained in the Buddhist histories are too late to be of any relevance. He left no writings but remains nevertheless the only one of Hongren's disciples, except Huineng, whom later sectarian historians have not completely ignored or otherwise demoted (as happened to Shenxiu, Faru, and their followers).

Xuanze's lineage, which seeks to establish Xuanze as one of the main disciples of Hongren, is set forth in the *Records of Men and Methods [in the Transmission] of the Laṅkāvatāra*. However, it is not clear that Xuanze was a very prominent master in his own time, and it seems likely that the compiler of the *Records of Men and Methods,* Jingjue, who was Xuanze's disciple, tried to promote him to further his own standing.[34]

In contrast to the political agendas separating the different lineages of Northern Chan, there appears to have been a significant consensus on the philosophy and methods of meditation the lineages employed. Common to all of them was a rhetoric of the absolute, nondual reality of Buddhist enlightenment, but in actuality they all appear to have followed a rather traditional path of gradual practice. This is evident in the terminology and instructions relating to meditation in the surviving works of these figures. The practices behind such notions as *linian* (removed from thought), *kanjing* (beholding purity) and *shouyi* (maintaining one-pointed concentration), all cardinal aspects of Northern Chan meditation, do not seem to indicate a program centered on sudden enlightenment or nondualistic practice.[35]

Although meditation clearly was the focus of the spiritual endeavors of the collateral lineages of Northern Chan, nevertheless all of them maintained a close doctrinal connection with the scriptural tradition of Mahāyāna Buddhism. This is evident in the large number of mainstream scriptures quoted in the writings of the masters of Northern Chan,[36] who invoked a diverse selection of canonical and apocryphal scriptures to support their views. More importantly, the manner in which these scriptures were used clearly indicates that Northern Chan, and Shenxiu's branch in particular, was no less concerned with doctrinal orthodoxy or scripture than were the followers of, for example, the Tiantai school. Clearly, the notion of a "transmission outside the scriptural teaching" that characterizes the later Chan tradition had not yet formed at this stage of its history.

SHENXIU'S DISCIPLES AND SHENHUI'S ATTACKS ON NORTHERN CHAN

The first Chan histories discussed at the beginning of this chapter grew out of the power struggle that developed as the leading disciples of Hongren began establishing their respective centers of teaching. It was customary for a master to have several recognized heirs, as seems to have been the case with Hongren. But as the groups around his disciples and his disciples' disciples began to compete for patronage, the question of who was the real Sixth Patriarch of Chan took on paramount importance. The answer could not only secure an enduring place in the history of Chan Buddhism for a Chan master and his disciples and give them considerable political influence, but could also determine the nature of orthodox Chan practice.

After the passing of Shenxiu during the early years of the eighth century, the scene was mainly left to the second-generation followers of the collateral branches of Northern Chan. In particular, Lao'an's and Shenxiu's disciples, including Jingzang (675–746), belonging to the former's lineage,[37] and Puji (651–739) and Yifu (661–736), of the latter's lineage, became greatly influential in the area of the twin capitals (Chang'an and Luoyang) of the Tang empire.[38] As far as the sources allow us to conclude, in terms of meditation methods and doctrinal views, the branches were by and large similar in their interpretation of the Buddhist path. It was in this phase in the history of the Chan tradition that sectarian writings and compilation of lineage histories and doctrinal tracts began in earnest, as seen in the *Annals of the Transmission of the Dharma Treasure* and the *Records of Masters and Disciples [in the Transmission] of the Laṅkāvatāra.*

During the early 730s a monk appeared in the central plains with a radical new interpretation of Chan history and practice. This was Shenhui (684–758), a charismatic Chan monk, clever organizer, and astute thinker whose mission in life was to establish the virtually unknown Huineng, an allegedly uncouth "barbarian" from remote Shaozhou in Guangdong (Lingnan), as the true Sixth Patriarch.[39] Shenhui repeatedly attacked the established view of patriarchal succession as claimed by the collateral branches of Northern Chan established by Shenxiu's successors, rejecting Shenxiu as the Sixth Patriarch in the transmission.

But Shenhui not only attacked the Northern Chan transmission lineage. In the process of bolstering Huineng as the authentic Sixth Patriarch, he attempted to thoroughly demolish the doctrines and practices of Northern Chan. Even the practice of meditation itself, the core of Chan Buddhism, was rejected as mental agitation, in line with his uncompromising, nondual approach to enlightenment.[40]

Shenhui's own training is somewhat obscure, but it would appear that he had absorbed or borrowed a significant amount of his Chan Buddhism from followers of the Niutou (Oxhead) School, another branch of Chan that had arisen in south China, which (spuriously) claimed a lineage descending from Daoxin. The Niutou School taught a type of Chan based on a radical, highly practical interpretation of the philosophy of the perfection of wisdom mixed with elements of Daoist philosophy (based on the *Daode jing* and the *Zhuangzi*).[41] It is an open question whether the Niutou School of Chan inspired Shenhui to formulate the doctrines of nonaction (*wuwei*) and sudden enlightenment (*dunwu*), but clearly these devices enabled him to successfully reject Northern Chan's methods of meditation as being gradual and dualistic in nature. As John Jorgensen discusses in his chapter, Shenhui almost certainly did not study with Huineng—or even ever meet him—and it seems unlikely that Shenhui's ideas had any basis in teachings formulated by Huineng. The fact remains that we simply do not know anything for certain about what Huineng taught.

The success of Shenhui's campaign hinged on a combination of political and religious events, all of which worked to his advantage. First, the rise to prominence of the Northern School had been a result of direct imperial favor bestowed upon Shenxiu by Empress Wu. Even after her demise, the continued success of the Northern Chan lineages was secured through their close relationship with the powerful families of the aristocracy. By 730, when Shenhui mounted the first in a series of attacks against Northern Chan, the time was still not ripe, partly because the power base of Shenxiu's successors was still largely intact, and also because Shenhui was operating in the provinces far from the capital area. Hence, Shenhui's efforts at first seem to have failed. However, in 745 he was appointed to a monastery in the region of the capital cities, where he again started agitating against Northern Chan. This time he was far more successful and drew huge crowds to his sermons, perhaps also administering precepts to both laypeople and monastics. But he had to suffer another setback before being able to prevail: in 753, after an audience with the emperor, he was sent into exile for disturbing the peace.

By the time of the An Lushan rebellion of the mid-750s, which devastated large parts of central China, a general shift in the political structure as well as in the religious climate had taken place.[42] In this new situation many of the old aristocratic families had lost their power, consequently weakening the position of Northern Chan. The An Lushan rebellion created a financial crisis for the Tang dynasty. The government sought, among other measures, to raise money from the sale of Buddhist ordination certificates. This device worked as a kind of government bond offering, bringing money to the state in exchange for tax exemptions granted to those with monastic status. In 756, Shenhui was called back from exile and given the task of selling these certificates because of his oratory skills. He was so successful in filling the state coffers that he received official recognition and support from the Tang emperor.[43] Moreover, all of Shenxiu's influential disciples had passed away, leaving a vacuum for Shenhui to fill. Lastly, Shenhui's penetrating, abstruse teachings of sudden enlightenment appear to have had broad appeal.

THE ROLE OF THE *PLATFORM SŪTRA* IN THE SUCCESS OF SOUTHERN CHAN

It has long been thought that the *Platform Sūtra* was created by Shenhui or someone among his followers as part of an attack on Shenxiu's Northern Chan. However, although it is possible that people in Shenhui's camp first composed the text, the earliest version we now have (the Dunhuang version) cannot be their direct product. Although the *Platform Sūtra* and the extant writings of Shenhui have important things in common, including basic ideas and overall approach to the path, there are also enough contradictions and differences in terminology, citations, and lists of Indian patriarchs to suggest that the sūtra as it now stands was not created by Shenhui's school. Interestingly, and perhaps most significantly, the *Platform Sūtra* mentions Shenhui in a way that is not always flattering, at times placing him in a rather critical light. This points to the involvement of a competing Chan lineage—another group that claimed descent from Huineng but also accepted Shenhui's importance. This does not rule out that

Shenhui or his disciples could have compiled an ur-version of the *Platform Sūtra* that was later modified and added to by other Chan practitioners. However, in the light of the data available today, I do not believe such a scenario is very likely. (For a different evaluation, see the chapter in this book by John Jorgensen.)

Although it was by and large Shenhui's attacks on the Northern School that brought about the shift in Chan that paved the way for the *Platform Sūtra*, neither he nor his successors were to reap the ultimate benefit of their efforts. Within two generations after Shenhui's death, his lineage had all but vanished and the "transmission of the patriarch's lamp" had instead gone to two provincial groups of Chan practitioners. One was in south China under the leadership of one Mazu Daoyi (709–788) and his Hongzhou School,[44] and the other was located in Sichuan and known as the Baotang School. As Wendi Adamek's chapter in this book demonstrates, both of these Chan traditions taught sudden enlightenment and maintained distinct views on the orthodox patriarchal succession. In a manner of speaking, the *Platform Sūtra*'s listing of the Chan patriarchal succession provided the final and definitive version of the orthodox history of Chan up to Huineng, and both of these new Chan groups can be seen as upholders of this norm. Although Shenhui does appear as a minor figure—after all, it was not possible to completely erase his role as de facto creator of Huineng—Shenxiu and the Northern School of Chan were completely ignored.

With the formal establishment of Huineng as the Sixth Patriarch of Chan, the protracted period of sectarian strife in Chan, which had lasted a good part of the eighth century, was finally over. A new age was dawning in which Southern Chan, particularly those lineages represented by Mazu's Hongzhou School and other collateral branches claiming descent from Huineng, was dominant, setting the course for the future development of Chan Buddhism in China. During the ninth and tenth centuries, Huineng's Chan was understood to have branched out into five schools: the Weiyang, Linji, Caodong, Yunmen, and Fayan. All of them hailed Bodhidharma as the founder of the tradition in China and Huineng as the Sixth Patriarch and final master in the orthodox line of succession. By this time all other lineages of Chan had died out.

APPENDIX: THE PATRIARCHAL TRANSMISSION ACCORDING TO EARLY CHAN LITERATURE

A. "Tang Zhongyue shamen Shi Faru Chanshi xingzhuang" (The Account of the Activities of the Monk, Chan Master Faru from Zhongyue of the Tang Dynasty). Contained on Faru's funerary stele. Lineage: (1) Bodhidharma, (2) Huike, (3) Sengcan, (4) Daoxin, (5) Hongren, (6) Faru. As the oldest written record setting out the Northern Chan transmission from Bodhidharma, this inscription is the de facto progenitor of all later transmission lineages in Chan history. It is intended to promote Faru as the foremost among Hongren's disciples.

B. *Chuan fabao ji* (*Annals of the Transmission of the Dharma Treasure*). Lineage: (1) Bodhidharma, (2) Huike, (3) Sengcan, (4) Daoxin, (5) Hongren, (6a) Faru, (6b) Shenxiu. This lineage was meant to favor both Faru and Shenxiu as the leading disciples of Hongren. In a rather strange move, the text claims that the patriarchy went in a lateral move to Shenxiu after Faru's death. It seems the main thrust is to prove that Shenxiu received the transmission, but because of Faru's inscription ("Tang Zhongyue shamen Shi Faru Chanshi xingzhuang," noted above), the text also had to include him.

C. *Lengqie ren fa zhi* (*Records of Men and Methods [in the Transmission] of the Laṅkāvatāra*). Lineage: [1] Bodhidharma, [2] Huike, [3] Sengcan, [4] Daoxin, (5) Hongren, (6) Xuanze/Shenxiu. This lineage history is only known from a partial quotation in the *Lengqie shizi ji* (see below), and we cannot be certain about the earlier parts of the lineage (the first four patriarchs, with numbers in brackets) it presented. Here we find the earliest mention of Huineng (as a local teacher in the south) in a list of ten disciples of Hongren. Hongren is also cited as stating that Shenxiu and Xuanze were his most important disciples.

D. *Lengqie shizi ji (Records of Masters and Disciples [in the Transmission] of the Laṅkāvatāra)*. Lineage: (1) Guṇabhadra, (2) Bodhidharma, (3) Huike, (4) Sengcan, (5) Daoxin, (6) Hongren, (7) Shenxiu/ Xuanze/Lao'an, (8) four disciples of Shenxiu. This lineage history was meant to favor Shenxiu's Northern Chan transmission as well as that of his direct disciples, but still also includes Xuanze and Lao'an as recipients of Hongren's transmission. Until the advent of Shenhui and the *Platform Sūtra*, this was the commonly accepted lineage of succession.

E. *Platform Sūtra*. Lineage: (1) Bodhidharma, (2) Huike, (3) Sengcan, (4) Daoxin, (5) Hongren, (6) Huineng. Meant to demonstrate the orthodoxy and spiritual supremacy of Huineng's Southern Chan, this genealogy completely ignores all the transmission lineages of Northern Chan. Although it does favor Shenhui, the Dunhuang version of the text also attributes authenticity to the Fahai lineage, a local tradition at Caoqi, since Fahai is said to have received the *Platform Sūtra* from Huineng.

NOTES

1. A similar model of interpretation can be found in Charles D. Orzech, *Politics and Transcendent Wisdom: The Scripture for Humane Kings in the Creation of Chinese Buddhism*, Hermeneutics: Studies in the History of Religions (University Park: Pennsylvania State University Press, 1998), 42–50.

2. See also John Jorgensen, "The 'Imperial' Lineage of Ch'an Buddhism: The Role of Confucian Ritual and Ancestor Worship in Ch'an's Search for Legitimation in the Mid-Tang Dynasty," *Papers on Far Eastern History* 35 (1987): 89–133; and *Inventing Hui-neng, the Sixth Patriarch: Hagiography and Biography in Early Ch'an*, Sinica Leidensia, 68 (Leiden: Brill, 2005), 274–321.

3. These concepts do appear in Indian Buddhist sources, but they are not very prominent. In fact, the strong ontological reading commonly associated with their use in the Chinese Chan material suggests that they underwent considerable modification and philosophical development in China.

4. The dates of early Chan figures are all tentative, and some of the figures may indeed be entirely fictive.

5. "Tang Zhongyue shamen Shi Faru Chanshi xingzhuang" (Account of the Activities of the Monk, Chan Master Faru from Zhongyue of the Tang Dynasty). For the rubbing of the actual stele and an edited version, see Yanagida Seizan, *Shoki zenshū shisho no kenkyū* (Kyoto: Hōzōkan, 1967), 487–96, pl. 1. For further details, see the appendix to this chapter, "The Patriarchal Transmission According to Early Chan Literature."

6. A complete translation can be found in John McRae, *The Northern School and the Formation of Early Ch'an Buddhism*, Kuroda Institute, Studies in East Asian Buddhism, 3 (Honolulu: University of Hawai'i Press, 1986), 226–69; see also Jorgensen, *Inventing Hui-neng*, 536–42.

7. No longer extant. It only exists in the form of quotations found in the *Records of Masters and Disciples [in the Transmission] of the Laṅkāvatāra*.

8. See the somewhat problematic translation in J. C. Cleary, *Zen Dawn: Early Zen Texts from Tun Huang* (Boston: Shambhala, 1986), 17–78.

9. See McRae, *The Northern School*, 41, which notes that Hongren "taught meditation and nothing else."

10. For a thorough discussion of this term, see Robert B. Zeuschner, "The Concept of Li-nien ('Being Free from Thinking') in the Northern Line of Ch'an Buddhism," in *Early Ch'an in China and Tibet*, ed. Whalen Lai and Lewis R. Lancaster, Berkeley Buddhist Studies Series, 5 (Berkeley: Asian Humanities Press, 1983), 131–48. McRae reads *linian* as "transcending thought"; see *The Northern School*, 223. In the light of what the texts themselves reveal, such an interpretation is less likely.

11. See McRae, *The Northern School*, 136–38.

12. For the Three Treatise School's creation of its lineage, see Leon Hurvitz, "The First Systematizations of Buddhist Thought in China," *Journal of Chinese Philosophy* 2 (1975): 361–88. For the Tiantai school, see the classic study by Helwig Schmidt-Glintzer, *Die Identität der buddhistischen Schulen und die Kompilation buddhistischer Universalgeschichten in China*, Münchener Ostasiatische Studien, 26 (Wiesbaden: Franz Steiner, 1982), 64–74. For a discussion of later developments in Tiantai, see Koichi Shinohara, "From Local History to Universal History: The Construction of the Sung T'ien-t'ai Lineage," in *Buddhism in the Sung*, ed. Peter N. Gregory and Daniel A. Getz Jr., Kuroda Institute, Studies in East Asian Buddhism, 13 (Honolulu: University of Hawai'i Press, 1999), 524–76.

13. A reading of the history of early Chan from the perspective of power can be found in Bernard Faure, *The Will to Orthodoxy: A Critical Genealogy of Northern Chan Buddhism*, trans. Phyllis Brooks (Stanford: Stanford University Press, 1997), 145–59. For a radical reinterpretation of Chan history along these lines, see Alan Cole, *Fathering Your Father: The Zen of Fabrication in Tang Buddhism* (Berkeley: University of California Press, 2009).

14. For a survey of Huiyuan's meditation practices, see Kenneth Ch'en, *Buddhism in China: A Historical Survey* (Princeton: Princeton University Press, 1964), 108–10.

15. See Neal Donner, "The Mahayanization of Chinese Dhyāna," *The Eastern Buddhist* 10, no. 2 (1977): 49–64. Although dated, this study is nevertheless important for its discussion of the evolution of Chinese *dhyāna* practices in the pre-Tang period.

16. See the chapter entitled "Practice of Meditation" (*chanxi*) in *Xu gaoseng zhuan*, Daoxuan (596–667), *T* no. 2060, 50:550a–606c. On the genre of Buddhist biography, see John Kieschnick, *The Eminent Monk: Buddhist Ideals in Medieval Chinese Hagiography*, Kuroda Institute, Studies in East Asian Buddhism, 10 (Honolulu: University of Hawai'i Press, 1997).

17. *Luoyang qielan ji*, Yang Xuanzhi (ca. 493–547), *T* no. 2092, 51:1000b, 1004a; Yit'ung Wang, trans., *A Record of Buddhist Monasteries in Lo-yang* (Princeton: Princeton University Press, 1984), 20, 57.

18. *Xu gaoseng zhuan*, *T* 50:551b–c. There is much speculation over the issue of "wall contemplation" (*biguan*). Daoxuan's wording indicates that it simply means facing a wall while doing meditation in order to achieve tranquility of mind. Daoxuan also clearly states that it is a Mahāyāna practice (see *Xu gaoseng zhuan*, *T* 50:596c). For other interpretations, see McRae, *The Northern School*, 112–14.

19. For a discussion of the development of Bodhidharma's biography, see John McRae, *Seeing Through Zen: Encounter, Transformation, and Genealogy in Chinese Chan Buddhism* (Berkeley: University of California Press, 2003), 22–28. See also McRae, *The Northern School*, 101–17; and Jeffrey L. Broughton, *The Bodhidharma Anthology: The Earliest Records of Zen* (Berkeley: University of California Press, 1999).

20. *Xu gaoseng zhuan*, *T* 50:596c; see also Chen Jinhua, *Monks and Monarchs, Kinship and Kingship: Tanqian in Sui Buddhism and Politics*, Italian School of East Asian Studies, Essays, 3 (Kyoto: ISEAS, 2002), 156, 172.

21. *Xu gaoseng zhuan*, *T* 50:480c–81a. See also McRae, *The Northern School*, 278–80, notes 30–35.

22. Chen, *Monks and Monarchs*, 156, 174–78, 206–209. In Chan, the original Buddhist idea that all phenomena are the products of the thinking mind was modified to indicate a correlation, indeed an identification, between the mind's inherently enlightened nature, the buddha mind (*foxin*), and the nature of phenomena (*shi* or *fa*). A very useful overview of this issue can be found in Liu Ming-Wood, *Madhyamaka Thought in China*, Sinica Leidensia, 30 (Leiden: E. J. Brill, 1994).

23. See *Xu gaoseng zhuan*, *T* 50:552b, 666a–c. For an insight into the nature of the early translation of this important sūtra, see the recent translation: Gishin Tokiwa, *Laṅkāvatāra ratna sūtram: A Sanskrit Restoration, a Study of the Four-fascicle English and Japanese Translations with introduction, and the Collated Guṇabhadra Chinese Version with Japanese Reading* (Osaka: Gishin Tokiwa, 2003).

24. On the place of the *Laṅkāvatāra* in Northern Chan, see McRae, *The Northern School*, 27–29; and Faure, *The Will to Orthodoxy*, 145–59. The later flourishing of this legend probably explains why Guṇabhadra (ca. fifth c.), who made the first translation of this important sūtra, is made Bodhidharma's teacher in the *Lengqie shizi ji*, *T* no. 2837, 85:1283c.

25. On Sengcan, see McRae, *The Northern School*, 33–35, 118–21. On Daoxin, see McRae, *The Northern School*, 31–35; and David W. Chappell, "The Teachings of the Fourth Ch'an Patriarch Tao-hsin (580–651)," in *Early Ch'an in China and Tibet*, ed. Whalen Lai and Lewis R. Lancaster, Berkeley Buddhist Studies Series, 5 (Berkeley: Asian Humanities Press, 1983), 89–129. Note that Chappell accepts the attributions in the later Northern Chan material as authentic.

26. *Xu gaoseng zhuan*, T 50:606b.

27. McRae, *The Northern School*, 263.

28. On Hongren, see McRae, *Seeing Through Zen*, 33–35; and McRae, *The Northern School*, 35–43, 121–47.

29. Quoted in *Lengqie shizi ji*, T 85:1289c.

30. I use the term "Northern Chan" in this section to denote the early Chan lineages other than the one leading to Huineng, following Shenhui's usage.

31. Shenxiu's activities are described in detail in McRae, *Seeing Through Zen*, 55–73. The *Treatise on the Contemplation of the Mind* was once attributed to Bodhidharma; see McRae, *The Northern School*, 119. For a translation and discussion of *The Treatise on Complete Brightness*, see McRae, *The Northern School*, 149–71, 209–18.

32. For Faru's funerary inscription, see Yanagida Seizan, *Shoki zenshū shisho no kenkyū* (Kyoto: Hōzōkan, 1967), 487–96.

33. See the epitaph for his disciple Jingzang in *(Qinding) Quan Tang wen*, cited in McRae, *The Northern School*, 59.

34. Cole suggests that Xuanze is entirely fictional; see Cole, *Fathering Your Father*, 171–75.

35. There has been considerable discussion of the validity of the criticism leveled against Northern Chan (that it followed gradualism and taught a dualistic form of meditation) by Shenhui and the later followers of Southern Chan (and of course also the *Platform Sūtra*). McRae and others, following Yanagida's understanding of the problem, have argued that the approaches favored by Northern Chan were both "sudden" and "nondual"; see McRae, *The Northern School*, 196–232. However, while the doctrines of Northern Chan monks may have appeared more sudden than the manner in which the later Chan tradition has portrayed them, a closer look at the description of actual practices in Northern Chan works indicates otherwise. Hence, both Shenhui's critique as well as that of the *Platform Sūtra* and the later Chan tradition, as seen in the works of the important exegete (Guifeng) Zongmi (778–840), would appear justified in terms of the logic of sudden enlightenment and its hermeneutics. For a classic discussion of the different schools of Chan and their doctrinal positions, see Yün-hua Jan, "Tsung-mi: His Analysis of Ch'an Buddhism," *T'oung Pao* 58 (1972): 1–54.

36. Popular sūtras from which quotes can be found in the Northern Chan writings include, among others, the *Laṅkāvatāra* (translation by Tokiwa, noted above); the *Vimalakīrti Sūtra*, see Charles Luk, trans., *The Vimalakīrti Nirdeśa Sūtra (Wei Mo Chieh So Shuo Ching)* (Berkeley: Shambhala, 1972); the *Ratnakūṭa Sūtra*, see Garma C.C. Chang, trans., *Treasury of Mahayana Sūtras: Selections from the Maharatnakuta Sūtra* (University Park: Pennsylvania State University Press, 1983); the

Avataṁsaka Sūtra, see Thomas Cleary, trans., *The Flower Ornament Scripture* (Boston: Shambhala, 1993); the *Suvarṇaprabhāsa Sūtra*, see R. E. Emmerick, trans., *The Sūtra of Golden Light: Being a Translation of the Suvarṇaprabhāsottamasūtra*, Sacred Books of the Buddhists, 27 (London: Luzac, 1970); the *Mahāparinirvāṇa Sūtra*, see Kosho Yamamoto, trans., *The Mahayana Mahaparinirvana-sūtra*, 3 vols., Karin Buddhological Series, 5 (Ube: Karin bunko, 1973); the *Sukhāvatīvyūha*, see Luis O. Gómez, trans., *The Land of Bliss: The Paradise of the Buddha of Measureless Light* (Honolulu: University of Hawai'i Press, 1996); the *Saddharmapuṇḍarīka*, see Burton Watson, trans., *The Lotus Sutra*, Translations from the Asian Classics (New York: Columbia University Press, 1993). Scriptures of the *prajñāpāramitā* class include the important *Vajracchedikā*, see Charles Luk [Lu K'uan Yü], trans., *The Heart Sutra and the Diamond Sutra* (Hong Kong: World Fellowship of Buddhists, 1960); the *Pañcaviṁśatisāhasrikā-prajñāpāramitā*, partly translated in Edward Conze, trans., *The Large Sūtra on Perfect Wisdom* (Berkeley: University of California Press, 1975); and the *Saptaśatikā-prajñāpāramitā Sūtra*, see Edward Conze, trans., *The Short Prajñāpāramitā Texts* (London: Luzac, 1973), 79–107. In addition to the Indian scriptures we have a number of Chinese compositions, including apocryphal works, such as the *Jingang sanmei jing* (*Vajrasamādhi*), see Robert E. Buswell Jr., *The Formation of Ch'an Ideology in China and Korea: The Vajrasamādhi-Sūtra*, *A Buddhist Apocryphon* (Princeton: Princeton University Press, 1989), 185–251.

37. Cf. McRae, *The Northern School*, 58–59.

38. McRae, *The Northern School*, 64–67.

39. For a discussion of Shenhui and his creation of Southern Chan, see McRae, *Seeing Through Zen*.

40. Cf. John McRae, "Shen-hui and the Teaching of Sudden Enlightenment in Early Ch'an Buddhism," in *Sudden and Gradual Approaches to Enlightenment in Chinese Thought*, ed. Peter N. Gregory, Kuroda Institute, Studies in East Asian Buddhism, 5 (Honolulu: University of Hawai'i Press, 1987), 227–78.

41. This is among other places evident in the *Jueguan lun* (*Treatise on the Cessation of Contemplation*). See Gishin Tokiwa, trans., *A Dialogue on the Contemplation-Extinguished, Translated from the Chüeh-kuan Lun, An Early Chinese Zen Text from Tun Huang* (Kyoto: The Institute for Zen Studies, 1973). See also the discussion in John McRae, "The Ox-head School of Chinese Ch'an Buddhism: From Early Ch'an to the Golden Age," in *Studies in Ch'an and Hua-yen*, ed. Robert M. Gimello and Peter N. Gregory, Kuroda Institute, Studies in East Asian Buddhism, 1 (Honolulu: University of Hawai'i Press, 1983), 211–17.

42. For a discussion of this rebellion and its impact see Denis C. Twitchett, ed., *The Cambridge History of China*, Volume 3, *Sui and T'ang China* (Cambridge: Cambridge University Press, 1979), 333–560.

43. See McRae, *Seeing Through Zen*, 101–18; and the classic article by Hu Shih, "Ch'an (Zen) Buddhism in China, Its History and Method," *Philosophy East and West* 3, no. 1 (1953): 3–24.

44. For recent studies on Mazu's Chan, see Mario Poceski, *Ordinary Mind as the Way: The Hongzhou School and the Growth of Chan Buddhism* (Oxford: Oxford Univer-

sity Press, 2007); and Jinhua Jia, *The Hongzhou School of Chan Buddhism in Eighth-Through Tenth-Century China* (Albany: State University of New York Press, 2006). A detailed treatment of the Baotang School and a translation of its key text can be found in Wendi L. Adamek, *The Mystique of Transmission: On an Early Chan History and Its Contexts* (New York: Columbia University Press, 2007).

4

THE *PLATFORM SŪTRA*
AS THE SUDDEN TEACHING

· · · · · · · · · ·

PETER N. GREGORY

The full title of the *Platform Sūtra* proclaims it as the sudden teaching. This chapter will try to unpack what that means by focusing on a close reading of the first two segments of the text: the story of the poetry contest for the mantle of the Sixth Patriarch related in the opening autobiographical portion (Yampolsky, secs. 2–11) and the core section of Huineng's sermon that follows (secs. 12–19). I will argue that the sudden teaching is both a teaching and a method. Its doctrinal content is the teaching of nondualism. As a method, it entails the rejection of all expedient means (*fangbian*; Skt.: *upāya*).

The *Platform Sūtra* must be understood as a skillfully crafted literary creation that proves that Huineng was the real Sixth Patriarch and attributes to him a teaching that in many ways must have been seen as new and radical by its intended audience. The dramatic story of the exchange of verses on the south corridor wall is surely the most famous episode in the *Platform Sūtra*. It is the pivotal event on which the transmission story turns, explaining how and why the patriarchate was passed on to Huineng and not Shenxiu, thereby sealing the triumph of the Southern line over the Northern line as the orthodox Chan tradition. Since the verses exemplify the sudden and gradual approaches to meditation practice, represented by Huineng and Shenxiu, this episode is also generally taken to be the locus classicus for the distinction between sudden and gradual in Chan.[1] The sermon lays out some of the most important and characteristic teachings of the *Platform Sūtra*, such as the oneness of concentration and wisdom, straightforward mind, no-thought, nonform, and nonabiding. Since these later came to define the sudden teaching as Chan orthodoxy, the sermon is especially critical for understanding the message of the text. My understanding of this portion of the text differs in important ways from that of Philip B. Yampolsky, so below I offer alternative translations of several sections.

Although Huineng is portrayed as an illiterate menial from a "barbarian" region in the south, his teaching as presented in the *Platform Sūtra* rests on a large body of Mahāyāna texts that comprised the common frame of reference for Chinese Buddhists in the eighth century. The basic doctrinal orientation of the *Platform Sūtra* is suggested by its identification of its teaching with the "perfection of wisdom" (*prajñāpāramitā*), which refers to a body of Mahāyāna Buddhist scriptures, a practice, and a teaching. These texts teach the perfection of wisdom, the final of the six perfections that must be cultivated by the bodhisattva on the path to buddhahood. The literature emphasizes wisdom above all the other perfections, stressing that when it is perfected, the other five are as well. Wisdom is therefore said to be the mother from which all buddhas are born. The particular kind of wisdom (*prajñā*) that is perfected consists of a thoroughgoing insight into the emptiness of all things.

The prominent place accorded the perfection of wisdom in the *Platform Sūtra* is signaled from the very beginning: it is mentioned in the full title of the text, it is invoked in the opening sentence, and it is contained in the first words spoken by Huineng: "Good friends, purify your minds and concentrate on the dharma of the great perfection of wisdom" (Yampolsky, 126). Huineng's sermon explains it at length (secs. 24–26), links it to the *Diamond Sūtra* (sec. 28)—a popular scripture expounding the perfection of wisdom—and emphasizes its practice (sec. 29).

Unlike texts of the so-called Northern Chan school or even the writings of Shenhui, which cite a relatively wide range of Mahāyāna Buddhist canonical sources, the *Platform Sūtra* only mentions a few scriptures. The *Vimalakīrti Sūtra* is quoted, paraphrased, or explicitly alluded to more than any other text. The *Diamond Sūtra* is mentioned four times, alluded to once, and quoted once. The *Laṅkāvatāra Sūtra* is implicitly alluded to twice (Yampolsky, 129, 130). The same passage from the *Brahma's Net Sūtra* (*Fanwang jing*) on the intrinsic purity of one's own nature is quoted two times (Yampolsky, 141, 151). The meaning of the *Lotus Sūtra* is discussed at length in section 42, where a point is made of Huineng's illiteracy. And four words are quoted from the *Sūtra on the Contemplation of Amitāyus* (Yampolsky, 156) in a discussion of the true location of the pure land. The paucity of references to other Buddhist texts is in keeping with the character of Huineng as portrayed in the *Platform Sūtra*. As a natural religious genius, he has an understanding based on direct insight into the original nature of his own mind rather than on written texts; this illustrates the claim that Chan teaching is founded on a direct transmission of mind rather than words and letters.

The importance of a direct insight into the original nature of the mind points to the centrality of another body of canonical texts— those associated with buddha nature (*foxing*), or the "storehouse of the thus-come" (*rulaizang*, Skt.: *tathāgata-garbha*) as it is known in more technical nomenclature. Although not explicitly mentioned, this literature provides the ontological substratum on which some of the cardinal teachings of the *Platform Sūtra* are based—such as "seeing the nature" (*jianxing*) and the innateness of wisdom. Especially important in this regard is the doctrine of original awakening (*benjue*) found in the *Treatise on the Awakening of Faith in the Mahāyāna* (*Dasheng qixin lun*, hereafter the *Awakening of Faith*).[2] The explicit emphasis on the perfection of wisdom thus needs to be counterbalanced by a recognition of the importance of the *tathāgata-garbha* doctrine. Indeed, the teachings of the *Platform Sūtra* represent a blending of the two doctrinal traditions. The *prajñāpāramitā* teachings provide the principle of the emptiness of the defilements (*fan-nao*, Skt.: *kleśa*, often translated as "afflictions" or "passions"), and the *tathāgata-garbha* tradition provides the ontological ground for awakening.

THE *DIAMOND SŪTRA* AND THE TRANSMISSION STORY

The displacement of the allegedly gradual teaching of Northern Chan by the sudden teaching of Southern Chan is symbolized in the *Platform Sūtra* by a shift away from the *Laṅkāvatāra Sūtra* toward the *Diamond Sūtra*. Of course, we need to remember that the "Northern Chan" depicted in the *Platform Sūtra* is a polemical construction. The positions attributed to Huineng's rivals in the text are intended to show his superiority and cannot be understood to accurately describe other Chan teachings.

The early Chan movement had identified itself with the *Laṅkāvatāra Sūtra*, which was believed to have been transmitted from Bodhidharma to his Chinese successor, Huike. It styled itself the Laṅka School because it claimed to be based on the transmission of the *Laṅkāvatāra Sūtra*, as reflected in the title of one of its genealogical histories, *Records of Masters and Disciples [in the Transmission] of the Laṅkāvatāra*.[3] The importance of the *Laṅkāvatāra Sūtra* in establishing a lineal connection with Bodhidharma far outweighs its role in defining the doctrinal orientation of Northern Chan teachings, although the text does contain *tathāgata-garbha* teachings and expounds the identity of *saṃsāra* and *nirvāṇa*. The *Records of Masters and Disciples [in the Transmission] of the Laṅkāvatāra* explicitly links Hongren's teaching, and his transmission of it to Shenxiu, with the *Laṅkāvatāra*.[4] In its overturning of Northern Chan claims to orthodoxy, the *Platform Sūtra* thus had to dissociate the patriarchal transmission from the *Laṅkāvatāra*. It did this by explicitly joining Hongren's teaching, and his transmission of it to Huineng, to the *Diamond Sūtra*, a text with no prior sectarian affiliation.

Despite aligning itself with the *Diamond Sūtra*, the *Platform Sūtra* only mentions that text in a clearly delimited set of circumstances: it is only invoked at critical junctures in the transmission story, and it is never cited in those passages where Huineng expounds his most distinctive teachings. Huineng's initial inspiration that sets him on the path to becoming the Sixth Patriarch occurs upon overhearing someone reciting the *Diamond Sūtra*. Learning that the Fifth Patriarch Hongren urges his disciples to uphold the text in order "to see into their own natures" and "to realize buddhahood" (cf. Yampolsky, 127), Huineng decides to set out for the Fifth Patriarch's monastery. Later, in a secret midnight meeting with the Fifth Patriarch, Huineng immediately understands the *Diamond Sūtra* upon hearing Hongren expound it. The Fifth Patriarch then transmits the sudden teaching and the patriarchal robe to him and recognizes Huineng as the Sixth Patriarch (Yampolsky, sec. 9). In the concluding sections of his sermon, Huineng twice mentions the *Diamond Sūtra* as integral to the sudden teaching he transmits, linking it, as did Hongren, with seeing the nature (Yampolsky, 149). He then alludes to his earlier experience of "great insight, in which he suddenly saw the original nature of true reality" (cf. Yampolsky, 151–52) upon hearing Hongren expound it. The *Diamond Sūtra* is thus associated with seeing own's own nature, the sudden teaching, and the patriarchal transmission.

The displacement of the *Laṅkāvatāra Sūtra* by the *Diamond Sūtra* is dramatically enacted in a telling detail skillfully included in the opening autobiographical section of the *Platform Sūtra*.[5] The episode takes place just after Hongren has charged his disciples with composing a verse expressing their understanding so that he can determine on whom to confer the mantle of Sixth Patriarch.

At that time there was a three-sectioned corridor in front of the Master's hall. On the walls were to be painted illustrations of the *Laṅka* together with a picture in commemoration of the five patriarchs transmitting the robe and dharma, in order to disseminate them to later generations and preserve a record of them. The artist, Lu Zhen, had examined the wall and was to start work the next day. (Cf. Yampolsky, 128–29.)

It is on this wall that Shenxiu anonymously writes his verse in the middle of the night in secret. The next day at dawn the Fifth Patriarch summons the artist to paint illustrations of the *Lanka*. Seeing Shenxiu's verse, however, he dismisses the painter, saying:

> I will give you thirty thousand cash. You have come a long distance to do this arduous work, but I have decided not to have the pictures painted after all. It is said in the *Diamond Sūtra*: "All forms everywhere are unreal and false."[6] It would be best to leave this verse here and to have the deluded ones recite it. If they practice in accordance with it they will not fall into the three woeful paths [of rebirth]. Those who practice by it will gain great benefit. (Cf. Yampolsky, 130.)

It is on this wall again that Huineng later has someone write his verse (Yampolsky, sec. 8). The south corridor wall in Hongren's monastery is thus not only the site where the contest over the patriarchate takes place but also where old conceptions about the Chan transmission lineage are literally overwritten by a new vision.

Although the *Platform Sūtra* identifies Hongren's teaching and his transmission of it to Huineng with the *Diamond Sūtra*, the preceding passage is the only one in the entire text in which the *Diamond Sūtra* is actually quoted. This is particularly significant given the symbolic nature of the episode: the words of the *Diamond Sūtra* about the unreality of forms (*xiang*) are quoted to dismiss the older representation of the lineage in order to create the space on which the new one that supplants it can be written. It is also significant that the *Diamond Sūtra* is not quoted elsewhere, suggesting that its importance for the *Platform Sūtra* is largely emblematic. Although the quotation resonates with the emphasis on formlessness (*wuxiang*) throughout the *Platform Sūtra*, this is a pervasive theme in many Mahāyāna sūtras within the perfection of wisdom corpus to which the *Diamond Sūtra* belongs. Aside from what is generic to the perfection of wisdom texts, there is little that is specific to the *Diamond Sūtra* that informs the doctrinal content of the *Platform Sūtra*. The identification of Northern Chan with the transmission of the *Laṅkāvatāra Sūtra* and Southern Chan with the transmission of the *Diamond Sūtra* thus tells us more about the way competing groups within Chan constructed their identity than it does about the content of any actual teachings.

THE *VIMALAKĪRTI SŪTRA* AND NONDUALITY

The scripture that had the biggest impact on the form and content of the *Platform Sūtra* is the *Vimalakīrti Sūtra*.[7] It is quoted or paraphrased more than any other text in the *Platform Sūtra*,[8] where its authority is invoked as part of a broad critique of all dualistic approaches to practice, often, but not always, attributed to Northern Chan. It is frequently cited at those very junctures in which the *Platform Sūtra* expounds some of its best-known teachings. In all cases, what is criticized is the deep-rooted tendency of humans to objectify a teaching or a practice. Any such objectification, where the teaching or the practice is taken as the object of understanding or practice, necessarily presupposes a separation between subject (e.g., a deluded, bound sentient being) and object (e.g., awakening, liberation) and is therefore dualistic.

The *Vimalakīrti Sūtra* and the *Platform Sūtra* thus both champion the teaching of nonduality. Since the truth is nondual, the *Vimalakīrti Sūtra* repeatedly emphasizes that the dharma can never be grasped as an object. It is therefore ultimately inexpressible and inconceivable. Of course, even to say that the dharma is inexpressible is to make a statement about it. Hence there can be no teaching in regard to such a dharma, as Vimalakīrti tells Maudgalyāyana in chapter 3 of the *Vimalakīrti Sūtra*.[9] Teaching the nature of nonduality thus requires special strategies. Vimalakīrti accordingly deploys a panoply of expedient means (*fangbian*; Skt.: *upāya*) to express the inexpressible.[10] Likewise, the text skillfully uses a dazzling array of literary devices to dramatize the philosophical points that its arguments demonstrate cannot be made discursively.

Any attempt to teach nonduality is therefore inherently paradoxical. The paradox involves a logical point about the meaning of nonduality and has important ramifications for the rhetorical strategies needed to teach a teaching that cannot be taught. Nondualism, of course, is defined in opposition to dualism, and its meaning can only be established in reference to dualism. That is, it requires dualism as the object of its negation. There is thus the further paradox that nondualism itself inevitably forms a duality with dualism. In the *Platform Sūtra*, it is this higher-order duality that is expressed in the distinction between "gradual" (*jian*) and "sudden" (*dun*), which stand for dual and nondual respectively. Whereas the *Vimalakīrti Sūtra* suggests ways this higher duality might be transcended, the *Platform Sūtra* tends to reify it by making the sudden teaching into an ideology.

The *Vimalakīrti Sūtra*, like the *Platform Sūtra*, is a polemical text. It engages in a pointed critique of Hīnayāna dualism, often focused on the figure of Śāriputra, one of the Buddha's most outstanding disciples, known as "the foremost of the wise," who becomes a foil against whom Vimalakīrti is able to display the superiority of Mahāyāna nondualism. The *Platform Sūtra*'s critique of Northern Chan gradualism parallels the *Vimalakīrti Sūtra*'s critique of Hīnayāna dualism. Northern Chan is thus the rhetorical equivalent of Hīnayāna. Moreover, just as Śāriputra is singled out for special criticism precisely because he stands above his peers, so too is Shenxiu, who in real life was a famous Chan master and here is depicted as the head monk at the Fifth Patriarch's monastery, looked up to by the other monks as their teacher. Vimalakīrti also provides a general model for Huineng. Both are laymen who demonstrate their superior understanding vis-à-vis conventional representations of monastic authority. In different ways, both also embody nondualism. The exemplary role that Vimalakīrti and Huineng play in their respective texts reveals that their representation is designed to serve a larger narrative and pedagogic purpose. The same can be said for Śāriputra and Shenxiu. Each in his own way embodies an ideal religious type rather than a historical reality. The *Platform Sūtra*'s critique of Northern Chan should thus be read as targeting a generic approach to meditation practice rather than as an account of actual early Chan practices.

A good example of the *Platform Sūtra*'s use of the *Vimalakīrti Sūtra* in its critique of Northern Chan practice can be seen in Huineng's sermon on "the samādhi of the practice of oneness" (*yixing sanmei*, Yampolsky, sec. 14), which invokes the scripture three times. The passage uses the *Vimalakīrti Sūtra* to redefine seated meditation, as part of its critique of the dualistic (i.e., gradualistic) approach to meditation practice attributed to Northern Chan. In particular, it uses the *Vimalakīrti Sūtra* to redefine the *samādhi* of the practice of oneness, which in Chan circles in the eighth century had come to be understood to refer to seated meditation, as an attitude of mind ("straightforward mind," *zhixin*) rather than a physical activity.[11] As Huineng says: "The *samādhi* of the practice of oneness is the constant practice of straightforward mind in all circumstances, whether walking, standing, sitting, or lying" (cf. Yampolsky, 136). The word translated as "straightforward" (*zhi*) means "direct" or "unmediated," and as such it represents the "sudden" approach to practice. It is taken from the *Vimalakīrti Sūtra*, as the *Platform Sūtra* makes clear: "The *Vimalakīrti Sūtra* says: 'Straightforward mind is the place where the Way is realized. Straightforward mind is the pure land'" (cf. Yampolsky, 136).[12] This reinterpretation of the *samādhi* of the practice of oneness is part of the strategy seen throughout both the *Vimalakīrti Sūtra* and the *Platform Sūtra* to define the meaning of a particular practice in terms of an attitude of mind rather than a specific activity—such practice is therefore formless. "The place where the Way is realized" (*daochang*) translates the Sanskrit term *bodhimaṇḍa*, which literally refers to the place where the Buddha attained enlightenment or, more broadly, any place where enlightenment ("the Way") can be realized. The *Vimalakīrti Sūtra* quote thus shifts the reference from a place (or a place where specific practices are to be carried out) to a state of mind. The pure land is likewise redefined—it is no longer a place where one aspires to be reborn but a state that can be immediately realized in one's mind. These two quotes exemplify the governing hermeneutical strategy repeated throughout the *Vimalakīrti Sūtra* and adopted by the *Platform Sūtra*—that is, to shift the reference away from any practice that has specific attributes ("form," *xiang*) to a state that is empty of all characteristics and is therefore formless (*wuxiang*). This entails the rejection of all externalized approaches to practice.

This hermeneutic strategy thus moves the practice of seated meditation into an utterly formless realm of discourse, where it can no longer be defined by any specific mental or physical activity, and is part of the critique of the Northern Chan approach in the remainder of the passage. In the *Records of Masters and Disciples [in the Transmission] of the Laṅkāvatāra*, both Daoxin and Shenxiu identify this *samādhi* as a core teaching of Northern Chan.[13] The mention of the *samādhi* of the practice of oneness thus signals that the *Platform Sūtra* passage is targeting the Northern Chan interpretation of meditation. This point is substantiated in the rest of the passage, which lists a stock set of practices that had come to be associated with Northern Chan: sitting without moving (*zuo budong*), getting rid of falsehood (*chuwang*), and not giving rise to thoughts (*buqixin*). The *Platform Sūtra* then introduces its own position of not abiding (*buzhu*), elaborated more fully below (Yampolsky, sec. 17), where it is linked with and used to explain the core teaching of no-thought (*wunian*).

The passage concludes by once more citing the example of Vimalakīrti: "If sitting without moving were good, Vimalakīrti should not have upbraided Śāriputra for sitting in meditation in the forest" (cf. Yampolsky, 137). This episode is one of the most famous in the *Vimalakīrti Sūtra* and would have been well known to the readership of the *Platform Sūtra*. One day when Vimalakīrti comes across Śāriputra seated under a tree absorbed in meditation, he upbraids him, telling him that meditation does not necessarily entail sitting.[14] Vimalakīrti then makes six points to explain how one should practice meditation. The doctrinal details of these points need not detain us here. What is important to note is that each involves doing something that appears to be a contradiction in terms and by conventional standards is clearly impossible. What they all have in common is that the very way a bodhisattva manifests himself in the world embodies nondualism. The main point of Vimalakīrti's homily to Śāriputra could be summed up by saying that the bodhisattva neither abides in the world of bondage (saṃsāra) nor abides in the world of liberation (nirvāṇa). Similarly, in the language of the *Platform Sūtra*, the Chan practitioner's meditation is not defined by the physical activity of sitting but is expressed in the formless practice of no-thought, in which he does not think while in the midst of thoughts.

The *Platform Sūtra* and the *Vimalakīrti Sūtra* thus share the basic standpoint of nonduality and deploy similar rhetorical strategies to teach it. Nevertheless, there is a crucial difference in the way that the texts use and valorize expedient means. The *Vimalakīrti Sūtra* celebrates expedient means as the supreme expression of the wisdom and compassion of the bodhisattva working in unison to liberate all sentient beings. All teachings—including that of nonduality—are part of the limitless panoply of expedients used by the bodhisattva in his liberative activity in the world. The "truth" of a teaching thus lies not in the profundity of its doctrinal content or the cogency of its philosophical formulation, but in its effectiveness in freeing beings from the particular attachments by which they are bound. Its effectiveness is always determined by whether it is appropriate to the particular circumstances at hand.

The *Platform Sūtra*, however, uses expedient means in a very different way, as the primary criterion by which the distinction between the gradual and sudden positions is drawn. The gradual teaching or approach uses expedients, and the sudden teaching does not. Gradual teachings are dualistic precisely because they employ an instrumental approach to practice, in which a teaching or practice is used as a means to realize a goal. By contrast, the sudden teaching is nondual precisely because it discards all means and directly addresses the ultimate nature of reality without any mediation. The label of "gradual" thus marks the Northern approach to Chan practice as inferior to the "sudden" approach championed in the *Platform Sūtra*. In the end, nondualism—as exemplified by the sudden teaching—becomes an ideological position with which the *Platform Sūtra* identifies itself.

THE POETRY CONTEST AND THE SUDDEN TEACHING

Since the story of the exchange of verses on the south corridor wall is generally taken to be the locus classicus for understanding the sudden and gradual approaches to meditation practice represented by Huineng and Shenxiu, it is a good place to begin to examine in more detail how the sudden teaching is understood in the *Platform Sūtra*.

Before analyzing the content of the verses, it is instructive to compare them structurally. Curiously, the Dunhuang text of the *Platform Sūtra* gives two verses by Huineng, indicating that at the time it was compiled in the late eighth century, there were two different versions of Huineng's verse in circulation. This awkward fact is remedied in later versions of the text, which delete Huineng's second verse. In later versions, the third line of his first verse also gets changed to read: "From the beginning there is not a single thing." Here are the poems presented in the Dunhuang text (cf. Yampolsky, 130 and 132):

SHENXIU'S VERSE	HUINENG'S FIRST VERSE	HUINENG'S SECOND VERSE
The body is the bodhi tree;	From the beginning *bodhi* has no tree;	The mind is the bodhi tree;
The mind is like a luminous mirror (stand).	The luminous mirror also has no stand.	The body is like a luminous mirror's stand.
Constantly strive to keep it polished and pure.	Buddha nature is always pure.	From the beginning the luminous mirror is clear.
And never let dust collect.	Where could dust settle?	Where could it be stained by dust?

The first thing that is apparent, and also clear from the narrative context, is that Huineng's verse is a comment on Shenxiu's and cannot stand on its own, just as the position of nondualism can only be established in reference to dualism. The two versions of Huineng's verse either negate or invert the terms of comparison in the first two lines of Shenxiu's verse. The bodhi tree is the tree under which the Buddha sat when he attained enlightenment (*bodhi*). The translation of the second line of Shenxiu's verse has been deliberately hedged to clarify Huineng's response in the first version of his verse. The function of *tai* (stand), the fifth and last word in this line in Shenxiu's verse, is not entirely clear, but it seems the compound of *jing* (mirror) and *tai* simply means "mirror" here. (The *tai* is also needed for the rhyme.) Even though the meaning of the verse clearly hinges on the metaphor of the mind as mirror (hence "stand" appears in parentheses), Huineng's response treats "tree" and "stand" in the same way, giving "stand" a weight that it does not seem to have had in Shenxiu's poem. In the comparison on which the meaning of the verse rests, it is the mirror (as opposed to its "stand") that must be polished to keep its reflective surface bright.[15]

Huineng's first verse further suggests that both enlightenment and the luminosity of the mind ultimately have nothing on which they depend for their existence—they exist in and of themselves. Here it is important to note that Huineng uses the term *ben* (literally "root," translated here as "from the beginning"; in Yampolsky's translation, "originally") in the first line, indicating that he is speaking from the ultimate or ontological perspective. That which is *ben* exists from the beginning and therefore does not depend on anything. The clear implication, then, is that neither enlightenment (*bodhi*) nor the luminosity of the mind depends on practice to be realized—they are already fully present. For ease of reference, we could refer to this position as the doctrine of innateness.

Huineng's second verse inverts the comparison that Shenxiu makes in the first two lines. Whereas Shenxiu identifies the body with the bodhi tree and likens the mind to a luminous mirror, Huineng identifies the mind with the bodhi tree and likens the body to a luminous mirror's stand. Huineng's inversion of the terms of Shenxiu's comparison makes sense for the first two lines, but the comparison of the body with a luminous mirror's stand becomes strained in the third line, since now both the luminous mirror and the bodhi tree are references to the mind or buddha nature.

In the last two lines, Shenxiu's verse implies the need for constant effort to keep the mirror of the mind free from dust, whereas Huineng's verse emphasizes the intrinsic purity of the buddha nature (or the luminous mirror)—thus it concludes with the rhetorical question: "Where could the dust settle?" The third and fourth lines also make clear that the doctrinal meaning of the verse hinges on the interpretation of buddha nature (*foxing*) and the nature of the defilements (*fannao*, Skt.: *kleśa*) that cover it, like the dust on the metaphorical mirror.

The *tathāgata-garbha* is often defined as the dharma body (*fashen*; Skt.: *dharmakāya*) covered over by defilements. Although scholastic literature distinguishes 108 kinds of defilements, in the simplest formulations they refer to the three poisons of greed (Skt.: *rāga*), anger (Skt.: *dveśa*), and confusion (Skt.: *moha*). The *Platform Sūtra* uses "defilements" in conjunction or interchangeably with *chenlao*, translated here as "afflictions." The first character in the latter binome is "dust" (*chen*), reminding us that the defilements are often described as "adventitious defilements" (*kechen fannao*; Skt.: *āgantukakleśa*)—meaning that they are extrinsic to the mind. Defilements come from without, like the dust that settles on the surface of the mirror, but the nature of the mind is originally pure.

Whereas Shenxiu's verse as presented in the *Platform Sūtra* may be said to represent buddha nature covered over by defilements, Huineng's asserts that buddha nature is empty of defilements. Shenxiu's accordingly emphasizes the constant effort needed to purify the mind, while Huineng's holds that no effort is needed because from the beginning there is nothing to purify, since the mind is originally pure and the defilements that appear to cover it are merely illusory.

The attitude of the *Platform Sūtra* toward the defilements thus melds the perspectives of *tathāgata-garbha* and perfection of wisdom. Whereas *tathāta-garbha* theory holds that buddha nature is empty of defilements (which are adventitious), perfection of wisdom texts maintain that the defilements themselves are empty—they are said to be "unreal" (*xu*) and "false" (*wang*) (Yampolsky, 144). That is, they have no inherent reality of their own but are merely illusory creations of deluded thought. Regarding them as something to be removed gives them seeming substance by objectifying them. Any attempt to remove the defilements is therefore counterproductive because it imputes to them an objective reality that they lack and only increases the delusory activity of the mind, which is precisely what the defilements consist in. To see the nature is to see the original purity of the mind, which itself entails seeing through the illusory character of the defilements—the presumption being that an illusion is dispelled as soon as it is seen as illusory.

Tathāta-garbha theory further holds that buddha nature is also not empty (*bukong*; Skt.: *aśūnya*) of all the supernal qualities of buddhahood. For the *Platform Sūtra*, this "not empty" aspect is reflected in the importance of the doctrine of the innateness of wisdom, which more generally reflects the theory of original awakening developed in the *Awakening of Faith*. This position is stated clearly at the very beginning of Huineng's sermon: "The wisdom of *bodhi* [enlightenment] and *prajñā* [wisdom] are from the outset [*ben*] naturally possessed by people of the world. It is only because their minds are deluded that they cannot realize it for themselves" (cf. Yampolsky, 135).[16]

Even though Shenxiu's verse could be interpreted in more favorable ways, the narrative context compels us to read it critically, clearly marking his verse as inferior and Huineng's as superior. Here it is particularly important to note Hongren's comments. As he remarks upon first seeing Shenxiu's verse, if those who are deluded "practice in accordance with it, they will not fall into the three woeful paths of rebirth" and "will gain great benefit." He then calls his disciples together and tells them, "you should all recite this verse so that you will be able to see into your own natures. With this practice you will not fall into the three woeful paths of rebirth" (cf. Yampolsky, 130). Later, in the privacy of his quarters, Hongren tells Shenxiu:

This verse you wrote shows that you still have not reached true understanding. You have merely arrived at the front of the gate but have yet to be able to enter it. If common people practice according to your verse they will not fall [into woeful paths of rebirth]. But in seeking enlightenment [*bodhi*] one will not succeed with such an understanding. You must enter the gate and see your own original nature. Go and think about it for a day or two and then make another verse and present it to me. If you have been able to enter the gate and see your own original nature, then I will give you the robe and the dharma. (Cf. Yampolsky, 131.)

Shenxiu's initial pondering and doubt, and his later inability to compose a verse that displays deeper insight, are in marked contrast to Huineng, who spontaneously dictates his verse on the spot immediately after Shenxiu's verse is read to him. The contrasting manner in which the verses are composed reflects the difference between the gradual and the sudden approaches exemplified by their authors. Whereas Shenxiu's poem is produced through an inner deliberative struggle, Huineng's is a natural and spontaneous expression of his innate wisdom. One is mediated through a complex set of psychological and cognitive processes; the other is not.

This story also tells us that the understanding expressed in Shenxiu's verse is not utterly mistaken; it is just incomplete. It is appropriate for those who are still deluded. They will not go wrong if they practice according to it. In fact, it is meritorious and will prevent them from falling into the three woeful paths of rebirth (i.e., the realms of hell, hungry ghosts, and animals). It will never lead to liberation, however, because it does not express the cardinal point (*dayi*). No matter how meritorious or beneficial, all such activities still produce karma and therefore keep beings bound to the wheel of rebirth. Although the Fifth Patriarch's remarks thus seem to leave some slight opening for gradualism, they make it abundantly clear that such gradual practices are decidedly inferior and only suited for those of lower spiritual capacity. The verses by Shenxiu and Huineng thus express an understanding of practice and enlightenment seen from two seemingly incommensurate perspectives: of those who have not yet seen the original nature of their mind and of those who have.

What, then, is it about these verses that makes them "gradual" and "sudden"?

We can begin to answer this question by observing that in the *Platform Sūtra* the two terms are preponderantly used as adjectives, occasionally as adverbs, but only rarely, if ever as nouns. The question, then, is: "sudden" or "gradual" what? A simple inventory of how the term for "sudden" is used yields some surprising insights. It is used a total of twenty-five times in the Dunhuang edition of the *Platform Sūtra*, and fifteen of those times it explicitly refers to a teaching ("sudden teaching," *dunjiao* = 4; "sudden dharma," *dunfa* = 4; "dharma of the sudden teaching," *dunjiaofa* = 5; "sudden dharma gate," *dunfamen* = 2); it is used four times in conjunction with gradual (*dunjian*), where the point of reference is the dharma, which lacks "suddenness" or "gradualness" in contradistinction to human beings, whose capacities can be "sharp" or "dull" (Yampolsky, 137, 163) or whose seeing can be "fast" or "slow" (163); and it is used twice to refer to practice (*dunxiu*) (Yampolsky, 137, 164), where "sudden" means nondual or unmediated. It is used twice to refer to seeing (*dunjian*), and, surprisingly, it is used only twice to refer to what is often, but somewhat misleadingly, translated as "enlightenment" (*dunwu*).

This inventory reveals that the primary reference of "sudden" is to a teaching—or what we could more generally style as an approach—rather than to "enlightenment." In fact, it would be more appropriate to see so-called "sudden enlightenment" as a corollary to the sudden teaching, practice, or approach. We should not forget that the full title of the *Platform Sūtra* begins with the words "The Sūtra of the Perfection of Wisdom of the Supreme Vehicle of the *Sudden Teaching* of the Southern Tradition." Clearly the verses of Shenxiu and Huineng have to do primarily with gradual and sudden approaches to practice, not with gradual and sudden "enlightenment."

This point deserves highlighting because the main message of the text has often been said to be Huineng's teaching of "sudden enlightenment." This characterization is misleading on two counts. First, it distorts the primary point of reference of the term "sudden." Second, the English word "enlightenment" is problematic as a translation of the Chinese word *wu* (*satoru* in Japanese). Where "sudden" is used to modify *wu* or "seeing" (*jian*), it functions as an adverb, and *wu* and "seeing" are both verbs. Indeed, *wu* is the cognitive correlate to the perceptual act of seeing. Like "seeing," *wu* is often used as a transitive verb with an object, and its most fundamental meaning is "to awaken (to)." "Enlightenment," however, refers to a state or condition and cannot be easily bent into use in English as a transitive verb. *Wu*, by contrast, denotes a certain kind of cognitive act that might best be translated as "to realize" or "to understand," as when one realizes, understands, or "gets" the point of something; there is a shift in perspective in which what was formerly unclear suddenly becomes clear. But what is realized or understood is not predetermined and can range from the point of a story or the meaning of a scriptural passage to the ultimate nature of reality. It is the mode in which that realizing or seeing takes place—directly, immediately, or nondiscursively—that is "sudden." It is not mediated by any other process (such as thinking, reasoning, deliberation, etc.). The term that is most aptly translated as "enlightenment" in the *Platform Sūtra* is *puti* (the Chinese pronunciation of the Sanskrit word for wisdom, *bodhi*), which is always used as a noun.

"Suddenly realizing" and "suddenly seeing" are interchangeable, suggesting further that *dunwu* is often synonymous with "seeing the nature," "seeing one's own nature," or "seeing one's own original nature." In doctrinal terms, the nature, of course, is buddha nature, the original nature of the mind that is from the beginning intrinsically pure. Seeing buddha nature, moreover, is the realization that one has always been fully endowed with the wisdom of the Buddha and that there is fundamentally no difference whatsoever between oneself and the Buddha. As expressed in the *Platform Sūtra*, it is realizing that the wisdom of *prajñā* has always been present. There is no way to attain what one already has, hence all means must be discarded. As long as wisdom is objectified as something to attain, it can never be attained—in fact, such objectification is precisely the problem.

THE CORE TEACHINGS IN HUINENG'S SERMON

The core section of Huineng's sermon (Yampolsky, secs. 12–19) contains some of the signature teachings of the *Platform Sūtra* that came to define the sudden teaching as the orthodox position of the Chan tradition. The sermon can also be read as offering an interpretation of the verses, and it is therefore a good place to continue our discussion of the sudden/gradual polarity. The criticisms of meditation practices associated with Northern Chan (such as viewing the mind, viewing purity, sitting without moving, and not giving rise to thoughts) help clarify wherein Shenxiu's verse represents a gradual approach as well as how the use or rejection of expedient means functions as the criterion defining the difference between the gradual and sudden approaches. Expedient means, as already noted, is based on a means-end model. Any practice that would take meditation as a means to an end (enlightenment) is ipso facto gradualist. The cultivation of meditation (Skt.: *dhyāna*) or meditative concentration (Skt.: *samādhi,* as in "the *samādhi* of the practice of oneness," below referred to as "concentration") as a means to awakening wisdom (*prajñā*) would be a prime example.

Huineng, by contrast, stresses the oneness of meditative concentration and wisdom:

> Good friends, this teaching of mine takes [meditative] concentration [*ding*; Skt.: *samādhi*] and wisdom [*hui*; Skt.: *prajñā*] as its basis [*ben*]. Above all never deludedly say that concentration and wisdom are separate. Concentration and wisdom in essence are one, not two. Concentration itself is the essence [*ti*] of wisdom,

and wisdom itself is the functioning [*yong*] of concentration. As soon as there is wisdom, concentration exists within wisdom, and as soon as there is concentration, wisdom exists within concentration. Good friends, this means that concentration and wisdom are concurrent [*deng*]. (Cf. Yampolsky, 135, who translates *ding* as "meditation.")

Neither concentration nor wisdom is defined in this passage. Elsewhere (Yampolsky, 140), concentration is defined as not being distracted internally, which is related to being free from form externally. As the chapter in this volume by Brook Ziporyn explains in greater detail, "essence" (*ti*) implies that concentration is a state, whereas "function" (*yong*) implies that wisdom is an activity. The passage might best be understood here to connote seeing one's own nature or realizing true reality; it does not refer to the knowledge that forms the content of wisdom.

Huineng continues, using the analogy of a lamp and its light to illustrate the oneness of concentration and wisdom. The analogy presumes that the lamp is lit, likening concentration to the lamp and wisdom to its light:

Good friends, how are concentration and wisdom concurrent? It is like a lamp and its light. [Only] when there is a lamp, is there light; without a lamp there is no light. The lamp is the essence [*ti*] of the light, and the light is the functioning [*yong*] of the lamp. Although they have two names, in essence they are not two. (Cf. Yampolsky, 137.)

Both of these passages use the polarity of essence and function to explain the relationship of concentration and wisdom. This polarity expresses their inseparability and mutuality: they are different aspects of each other. Since they are contained within each other, they are said to be "concurrent" (*deng*)—that is, they exist simultaneously, one does not precede or follow the other. The oneness of concentration and wisdom is the sudden practice because it does not treat concentration as a means to achieving wisdom. To do so necessarily involves a dualistic understanding of the dharma and is therefore gradualistic; it also locates liberation or enlightenment as something to be realized in the future and thereby fails to recognize that it is already fully present. As Huineng states,

> Students of the Way, be careful not to say that wisdom issues from concentration, or that concentration issues from wisdom, or that concentration and wisdom are different from one another. For those who hold this view, the dharma has a dual character. (Cf. Yampolsky, 135.)

Huineng's sermon continues, expressing sudden practice in terms of straightforward mind and the *samādhi* of the practice of oneness:

> Only practicing straightforward mind without clinging to anything at all is called the *samādhi* of the practice of oneness. The deluded person, attached to the characteristics of things, clings to the *samādhi* of the practice of oneness, and just says that sitting without moving, getting rid of falsehood, and not giving rise to thoughts is the *samādhi* of the practice of oneness. This kind of practice is the same as insentiency and the cause for obstructing the Way. The Way should flow freely; how could it be obstructed? If the mind does not abide [*buzhu*] in things, the Way flows freely. (Cf. Yampolsky, 136.)

This passage makes several points worth noting. The sudden practice is the practice that does not cling to anything at all. Nor can it be objectified. The criticism that practices such as sitting without moving, getting rid of falsehood, and not giving rise to thoughts lead to a blocking out of conscious awareness (insentiency) is particularly important. If conscious awareness (sentiency) is cut off, there can be no seeing one's own nature or realizing (*wu*) true reality—a point that provides a key for understanding the explanation of no-thought (*wunian*). It makes clear that no-thought does not mean a blanking of the mind. The mention of the Way (*dao*) provides another important key for understanding ideas elaborated later in the sermon. "Clinging" (*zhizhu*) or "abiding" (*zhu*) in things obstructs the Way and, as we shall see, is what is meant by bondage. No-thought is like the Way: it flows freely and does not abide in anything.

This passage adds viewing the mind (*kanxin*) and viewing purity (*kanjing*) to the list of mistaken practices. Huineng soon proceeds to explain the error of these two practices:

Good friends, in this teaching seated meditation, from the beginning, is not attached to the mind nor is it attached to purity, nor do we talk about immobility. If viewing the mind is spoken of, the mind [in question] is of itself delusory, and as delusions are like magical illusions, there is nothing [real] to be seen. If viewing purity is spoken of, human nature is originally pure, and it is only because of deluded thoughts that true reality is covered over. Being free from deluded thoughts, your original nature is pure. If you activate your mind to view purity without realizing that your original nature is itself pure, then you only produce delusions of purity. Since such delusions are without basis, you should realize that [the activity of] viewing is only a delusion. Purity has no form or shape, yet [some people] postulate the form of purity and say that is what we should direct our efforts toward. People who hold this view obscure their own original nature and are bound by purity. . . . Viewing the mind and viewing purity are only causes for the obstruction of the Way. (Cf. Yampolsky, 139–40.)

Both viewing the mind and viewing purity are dualistic in that they posit something as an object of contemplation. The criticism of viewing purity, in particular, can be taken as an elucidation of Huineng's verse. Because one's original nature is pure, activating one's mind to view it entails taking purity as an object to be viewed, and such objectification posits purity as something outside of oneself. But such objectification is delusory (*wang*), and it is precisely such deluded thoughts that cover the original purity of the mind so that it cannot be seen. The most important ideas for which the *Platform Sūtra* is known are elaborated in section 17. Huineng begins by stating the centrality of the three key interrelated doctrines of no-thought (*wunian*), nonform (*wuxiang*), and nonabiding (*wuzhu*), followed by brief definitions of each:

> Good friends, in this teaching of mine, from ancient times up to the present, all have established no-thought as the cardinal principle [*zong*], nonform as the essence [*ti*], and nonabiding as the basis [*ben*]. Nonform is to be free from form while in the midst of form. No-thought is not to think in regard to thoughts. Nonabiding is the original nature of human beings. (Cf. Yampolsky, 137–38.)

Huineng then explains each of these doctrines in turn, beginning (in reverse order) with nonabiding:

> Thoughts follow each other but do not abide; past, present, and future thoughts follow one after the other without interruption. If a single moment of thought were interrupted, the dharma body would become detached from the physical body. As thoughts follow each other they do not abide in anything. If a single moment of thought abides [in something], then successive thoughts will abide—that is what is meant by bondage. If successive thoughts follow one another without abiding in anything, then you will be free from bonds. Therefore nonabiding is the basis. (Cf. Yampolsky, 138.)

Earlier Huineng associated nonabiding with the Way, which implies that it is part of the natural order of things. The uninterrupted flow of thoughts from moment to moment is the natural functioning of the original nature. Hence nonabiding is defined as the original nature of human beings. The natural flow of thought is interrupted when the mind abides in things, which here is said to cause a separation of the dharma body and the physical body. This is tantamount to separating oneself from one's own nature, as later in the sermon Huineng identifies one's own nature with the dharma body. He also enjoins the assembly to take refuge in the dharma body of the Buddha in their own physical bodies. Even though everyone possesses the dharma body within their own nature, the deluded do not see it and seek it outside instead. The association of nonabiding with the Way implies that liberation is the natural state of human beings. Hence it is said to be *ben* ("the basis"), a term that in other contexts is rendered as "original" (as in "original nature"). *Ben* thus relates nonabiding to the ontological basis of the teaching of the *Platform Sūtra*.

Huineng continues with the discussion of nonform: "Good friends, externally to be free from all forms is [what is meant by] nonform. Only by being free from form is the essence of the nature pure. Therefore nonform is the essence" (cf. Yampolsky, 138). We have already noted the emphasis placed on formlessness (*wuxiang*) throughout the *Platform Sūtra*. Here "form" (*xiang*) refers to the characteristics by which something can be known or discerned. It thus implies objectification. As the external characteristics of things, form (*xiang*) is often contrasted with "nature" (*xing*), which refers to what is intrinsic (*ben*). In the context of this passage, nonform can be treated as synonymous with no-thought, as implied in its definition earlier ("non-form is to be free from form while in the midst of form," Yampolsky, 138).

Before discussing the lengthy explanation of no-thought that follows, it might be useful to recall the definition given in the beginning of this section: "No-thought is not to think in regard to thoughts." To make sense of this definition and the explanation that ensues, it is helpful to note that the word translated as "thought" (*nian*) is being used in two different senses. In its primary sense, "thought" (T_1) refers to the entire spectrum of mental activity, which includes everything that we see, hear, perceive, and are aware of. This is the thought that continues without interruption from moment to moment without abiding. In its secondary sense, "thought" (T_2) refers to the mental act of interrupting the natural flow of thoughts and taking one of those moments of thought as an object, as when we "think on" or "dwell on" something. Hence the definition of no-thought could be glossed: "No-thought means not to think (T_2) in the midst of thoughts (T_1)."

We are now ready to look at the explanation of no-thought. Huineng states:

> Not being stained by any external objects is [what is] referred to as no-thought. If you remain free from objects in your thought, you will not give rise to thoughts about anything. But do not stop thinking about everything and cast aside all thoughts. If a single moment of thought is cut off, you will die and be reborn somewhere else. (Cf. Yampolsky, 138.)

"External objects" (*jing*) is interchangeable with "form" (*xiang*) as used in the definition of nonform quoted above. "Not giving rise to thoughts about anything" is equivalent to not abiding in thoughts. The passage emphasizes, however, that no-thought does not mean casting aside all thoughts. Whatever the precise meaning of dying and being reborn somewhere else is, the context makes clear that it is not good. It suggests that if a single moment of thought is cut off, one will only continue the process of rebirth, which is the state of bondage (saṃsāra). No-thought, by contrast, is the state of liberation. Huineng continues:

> Students of the Way, take heed. You must understand the intent of the dharma. If you let yourself be in error, you will encourage delusion in others. If you do not yourself recognize your delusion, you will slander the teachings of the sūtras. Therefore I have established no-thought as the cardinal principle. Because deluded

people have thoughts in regard to external objects, false views arise from these thoughts, and all the afflictions and deluded thoughts accordingly are produced. Thus this teaching establishes no-thought as its cardinal principle. (Cf. Yampolsky, 138–39.)

Here no-thought is identified with the intent of the dharma (*fayi*) and is said to be established as the cardinal principle (*zong*) to serve as an antidote to mistaken views and their harmful effects. The passage clarifies that thoughts in regard to external objects give rise to false views, which produce afflictions and delusions. Huineng thus enjoins the assembly: "Men of the world, free yourself from views and don't give rise to thoughts."

The section concludes with the following explanation, which reveals the underlying ontological premise on which the teaching of no-thought is based:

> If there were no thoughts, then no-thought could not be established. The "no" is the "no" of what? "Thought" is ["the thought"] of what? "No" means to be free from the dualism [that produces] the afflictions. True reality is the essence [*ti*] of thought, and thought is the functioning [*yong*] of true reality. One's own nature gives rise to thoughts. Even though you see, hear, perceive, and are aware, if you are not stained by the myriad external objects, you will always remain free. The *Vimalakīrti Sūtra* says: "While externally clearly distinguishing the characteristics of things, internally he does not move away from the first principle." (Cf. Yampolsky, 139.)

The use of the essence/function paradigm in this passage is especially important. It clarifies the reason that the practice of no-thought does not entail the extinguishing of thoughts. The teaching of no-thought could not be established and the practice of no-thought could not be carried out if there were no thoughts. It is not just the logical point that nondualism can only be established in reference to dualism that is being made here. The passage also makes an ontological point that grounds thought in the ultimate nature of reality: true reality (*zhenru*) is said to be the essence of thought, and thought is said to be the functioning of true reality. This means that, if the sudden practice is about directly realizing true reality, true reality could never be realized if there were no thoughts. Since thoughts arise from one's own nature, cutting them off cuts off access to seeing one's own nature. Seeing thoughts as the functioning of true reality, moreover, entails the realization that they have no inherent reality of their own. Objectification, in contrast, is precisely the dualistic mode of consciousness that does not realize that thoughts are a manifestation of true reality.

We have seen that the essence/function paradigm was used earlier to emphasize that meditative concentration and wisdom are different aspects of each other. The same point could be said to apply here in the case of true reality and thought. Just as wisdom is the functioning of concentration, so thought is the functioning of true reality. By extension, we could say that without thought, there could be no wisdom.

The "no" in no-thought is glossed as the absence of dualism. "No" thus implies the nondual mode of the practice of no-thought, thematically resonating with the oneness of concentration and wisdom or straightforward mind. Hence no-thought is both a practice—albeit a formless one—and a characterization of the nature of true reality.

It is significant that the passage ends by quoting the *Vimalakīrti Sūtra*.[17] In terms of no-thought, "externally clearly distinguishing the characteristics of things" would correspond to being in the midst of objects (that is, not blocking them out of conscious awareness), while "internally not moving away from the first principle" would correspond to not being stained by objects (i.e., not abiding in thoughts).

Our earlier discussion of Vimalakīrti's homily to Śāriputra on the proper practice of meditation noted that the different points made by Vimalakīrti could be summed up by saying that the bodhisattva neither abides in the world of bondage nor abides in the world of liberation, and that that paralleled the Chan practitioner's practice of no-thought. Phrased in the language of the Platform Sūtra, we could say that no-thought involves neither abiding in thought (saṃsāra) nor eliminating thought (nirvāṇa). Here the last point made by Vimalakīrti might be singled out for further comment: the proper practice of meditation involves entering nirvāṇa without cutting off the defilements. In chapter 8, Vimalakīrti tells Mañjuśrī that all of the defilements constitute the seed of buddhahood. Just as the pure lotus flower can only grow in mud, so it is only within the mud of the defilements that sentient beings can give rise to the qualities of buddhahood. Likewise, in terms of the Platform Sūtra, we could say that it is only in the midst of thought that true reality can be realized. Here we must note Huineng's later statements: "The very defilements themselves are enlightenment," and "Don't drive away delusions; they themselves are the nature of true reality" (cf. Yampolsky, 148, 149).

The closing statement of Huineng's sermon (Yampolsky, sec. 31) ties together some of the key ideas in the core sections. It suggests how seeing one's original nature, which is the original nature of true reality, bridges the two aspects of no-thought. Understanding the teaching (fa) of no-thought makes its practice (xing) possible. The closing statement also equates no-thought with the sudden teaching. "If you recognize your original mind, then that is liberation. Once you have attained liberation, then that is prajñā-samādhi [bore sanmei]. When you have realized prajñā-samādhi, then that is no-thought" (cf. Yampolsky, 153).

This passage establishes a series of equivalents. Recognizing one's original mind (i.e., seeing one's original nature) is liberation. Liberation is the opposite of bondage, defined earlier as abiding in thoughts. Allowing the flow of successive thoughts (T_1) to follow one another without abiding in anything was thus said to be being free from bonds. Recognizing one's original mind thus enables one to be free from the bondage of objectifying thought (T_2). This recognition is equated with prajñā-samādhi, which, read as a single term, suggests the oneness of concentration (*samādhi*) and wisdom (*prajñā*) discussed earlier. *Prajñā-samādhi*, as the nonduality of concentration and wisdom (i.e., where one is not taken as a means to the other), is thus equated with no-thought.

The passage continues, amplifying the definition of no-thought given in the core sections. This passage seems to acknowledge the two uses of no-thought as a teaching (*fa*) and as a practice (*xing*). It again connects the practice of no-thought with *prajñā-samādhi*.

> What is no-thought? The teaching [*fa*] of no-thought means that while you see all things [also *fa*], you are not attached to anything, and while you are involved in all situations, you are not attached to any situation, and, always keeping your own nature pure, you cause the six thieves [i.e., the six sense consciousnesses] to exit through the six gates [i.e., the six sense organs]. Even though you are in the midst of the six dusts [i.e., the six types of sense objects], when you are neither apart from them nor stained by them and come and go freely—that is *prajñā-samādhi*. Being free and liberated is called the practice [*xing*] of no-thought. (Cf. Yampolsky, 153)

The passage concludes by identifying the teaching of no-thought with the sudden teaching and equating the realization of no-thought with buddhahood.

> If you stop thinking about everything and constantly cause your thoughts to be cut off, then that is being bound by things [*fa*], which is called a biased view. If you realize the teaching [*fa*] of no-thought, you will penetrate all things thoroughly and will see the realm of all buddhas. If you realize the sudden dharma [*dunfa*] of no-thought, you will have reached the status of buddha. (Cf. Yampolsky, 153)

By raising the sudden teaching as the banner of the new orthodoxy, the *Platform Sūtra* committed the Chan tradition to a radical rhetorical position. Its practice of no-thought redefined meditation in totally formless terms and rejected all means. As Carl Bielefeldt has pointed out, this move led to a curious paradox in which the tradition that touted itself as the "meditation tradition" could no longer, at least in its public professions, say anything concrete about the actual mechanics of the practice of meditation in which its monks daily engaged, because to do so would be to lapse into gradualism.[18] It did not, of course, mean that the tradition stopped practicing meditation. The *Platform Sūtra*, after all, claims that Huineng enjoined his disciples before his death that they should continue to sit in meditation (*duanzuo*) together as they had when he was alive (Yampolsky, 181). It only meant that the practice became, as it were, a house secret.

NOTES

1. See Peter N. Gregory, ed., *Sudden and Gradual: Approaches to Enlightenment in Chinese Thought*, Kuroda Institute, Studies in East Asian Buddhism, 5 (Honolulu: University of Hawai'i Press, 1987); and Bernard Faure, *The Rhetoric of Immediacy: A Cultural Critique of Chan/Zen Buddhism* (Princeton: Princeton University Press, 1991).

2. For an attempt to summarize the significance of *tathāgata-garbha*, buddha nature, and original awakening in Chinese Buddhism, see Peter N. Gregory, *Inquiry Into the Origin of Humanity: An Annotated Translation of Tsung-mi's "Yüan jen lun" with a Modern Commentary* (Honolulu: University of Hawai'i Press, 1995), 8–13.

3. For a translation of the *Lengqie shizi ji*, see J. C. Cleary, *Zen Dawn: Early Zen Texts from Tun Huang* (Boston: Shambhala, 1986), 19–78. As Bernard Faure notes, this text "was intended to establish the orthodox patriarchal tradition of Chan through the transmission of the *Laṅkāvatāra-sūtra*"; *The Will to Orthodoxy: A Critical Genealogy of Northern Chan Buddhism*, trans. Phyllis Brooks (Stanford: Stanford University Press, 1997), 145.

4. See Cleary, *Zen Dawn*, 68.

5. My attention was first drawn to the significance of this passage by Jan Fontein and Money L. Hickman, *Zen Painting and Calligraphy* (Boston: Museum of Fine Arts, 1970), xvi–xvii, who discuss this episode in reference to a drawing of *The Six Patriarchs of the Bodhidharma Sect* in the collection of Kōzanji (cat. No. 1, reproduced on p. 2).

6. *Jingang bore boluomi jing (Vajracchedikā)*, translated by Kumārajīva (Jiumoluoshi, 344–413), *T* no. 235, 8:749a24.

7. This text is one of the great masterpieces of Mahāyāna Buddhist literature. Its most accessible translation is that of Robert Thurman, *The Holy Teaching of Vimalakīrti* (University Park: Pennsylvania State University Press, 1976). Students interested in a more detailed and technical treatment of the text should consult Sara Boin's English translation of Étienne Lamotte's French translation, *The Teaching of Vimalakīrti (Vimalakīrtinirdeśa)* (London: The Pali Text Society, 1976). Both Thurman and Lamotte base their translation on the Tibetan text. For a translation of Kumārajīva's Chinese translation, see John R. McRae, *The Vimalakīrti Sūtra* (Berkeley: The Numata Center for Buddhist Translation and Research, 2004), available for free download at http://www.numatacenter.com/default.aspx?MPID=81. Although not as reliable, a readily found translation of the Chinese text is that of Burton Watson, *The Vimalakīrti Sūtra* (New York: Columbia University Press, 1997). For a probing discussion of the translations of this text, see Jan Nattier, "*The Teaching of Vimalakīrti (Vimalakīrinirdeśa)*: A Review of Four English Translations," *Buddhist Literature* 2 (2000): 234–58.

8. It is quoted, paraphrased, or explicitly referred to nine times—Yampolsky, 136 (3 times), 139, 141, 148, 151, 157, and 175. Its influence can be discerned in other places as well.

9. *Weimojie suoshuo jing (Vimalakīrtinirdeśa)*, translated by Kumārajīva (Jiumoluoshi, 344–413) in 406, *T* no. 475, 14:540a; cf. Thurman, *The Holy Teaching of Vimalakīrti*, 25–26.

10. Although seemingly idiosyncratic, Thurman's translation of *upāya* as "liberative technique(s)" gets at the meaning of this term in the *Vimalakīrti Sūtra* far better than its usual rendering as "expedient means."

11. For further discussion of this *samādhi*, see the three essays included in Peter N. Gregory, ed., *Traditions of Meditation in Chinese Buddhism*, Kuroda Institute, Studies in East Asian Buddhism, 4 (Honolulu: University of Hawai'i Press, 1986): Daniel B. Stevenson, "The Four Kinds of Samādhi in Early T'ien-t'ai Buddhism," esp. 55–58; Bernard Faure, "One-Practice Samādhi in Early Chan," 99–128; and David W. Chappell, "From Dispute to Dual Cultivation: Pure Land Responses to Ch'an Critics," esp. 164–169.

12. The quoted passages can be found in *Weimojie suoshuo jing*, *T* no. 475, 14:542c15 and 538b1, respectively. "Straightforward mind" translates Sanskrit *kalyāṇāśaya*, which Lamotte/Boin render as "good intentions" (16 and 95) and Thurman as "positive thought" (16 and 36).

13. See Cleary, *Zen Dawn*, 48 and 73.

14. Huineng himself is a prime example of someone for whom it was not necessary to sit. Wary of an antinomian reading, Zongmi adds the gloss: "Vimalakīrti said that it is not necessary to sit [in meditation], not that it is necessary not to sit [in meditation]"; *Zhuyuan zhuquanji duxu*, Zongmi (780–841), *T* no. 2015, 48: 403c20.

15. See John R. McRae, *Seeing Through Zen: Encounter, Transformation, and Genealogy in Chinese Chan Buddhism* (Berkeley: University of California Press, 2003), 60–67, for a different interpretation of the verses.

16. The natural innateness of wisdom is emphasized again in the *Platform Sūtra* in secs. 28 and 29.

17. The *Platform Sūtra* adds "externally" and internally" to the passage quoted from the *Vimalakīrti Sūtra* (*Weimojie suoshuo jing, T* 14:537c13). The passage is correctly quoted later in sec. 48. Thurman notes that whereas the Tibetan text "relates 'the deep analysis of things' (Skt.: *dharma-pravicaya*) to the teaching of the ultimate nature of reality," the Chinese text contrasts the two (110, n. 34); cf. Lamotte/Boin, *The Teaching of Vimalakīrti*, 9.

18. See Carl Bielefeldt, "Ch'ang-lu Tsung-tse's *Tso-ch'an I* and the 'Secret' of Zen Meditation," in *Traditions of Meditation in Chinese Buddhism*, ed. Peter N. Gregory, Kuroda Institute, Studies in East Asian Buddhism, 4 (Honolulu: University of Hawai'i Press, 1986), 129–61.

5

TRANSMITTING NOTIONS OF TRANSMISSION

. . . .

WENDI L. ADAMEK

THE PLATFORM IN THE *PLATFORM SŪTRA*

"Transmission" in the context or contexts that produced the *Platform Sūtra* is by no means a self-evident concept. There are at least three levels involved: transmission of a particular approach to the Buddhist teachings of liberation from suffering, transmission of the text itself as a kind of token or talisman conveying efficacy and authority, and transmission as part of an ideology legitimating a particular approach, efficacy, and authority. All of these levels involve contestation. If one approach to liberation, one form of Buddhist soteriology, is promoted, then others are explicitly or implicitly deemphasized or even dismissed. If a text or an object has a special aura attributed to it, then we must ask how and why it is invested with this privileged function. And finally, most subtly: when we identify transmission as an "ideology," what goes into that designation? The Chan notion of patriarchal transmission encompasses both the mystique of wordless rapport between master and disciple and the effectiveness of a political tool to invest a relatively small number of males (Chan masters) with spiritual and institutional authority. When we label Chan transmission as an ideology, we take the mystique as a function of the politics and focus on competitive relationships and rhetorical strategies. However, throughout this exploration of the meanings of transmission at work in and around the *Platform Sūtra*, I would like us to remain reflexively aware of the rhetorical work involved in the exploration itself. What do we transmit, intentionally or otherwise, when we choose to focus on the soteriology, the ritual magic, or the competitive politics? Do we implicitly or explicitly claim that one level is more real than the others? Can they be separated?

Let us begin on the level of the platform in the *Platform Sūtra*, with the first sentence: "The Master Huineng ascended the high seat at the lecture hall of the Dafan Temple and expounded the dharma of the great perfection of wisdom, and transmitted the precepts of formlessness" (Yampolsky, 125). The first thing we see is Chan Master Huineng stepping up and arranging himself on some sort of formal seat, placed on a stagelike elevation at the head of the dharma hall. As Huineng tells his story from this raised platform, the point is driven home that he was a laborer and not an ordained monk when he attained the realization and the transmission that gives him the authority to teach, and he is not even literate. This, then, is a version of the universally satisfying fairytale of the lowest of the low raised to eminence. However, there is a pivotal paradox embedded within this introduction to our patriarchal Cinderella.

What Huineng is teaching throughout the *Platform Sūtra* are variations on the theme that "form is emptiness, emptiness is form," as expounded in the *Heart Sūtra*, the most commonly recited of the perfection of wisdom (*prajñāpāramitā*) scriptures.[1] As explored in more detail in this and other chapters, for the Chan school this means that one's true nature is the buddha wisdom inherent in the realization of all things/forms as emptiness/interdependence. The only effective teaching is the "sudden" teaching that empties the forms of practice of their purposive presumptions. (You can't get there from here; you are always t/here.) This is why Huineng, rather than telling his audience, "Do not practice the precepts" (which would itself be a precept and a misconception), instead transmits the "precepts of formlessness," a concept discussed in Paul Groner's chapter in this book. Therefore, in the first line of the *Platform Sūtra* Huineng steps up to a position of authority by virtue of a realization that he tells his audience is their own intrinsic nature, gives an exposition on not being dependent on expositions, and transmits the efficacy of preceptless precepts.

The *Platform Sūtra* closes by recommending itself as a mark or token of transmission of this true dharma of formlessness or marklessness. In between the ascent to the platform and the handing down of the sūtra, the *Platform Sūtra* comprises four main parts: Huineng telling his own story, his subsequent lecture on buddha nature and formlessness, selected dialogues with questioners, and the scene of his impending death, including transmission of verses supposedly passed down by the previous patriarchs. We could dismiss this twelve-hundred-year-old text and its subsequent elaborations as "much ado about emptiness" and simply a product of factional rivalries. But what would that tell us about ourselves?

BUDDHISM AND TRANSMISSION:
WHERE'S THE DHARMA?

Buddhist traditions assert, in various forms, that under the right conditions a person has the capacity to realize truth directly. In the *Platform Sūtra* when the Fifth Patriarch Hongren (601–674) has transmitted the dharma to Huineng and bids him farewell, he says, "If one is able to open the mind, 'you' (and I) are no different" (cf. Yampolsky, 133). This should raise a number of questions. What is this realization, this "opening the mind"? Who has the authority to decide that someone has attained it? What is a trustworthy or effective method or guide for accomplishing it? Who is a legitimate judge of what is effective? These questions, in various forms, are at the heart of the issue of transmission in Buddhist traditions. How does the dharma, the Buddhist teachings, convey this potential realization, and how is its continuity maintained from one generation to the next and from one place to the next?

Buddhists often evoke the "Three Jewels" of the Buddha, the dharma, and the saṅgha (Buddhist community) as a means to designate what carries Buddhism across space and time.[2] Each of these jewels can be understood in both tangible and intangible terms. Traditionally, it is said that the Buddhist practitioner "takes refuge" in the Three Jewels in order to participate in the merit generated by Buddhist practice, and ultimately to be able to resolve the perplexing questions posed above through his or her own practice. Chan Buddhism, however, was radical in its rejection of the notion of taking refuge and accruing merit, recommending that the practitioner go straight to her or his own mind. In the *Platform Sūtra*, Huineng says: "Good friends, I urge you to take refuge in the Three Jewels (of your own nature). The Buddha is realization, the dharma is truth, and the saṅgha is purity" (cf. Yampolsky, 145). What does he mean by this? Let us examine the Three Jewels and their reformulation in the *Platform Sūtra* one by one.

Concretely, Śākyamuni is the physical representation of the Buddha jewel in this historical period. Over time, images of buddhas in text, painted images, wood, metal, and stone also came to represent the Buddha jewel. These images are considered sources of aid for devotees, and they also represent the potential for awakening (Skt.: *bodhi*) in each person. Thus, this refuge is both other—the salvific Buddha or bodhisattva (a buddha-in-the-making)—and one's own realization. Buddhism teaches that both physical bodies and images are illusions, but this does not negate their valid functions as potential vehicles of merit and realization. In an early Buddhist sūtra, Śākyamuni is said to have told his followers to take refuge in themselves. In the *Platform Sūtra*, Huineng says, "The sūtras say that oneself [as Buddha] takes refuge in the Buddha; they do not say to take refuge in other buddhas" (cf. Yampolsky, 146).

The second jewel, the dharma or teachings, can be considered concretely as Buddhist texts and lectures, but also ineffably as the

"Law," the nature of truth, to teach and realize itself. Early Buddhist scriptures are presented not as revelations or systematic compositions but as oral transmissions based on the memories of disciples who heard the Buddha speak. This is why early Buddhist sūtras begin with the phrase "Thus have I heard." However, each Buddhist country and era developed its own version of a Buddhist canon, and Buddhist texts written today may eventually become part of some future version of a Buddhist body of scriptures. Thus, a much longer and more elaborate version of the *Platform Sūtra* from the thirteenth century is included in the current East Asian Buddhist canon, as explained in Morten Schlütter's introduction to this book.

The *Platform Sūtra* itself teaches that everything in the scriptures is the nature of one's mind, but one may need the help of a teacher to activate it: "Therefore, although the buddhas of the three worlds and all the twelve divisions of the canon are within human nature, originally itself in complete possession [of the dharma], if one cannot awaken to one's own nature, one must obtain a good teacher to show one the way to see the nature. But if you awaken to yourself, do not depend on outside teachers" (cf. Yampolsky, 152).

The third jewel, the saṅgha or Buddhist community, is in its narrowest sense the community of ordained monks and nuns and in its broadest sense all Buddhist believers. Monks and nuns as a group are considered a refuge because they vow to live by a set of specific precepts mandating pure conduct, including celibacy.[3] This is why Huineng designates the saṅgha jewel as "purity," but he specifies that it is the innate purity of one's mind: "In your own mind take refuge in purity; although defilements and delusions are in one's own nature, one's own nature is not stained" (cf. Yampolsky, 145).

Chan/Zen teachings posed a challenge to traditional means of transmitting the Three Jewels. Yet challenge is intrinsic to the Buddhist teachings: there is always a potential conflict between the continuity of received forms and the new forms generated by individual awakening. Thus, the saṅgha's ability to transmit the dharma is illustrated by the metaphor of the monk or nun as a vessel. The monastic is the container and dispenser of something he or she has received but has made uniquely his or her own through practice and experience. In Mahāyāna Buddhism, that which the monastic contains is that which he or she has actualized by the realization that there is no container and nothing to contain. This paradoxical vessel, provisionally rule-bound and ultimately empty, was the means by which the dharma adapted to changing conditions in new places, like China.

FORMS OF TRANSMISSION IN
EARLY CHINESE BUDDHISM

In the early centuries of Buddhism's spread in China, transmission of certain forms of monastic rules, rituals, and texts gave authority and a sense of continuity. Transmission of *vinaya* texts, the rules for monks and nuns, gave practitioners the assurance that Buddhism in China was proceeding according to standards laid out by the Buddha. Rituals such as recitation of Buddhist scriptures, devotional offerings and liturgies, and vows to adhere to the practices of purity were events in which ordained clergy and the laity participated together, creating a sense of Buddhist community.

Lay devotees, both commoners and wealthy elites, were integral in maintaining the saṅgha in its daily needs as well as its spread from one region to the next. Lay patrons were responsible for commissioning the most durable monuments of Buddhism's early centuries in China, carved in stone and often painted: cave temples, Buddhist images, scenes and passages from the scriptures, memorial carvings of various types. These images were a fundamental means of transmitting Buddhism throughout China.

Scholarly traditions tend to focus on the translation and transmission of particular texts and doctrinal affiliations from one generation to the next. Traditions of textual transmission can be reconstructed from several kinds of sources, most importantly: prefaces to sūtra translations by the translator, his disciples, and later exegetes;

collections of biographies of eminent monks; and Chinese commentaries on South Asian and Central Asian sūtras and treatises. Doctrinal and text-based affiliations were often associated with particular places—the courts of pious emperors or the mountain temples of renowned monks.

Artistic representations as well as translation and reproduction of texts were facilitated by an important Buddhist tenet: the concept of merit (Skt.: *puṇya*). Early Buddhist scriptures taught that performing meritorious and virtuous deeds helps to improve one's future conditions by overcoming the negative effects of past actions. Practitioners, including monks and nuns, usually did not see any conflict between directing their merit-sweetened prayers toward mundane benefits like health and wealth and praying for the transmundane transfiguration of themselves and their loved ones into purer realms or conditions, such as Amitābha's pure land. In doctrinal terms, merit is not considered sufficient cause for enlightenment and liberation in and of itself, but is said to direct karmic momentum toward liberation, the realization that suffering arises from attachment to the illusion of a permanent and essential self. The practice of generosity is considered especially powerful in that it both generates merit and aids in overcoming the attachment to self. The most meritorious activities are those that support Buddhism by giving alms to monks and nuns, constructing temples and images, and commissioning the reproduction and dissemination of sūtras.

Merit was unquestionably a major motivation in the spread and growth of Buddhism in China. However, by the time the *Platform Sūtra* was compiled in the eighth century, it had become clear that Buddhism's power and prestige created problems as well as opportunities. Many emperors and members of the wealthy elite had funded the construction of spectacular temples and supported prominent Buddhist masters. As John Jorgensen's chapter in this volume explains, just before the time of Shenhui, Empress Wu (r. 690–705) spent lavishly on Buddhist building projects and showered famous monks with honors, no doubt in the hope of generating legitimacy and powerful merit for herself and her dynasty. This is why Huineng, in the *Platform Sūtra*, is depicted telling the story of Bodhidharma's rebuff to the merit-seeking Emperor Wu of the Liang dynasty (r. 502–549), declaring: "Building temples, giving alms, and making offerings are merely the practice of seeking after blessings. . . . In dharma nature itself there is merit" (Yampolsky, 156).

It is important to note the fictitious historical context: Huineng's criticism of merit seeking is conveyed through a mythical conversation between the First Patriarch of Chan, Bodhidharma, and one of the first historically verifiable imperial patrons of Buddhism, Emperor Wu of the Liang. The story is effective because it reflects a tension that continues to manifest in Buddhist associations to this day—attracting wealthy patrons is a sign of success, but also a sign of compromise. From the beginning of Buddhism's Chinese adventure, the relationship between the Chinese imperial state and the Buddhist saṅgha was empowering and threatening for both sides. At times state and saṅgha cooperated to the point of merging; at other times the wealth and power of Buddhism triggered regulatory measures and even persecutions. Regulating the growing Buddhist community presented difficulties even when Buddhism was just beginning to be established in China. As Buddhism underwent phenomenal expansion and bewildering diversification during the fifth through seventh centuries, there were periodic attempts at systematization and calls for reform from both within and outside the saṅgha.

This may have been one of the pressure points for the development of a distinctly Chan form of Buddhism. The notion of a mysterious patriarchy, a hidden line of teachers distinct from ordinary monks and nuns, was one means to address the problem of overproliferation. However, in order to create the mythos of a lineage of masters separate from the merely ordained, it was necessary to create a sense of privileged transmission that could not be reproduced through monastic rules and rituals, images, and texts. This lineage thus conferred an almost unprecedented degree of Buddhist authority on certain individuals and teachings and, as discussed in other chapters in this volume, became the central point of contention between different branches of Chan. We now turn to examine this special transmission as it is presented in the *Platform Sūtra*.

A SPECIAL TRANSMISSION:
SUDDEN VERSUS GRADUAL

As discussed in other chapters in this volume, the "Southern School" identified with Huineng is largely the creation of the Chan master Shenhui (684–758). Shenhui initiated a series of criticisms against the successors of the Chan master Shenxiu (606?–706).[4] In the *Platform Sūtra* Shenxiu is the head monk at the monastery of the Fifth Patriarch, Hongren, and all the other monks assume Shenxiu will receive transmission as the Sixth Patriarch. He is depicted as earnest but not very bright, although the actual Shenxiu appears to have been a highly respected monk of great integrity, acumen, and insight.[5]

Shenhui, the provocateur who promoted the notion of Huineng as the Sixth Patriarch, makes an appearance near the end of the *Platform Sūtra*. He is portrayed as a young monk praised by Huineng for being the only one to maintain equanimity in the face of his teacher's imminent death (Yampolsky, 174). However, though the historical Shenhui claimed to have received transmission from Huineng, in the *Platform Sūtra* Huineng does not reveal the name of his dharma heir (Yampolsky, 176). Instead, at the end it is claimed that the text was compiled by Fahai, who passed it to his fellow student Daoji (Yampolsky calls him Daocan), who on his deathbed passed it to his disciple Wuzhen (Daoji/Daocan and Wuzhen are otherwise unknown). It is said that the dharma they teach is sanctioned as Huineng's through the transmission of the *Platform Sūtra* itself (Yampolsky, 182).

Unlike the *Platform Sūtra*, none of Shenhui's own writings attained the status of a classic text. Nevertheless, he changed the course of

Buddhist history by linking the notions of sudden awakening and patriarchal lineage. As discussed elsewhere in this volume, Shenhui championed the notion of direct and spontaneous realization of the truth of one's own buddha nature/emptiness, accusing Shenxiu's followers of being gradualists. According to Shenhui, gradualists are those who delude people into thinking that awakening is a condition to be achieved through arduous meditation, rather than one's inherent reality. This is the import of the *Platform Sūtra*'s graffiti battle (Yampolsky, 129–31), the scene in which Shenxiu's and Huineng's competing verses are written on the temple walls. As Peter Gregory's chapter explains, Shenxiu's gradualist verse argues that one must strive to polish the mind daily, not letting the dust collect, while Huineng's sudden verse makes the point that there is nothing on which dust could collect.

Buddhist references to "no-thought" (*wunian*) predate this mythical conflict between the representatives of the so-called "Northern" and "Southern" Schools. In the context of the creation of this potent myth, however, no-thought came to refer to the nonconceptual realization of the nonseparation of practice and enlightenment. Huineng's verse supports the practice of not reifying *any* form of practice, including meditation, which was considered to be a form of polishing the mind like a mirror.

This begs the question: how do you teach and transmit such a teaching, such a practice, if you are supposed to not-think of it as anything in particular? This is the challenge that Chan presented to itself, how to transmit a tradition of no-tradition. In light of Chan's long and multifaceted history, we can see that impossible challenges may be an asset. This one has proved able to keep a large number of practitioners busy over the course of some twelve centuries.

Shenhui's contribution to this challenge was to formulate the notion that there was only one transmission of the true dharma of the sudden and direct. Moreover, this transmission was invested in only one patriarch per generation, and Huineng was the Sixth Patriarch to receive transmission on Chinese soil. Shenhui may well have been motivated by personal ambitions, but we should also keep in mind that Buddhism had become increasingly populous and diverse. In this context, many other clerics of the seventh and eighth centuries were also trying to devise exclusive means to define authoritative transmission of the Buddhist teachings.

BODHIDHARMA'S ROBE

According to Shenhui, the transmission of the true dharma went all the way back to Śākyamuni Buddha, who passed a special wordless transmission to his disciple Mahākāśyapa. This transmission continued through a lineage of single patriarchs until it reached Bodhidharma, the First Patriarch to transmit Chan in China. Shenhui claimed that this unique transmission was verified by a tangible token of authenticity: a robe passed down by Bodhidharma, first to his disciple, Huike, and then on to each of the Chinese patriarchs of Chan. Shenhui writes:

> The robe serves as verification of the dharma and the dharma is the robe lineage. Robe and dharma are transferred from one [patriarch] to another and are handed down without alteration. Without the robe one does not spread forth the dharma; without the dharma one does not receive the robe.[6]

Shenhui compared the transmission of the Chan "robe of verification" to the transmission of the regalia of a *cakravartin* (literally "wheel-turner"), a universal Buddhist monarch, to the next reigning prince. There are long-standing Buddhist associations between the consecration of a king and Buddhist ordination rituals. The notion of a sacred talisman signifying legitimate rule would also have made sense in the Chinese context: sacred heirlooms of jade and precious metals were believed to validate the reigning dynasty's mandate. These sacred heirlooms were supposed to protect the dynasty until the time had come for a new cycle and a new dynastic succession.

There are also Buddhist scriptural and anecdotal sources that would have provided material for the notion of a special robe as a symbol of transmission. In a work well known in China, *The Tang Dynasty Account of the Western Regions* (*Da Tang xiyu ji*), the famous pilgrim-monk Xuanzang (600–664) relates a version of the transmission of a robe from the Buddha to his disciple Mahākāśyapa.[7] The Buddha, about to enter *nirvāṇa,* entrusts his gold-embroidered robe to Mahākāśyapa and publicly invests him as leader of the saṅgha and successor to the transmission of the true dharma. The Buddha then predicts that twenty years after the first assembly, when Mahākāśyapa is on the point of entering nirvāṇa, he will enter the sacred Mount Kukkuṭapāda and stand holding the Buddha's robe in his arms. The mountain will enclose him and he will wait for eons for the advent of the future Buddha Maitreya. When Maitreya finally arrives, the mountain will open and Mahākāśyapa will transmit the robe to Maitreya in view of the assembled crowd. Mahākāśyapa will then ascend into the air and self-combust, entering nirvāṇa.[8]

There are magical properties associated even with ordinary monks' robes, so a special robe, the robe of the Buddha or the robe of Bodhidharma, was a powerful symbol of continuity in uncertain times. Nevertheless, placing such importance on a robe seems rather materialistic for a teaching based on realization of one's own buddha nature, just as the notion of patriarchy itself seems to run counter to the emphasis on one's own nonmediated access to the truth. However, Bodhidharma's robe can be viewed as a reassurance or guarantee that the power of the Three Jewels of Buddha, dharma, and saṅgha remained in force, tangibly invested in the patriarchs. The notion of Bodhidharma's robe as a guarantee soon became obsolete, along with the notion that there could be only one recipient of the transmission at a time: a generation after Shenhui, the robe had been demoted to a supplementary token. Yet the passing of the robe from Hongren to Huineng remains at the heart of the *Platform Sūtra* drama and is part of its lasting appeal.

HONGREN'S MIDNIGHT TRANSMISSION TO HUINENG: ROBE AND PATRIARCHY CONJOINED

In the *Platform Sūtra*, Huineng, seated on his platform, tells the assembly the story of how he received the robe and the dharma:

> At midnight the Fifth Patriarch called me into the hall and expounded the *Diamond Sūtra* to me. Hearing it but once, I was immediately awakened, and that night I received the dharma. None of the others knew anything about it. Then he transmitted to me the dharma of sudden enlightenment and the robe, saying: "I make you the Sixth Patriarch. The robe is the proof and is to be handed down from generation to generation. My dharma must be transmitted from mind to mind. You must make people awaken to themselves." The Fifth Patriarch told me: "From ancient times the transmission of the dharma has been as tenuous as a dangling thread. If you stay here there are people who will harm you. You must leave at once." (Yampolsky, 133)

Huineng is still a layperson when he receives this transmission in the *Platform Sūtra*. It is only later that he is ordained as a monk, as Paul Groner's chapter in this book discusses at greater length. Buddhism recognizes multiple sources of authority—the power of an individual's practice, the integrity of the collective saṅgha, and the transmission of texts and commentaries—but it was the fully ordained monk who was ritually invested with the authority to determine what would be taught and transmitted. Thus, the image of the Fifth Patriarch Hongren passing Bodhidharma's robe and the patriarchy to an outsider has the force of a radical challenge to tradition. Not only is Huineng illiterate, poor, and from a marginal area (he is called a *gelao* or "barbarian"), he is not even a monk! These shocking inversions of the norm serve to reinforce the notion that realization of buddha nature is accessible to anyone. At the same time, the aura of mystery and danger reinforces the notion that the patriarchy is attainable only by a special few.

Huineng tells his audience that following his midnight investiture as patriarch he fled south, pursued by a band of men wanting to steal the robe. In a dramatic mountaintop scene, the former general Huiming catches up with Huineng, who offers up the robe. However, Huiming is not interested in the token of patriarchy; he wants the dharma. After the mountaintop transmission he is awakened and goes on to become a teacher—but he does not receive the robe and become a patriarch (Yampolsky, 134).

While other Chan histories take the tale of the robe and the dharma into subsequent generations, in the *Platform Sūtra* the tale of the robe ends with Huineng. When he knows he is about to die and has been asked who will inherit the robe and the dharma, he says, "The robe may not be handed down. In case you do not trust in me, I shall recite the verses of the preceding five patriarchs, composed when they transmitted the robe and the dharma. If you depend on the meaning of the verse of the First Patriarch, Bodhidharma, then there is no need to hand down the robe" (Yampolsky, 176).

In constructing a vision of the future transmission of the dharma, the compilers of the *Platform Sūtra* thus placed more importance on the transmission of verses than on the transmission of the robe. Huineng, on the point of death, recites the verses supposedly passed down by each of the patriarchs active in China: Bodhidharma, Huike, Sengcan, Daoxin, and Hongren. He then recites two verses of his own, and the disciples leave thinking that their master is "not long for this world." However, before departing, Huineng still has several more important transmission statements to make. His next teaching concerns the lineage of patriarchs in India, linking his own transmission back to that of the Buddha in a single line of descent.

CONSTRUCTION OF A LINEAGE OF
INDIAN PATRIARCHS

The story of a master passing what he knows to a single disciple, who endures much hardship to prove himself, may be perennial.

However, it is noteworthy that current popular culture associates this motif with East Asia. Films like the *Star Wars* trilogies, *The Karate Kid*, and *The Matrix* draw on East Asian-style images of powerful masters, perplexed disciples, and the fate that binds them together. Vaguely East Asian fashion statements are associated with each of these films—robes continue to play important roles.

China has an indigenous tradition of master-disciple relations that goes back at least as far as the anecdotes about Confucius and his disciples found in the *Lunyu* (*The Analects*).[9] However, it may have been the blending of Buddhist traditions from India with Chinese notions of sympathetic resonance between fated individuals that gave birth to the compelling master-disciple narratives that abound in Chan lore.

There are long lists of names, evidently lineages of Indian masters and disciples, included in or appended to certain sūtra translations made in China in the fifth century. It seems clear that Indian Buddhists developed some form of genealogical record fairly early, specifying the first few generations after the Buddha's death and later recording the names of more recent masters associated with the transmission of a particular text. Narratives of master-disciple interactions would become increasingly detailed and dramatic in both India and China.

Other Buddhist groups and schools were also in the process of formulating specialized notions of lineage, most importantly the Tiantai school, which claimed Zhiyi (538–597) as founder. In a preface to Zhiyi's best-known work, the *Great Calming and Insight* (*Mohe zhiguan*), his disciple Guanding (561–632) created the foundation of a distinctive Tiantai lineage and transmission ideology. In this preface Guanding describes either end of a lineage that does not meet in the middle. The western line moves forward from Śākyamuni Buddha, and the eastern line moves backward from Zhiyi to his master, Huisi (515–577), and then to Huisi's master, Huiwen (ca. mid-sixth c.). There is no attempt to craft a "string of pearls" linking the two lines, but Nāgārjuna (ca. second–third centuries), the Thirteenth Patriarch in the western line, is evoked as the "high ancestral teacher."

Nāgārjuna becomes a spiritual ancestor not because there is a direct line of transmission, but because Huiwen's insights into a work believed to have been authored by Nāgārjuna become the source of the special method of cultivation that is passed down and explicated in Zhiyi's *Great Calming and Insight.*

As Tiantai scholar Linda Penkower points out, this is a creative solution to the problem of validating both the continuity of transmitted teachings and the innovations of individual insight. Linear time is represented in the western and eastern lineages, but spiritual affinities and karmic connections also permit transhistorical and even transtemporal relationships. In Guanding's biography of Zhiyi, Huisi is said to have claimed karmic connection with Zhiyi due to their having listened to the Buddha preach the *Lotus Sūtra* together in a past life. Guanding also refers to the *Lotus Sūtra*'s assurance that Śākyamuni is constantly preaching the *Lotus* in his "bliss body" or transcendent manifestation. Zhiyi's enlightenment experience through meditative study of the *Lotus Sūtra* is thus linked to both the past and the continued presence of direct transmission from the Buddha.[10]

The Tiantai notion of dual diachronic and synchronic transmission and the Chan ideology of strictly linear transmission drew on a common source: the *Account of the Transmission of the Dharma Treasury* (*Fu fazang zhuan*), a text of uncertain origins, which tells the stories of twenty-four Indian patriarchs. These stories contain episodes both dramatic and amusing, but the most violent moment comes at the end: Siṃha Bhikṣu, the Twenty-third Patriarch after the Buddha, is beheaded by a king in Kashmir and bleeds white milk instead of blood.[11] This is presented as both the truth of a clear line of transmission from the Buddha and a sign of the end of the era of the full power of the Buddha's teachings.

Buddhism includes in its teachings the recognition that the manifestations of the Buddhist teachings themselves are subject to cycles of impermanence. Eventually, there were a number of versions of the doctrine that there are three periods of the dharma taught by

Śākyamuni: the period of true dharma, when the Buddha's teachings are all available and people are able to study and understand them; the period of outward semblance of the dharma, when the Buddha's teachings have become obscured and very few people will be able to practice them; and the final age of the dharma (*mofa;* Ja.: *mappō*), when no one will be able to fully grasp the Buddha's teachings. The notion that the world had entered the final age of the decline of the dharma, when kings and monks were corrupt and true teachings difficult to encounter, took hold in China in the fifth and sixth centuries. An apocalyptic mood was not unwarranted, as China had been embroiled in violent warfare and divided into a multiplicity of short-lived dynasties for several centuries. The compiler of the *Account of the Transmission of the Dharma Treasury*, whether Indian, Central Asian, or Chinese, was clearly influenced by some form of the final age doctrine.

The *Account of the Transmission of the Dharma Treasury* was a major source for the version of the patriarchal lineage that is found in the *Platform Sūtra* and other Chan texts, but someone had to rework the ending in order to move the lineage along, on to Bodhidharma and the Chinese patriarchs. The unique contribution of Chan to the ideology of lineage was the myth of a *continuous* line of transmission from Śākyamuni to Huineng. The *Platform Sūtra* simply includes a list of the names of twenty-eight Indian patriarchs, but other Chan texts supplied extra narrative details in order to bridge the gap between the murdered patriarch Siṃha Bhikṣu and his successors.

The *Account of the Transmission of the Dharma Treasury* and the *Platform Sūtra* both stress, in different ways, that transmission is "dangling from a thread," as the Fifth Patriarch Hongren says (Yampolsky, 133). In these narratives the dharma is always about to be lost, and in the *Account of the Transmission of the Dharma Treasury* it in fact bleeds away. On the one hand, stories of transmission give reassuring evidence of the temporal extension of the Buddha's power. On the other hand, these stories underline the fragility of dharma transmission. In the *Platform Sūtra* and the other Chan works that promote rival versions of tales of the patriarchs, the take-home message is that Chan is a special transmission and one is extremely lucky to have access to it, especially if one is able to encounter the charisma of a patriarch.

DISPUTING TRANSMISSION: THE *RECORD OF THE DHARMA JEWEL THROUGH THE GENERATIONS*

Eighth-century Chan and "proto-Chan" sectarian histories each highlighted a distinctive form of practice attributed to the patriarchs whose teachings the work was designed to promote.[12] Competing claims to the most authentic practice went hand-in-hand with competing claims to the most authentic transmission. There was much at stake: a Chan group that could convince elites that its practices and transmission were the most genuine would be most likely to receive support, which would further the spread of its teachings.

How were these rival claims to authentic transmission advanced? In order to gain a deeper sense of the polemical aspects of transmission stories, let us take a look at a Chan history compiled around the same time as the *Platform Sūtra*, produced by a competing Chan lineage, known as the Baotang school. This text, the *Record of the Dharma Jewel Through the Generations* (*Lidai fabao ji*), was discredited by other Chan groups and lost in the mists of history, only to turn up again early in the twentieth century in the library cave at Dunhuang.[13] However, many of its stories were incorporated into later works that became part of the Chan/Zen orthodoxy.

While Huineng's death is the end of the line for the robe in the *Platform Sūtra*, for the compilers of the *Record of the Dharma Jewel Through the Generations* the story is just beginning to get interesting. In the *Record of the Dharma Jewel* version, when Huineng is asked about the robe, he says:

> Do not ask. After this, hardships will arise in great profusion. How often have I faced death on account of this *kāṣāya* robe? At Great

Master Xin's [i.e., the Fourth Patriarch Daoxin's] place it was stolen three times, at Great Master Ren's [i.e., the Fifth Patriarch
Hongren's] place it was stolen three times, and now at my place it
has been stolen six times. But at last no one will steal this robe of
mine, for a woman has taken it away. So don't ask me any more.[14]

The woman referred to is the famous Buddhist imperial patron-
ess, Empress Wu, and the authors of the *Record of the Dharma Jewel
Through the Generations* concoct an entertaining but convoluted account in which she receives Huineng's robe as a gift and passes it on
to a Master Zhishen (609–702), one of Hongren's disciples. Zhishen
is the great-grandfather in the dharma of Wuzhu, the Chan master whose teachings are promoted in the *Record of the Dharma Jewel
Through the Generations*. In the *Platform Sūtra*, Huineng and Hongren
meet only twice: at the beginning and then again nine months later,
when Hongren secretly conveys the dharma and the robe. In the
Record of the Dharma Jewel Through the Generations there is even less
direct contact between master and disciple. Wuzhu and Wuxiang
meet only once, and after that there is a kind of mind-reading or far-
seeing communication between them across the miles that separate
Wuxiang's temple in Chengdu and Wuzhu's retreat in the mountains.

Wuxiang and Wuzhu's long-distance relationship can be seen
as a device to explain away the fact that Wuzhu was never really
Wuxiang's disciple. At the same time, it is a powerful means of expressing the sudden teaching, not bound by physical presence or
monastic formalities. One could also consider the motif of their long-
distance relationship in light of the tension between the exclusive-
ness of mind-to-mind patriarchal transmission and the inclusiveness
of the teaching of innate buddha nature. This tension is symbolically
erased in the wordless bond between master and disciple.

The image of mysterious sympathetic resonance between pro-
tagonists who are destined to meet is not unique to Chan or to
Buddhism, but it was useful in solving one of the dilemmas of the
sudden teaching. Including an account of time spent studying with

the master *before* receiving dharma transmission would admit that the teaching is gradual; it implies that buddha nature is something learned. In other key Chan transmission narratives, this dilemma is solved by other means: the Second Patriarch Huike spends years with Bodhidharma *after* receiving initial transmission. Huineng spends nine months at Hongren's place, but they have only one encounter before Huineng receives the transmission. As noted, the *Record of the Dharma Jewel Through the Generations* story represents an extreme example of this motif: Wuzhu and Wuxiang meet face to face only once.

In the *Record of the Dharma Jewel Through the Generations*, transmission of the all-important talisman, the robe, is accomplished with a third person as an intermediary. Wuxiang (also known as the Venerable Kim) gives the robe to a servant, who is to convey it to Wuzhu:

> The Venerable Kim brought out a *kāṣāya* robe, [the one that] the rarest few among men have had in their keeping. He revealed it [and said], "This was given to the Venerable Shen by Empress [Wu] Zetian. The Venerable Shen gave it to the Venerable Tang, the Venerable Tang gave it to me, and I transmit it to Chan Master Wuzhu. This robe has long been cherished; don't let anyone know of it." When he finished speaking he became choked with sobbing and said, "This robe has been passed from legitimate heir to legitimate heir; one must make utmost effort, utmost effort!" Then he took from his own person his *kāṣāya*, under and outer robes, and sitting cloth. Altogether there were seventeen things. [He said,] "I am getting on in years. You take these things and convey them secretly to Chan Master Wuzhu, and transmit my words: Take good care of yourself, and make utmost effort, utmost effort! It is not yet time to leave the mountains. Wait three to five years longer, and only leave when a person of consequence welcomes you."[15]

Later, when his disciples ask him about the robe, Wuxiang says, "My Dharma has gone to the place of non-abiding. The robe is hanging

from the top of a tree, no one has got it."[16] This, however, is a pun—
the word for "nonabiding" in Chinese is "Wuzhu."

THE *PLATFORM SŪTRA* AS A TRANSMISSION DOCUMENT

Rather than continuing with an account of lineal transmission after Huineng, the *Platform Sūtra* appears to endorse the notion that
Huineng had ten disciples all qualified to pass on his teachings. Notably, their qualifications are to be sanctioned by possession of the
Platform Sūtra itself:

> The Master said: "You ten disciples, when later you transmit the
> dharma, hand down the teaching of the one roll of the *Platform
> Sūtra*; then you will not lose the basic teaching. Those who do not
> receive the *Platform Sūtra* do not have the essentials of my teaching.
> As of now you have received them; hand them down and spread
> them among later generations. If others are able to encounter the
> *Platform Sūtra*, it will be as if they received the teaching personally
> from me. (Yampolsky, 173)

The text then gives the date of Huineng's death (equivalent to
August 28, 713), followed by a lengthy account of his last words.
As noted, once he has recited a verse encapsulating his teachings,
Huineng gives the signature verses of each of the six patriarchs and
lists the Indian patriarchs. He then bids his disciples a final farewell with another long verse and gently expires. Miraculous signs,
well known to the audience from similar stories of the death of the
Buddha, occur after Huineng's demise. Following this is the above-
mentioned claim that Fahai compiled the text and passed it to his
fellow disciple Daoji, who passed it to Wuzhen. Finally, the *Platform Sūtra* once again recommends itself as an authentication of
transmission:

When [in the future] this dharma is to be handed down, it must be attained by a man of superior wisdom, one with a mind of faith in the Buddha-dharma, and one who embraces great compassion. Such a person is qualified to possess this sūtra, to make it a mark of the transmission, and to see that in this day it is not cut off. (Yampolsky, 182)

Thus, the *Platform Sūtra* presents itself as a kind of talisman, similar in function to the robe (though this remains ambiguous). Claiming to represent a teaching that is beyond ordinary textual transmission, the text invests itself with the status of a scripture. Many Mahāyāna scriptures end with similar injunctions about the effectiveness and sacredness of the text, and go into raptures about the merit accruing to anyone who would disseminate it. The *Platform Sūtra*'s admonitions also hark back to earlier Chinese traditions of transmission, in which initiation into the study of a particular scripture or commentary formed the basis for affiliation with a lineage or grouping of masters and disciples. However, the *Platform Sūtra* takes all of this to new heights when it claims that the very possession of a copy of itself is proof of having received the transmission. It seems likely that in the early days of the *Platform Sūtra* this involved inscribing the recipient's lineage in the text, as we see in the Dunhuang version (Fahai—Daoji—Wuzhen), but it also meant that later readers could feel themselves to be involved in Huineng's lineage simply because they were holding the text in their hands.

As Morten Schlütter has shown elsewhere, variations among the extant editions and fragments of the *Platform Sūtra* indicate that there were disputes over its transmission.[17] However, like the robe and the verses of the patriarchs, the *Platform Sūtra* probably played a more prominent role in the psycho-myth of mind-to-mind patriarchal transmission than it did in hand-to-hand patriarchal transactions. Yet such attempts helped to solidify notions of lineage and patriarchy and set textual patterns that could be elaborated upon and refined, leading to the production of massive branching genealogies like the *Records of the Transmission of the Lamp Compiled in the Jingde Era* (*Jingde chuandeng lu*) in the Song dynasty.

The precision and detail of the many-branched Chan genealogies of the Song dynasty and beyond must always be juxtaposed against the scarcity and fuzziness of lineage information in texts from the period the genealogies claim to represent. The fact that the Chan transmission narratives of the late eighth century tend to be vague about subsequent transmission points to a kind of built-in obsolescence within the ideology of the Chan patriarchy itself. The notion of one patriarch per generation was an effective way of bringing the dharma forward from the past, but it was untenable as a map of the future. As John Jorgensen points out in his chapter in this volume, the notion of the patriarchy mirrors the Chinese notion of dynastic succession, in which seven generations are necessary in order to establish a fully fledged dynasty.[18] However, while a dynasty is restricted to one emperor per generation, a flourishing school of Buddhism need not be so constrained. Once the "trunk" of six Chinese patriarchs had been established, the fact that there were several claimants to the title of Seventh Patriarch was nothing less than an indication that the school had begun to be. There was no "Chan school" in existence during the time of the first six Chinese patriarchs—it cannot even be said to begin with Shenhui, the one who shaped the linking of six names into a powerfully generative idea. However, once the imaginary line had been drawn in the sand of the past, it began to sprout real branches, and these continue to put forth new shoots even today.

NOTES

1. See Donald S. Lopez Jr., *Elaborations on Emptiness: Uses of the Heart Sūtra* (Princeton: Princeton University Press, 1996).
2. For surveys of Buddhism and its source texts, see Peter Harvey, *An Introduction to Buddhism: Teachings, History and Practices* (Cambridge: Cambridge University

Press, 1990); Donald S. Lopez Jr., *The Story of Buddhism: A Concise Guide to Its History and Teachings* (New York: HarperCollins, 2001); and John S. Strong, *The Experience of Buddhism: Sources and Interpretations* (Belmont, CA: Wadsworth/Thompson Learning, 2002).

3. For discussion of how monastic rules evolved in China, see Yifa, *The Origins of Buddhist Monastic Codes in China: An Annotated Translation and Study of the "Chanyuan Qinggui,"* Kuroda Institute, Classics of East Asian Buddhism (Honolulu: University of Hawai'i Press, 2002).

4. See John McRae, "Shenhui as Evangelist: Re-envisioning the Identity of a Chinese Buddhist Monk," *Journal of Chinese Religions* 30 (2002): 123–48.

5. On Shenxiu, see Bernard Faure, *The Will to Orthodoxy: A Critical Genealogy of Northern Chan Buddhism*, trans. Phyllis Brooks (Stanford: Stanford University Press, 1997); and John McRae, *The Northern School and the Formation of Early Ch'an Buddhism*, Kuroda Institute, Studies in East Asian Buddhism, 3 (Honolulu: University of Hawai'i Press, 1986).

6. *Dunwu wushang bore song*, S. 468. In Hu Shi, *Shenhui heshang yiji* (Taibei: Hu Shi jinianguan, 1970), 195.

7. Xuanzang's version of this transmission is different from both Indian and Chinese canonical sources, but it is likely to have been widely read in Buddhist circles.

8. *Da Tang xiyu ji*, Xuanzang (602–664). T no. 2087, 51:919b24–c24.

9. D. C. Lau, trans., *The Analects of Confucius* (New York: Penguin, 1999).

10. This discussion of Tiantai lineage is summarized from Linda Penkower, "In the Beginning . . . Guanding (561–632) and the Creation of Early Tiantai," *Journal of the International Association of Buddhist Studies* 23, no. 2 (2000): 245–96. See also Neal Donner and Daniel B. Stevenson, *The Great Calming and Contemplation: A Study and Annotated Translation of the First Chapter of Chih-i's "Mo-ho Chih-kuan"* (Honolulu: University of Hawai'i Press, 1993).

11. For more on the *Fu fazang zhuan*, see Wendi L. Adamek, *The Mystique of Transmission: On an Early Chan History and Its Contexts* (New York: Columbia University Press, 2007), 101–14.

12. Regarding eighth-century Chan works and polemics, see: Adamek, *The Mystique of Transmission*; Bernard Faure, *The Rhetoric of Immediacy: A Cultural Critique of Chan/Zen Buddhism* (Princeton: Princeton University Press, 1991); John Jorgensen, *Inventing Hui-neng, the Sixth Patriarch: Hagiography and Biography in Early Ch'an*, Sinica Leidensia, 68 (Leiden: Brill, 2005); and John McRae, *Seeing Through Zen: Encounter, Transformation, and Genealogy in Chinese Chan Buddhism* (Berkeley: University of California Press, 2003).

13. See Adamek, *The Mystique of Transmission*.

14. *Lidai fabao ji*, T. no 2075, 51:182c4–8; see Adamek, *The Mystique of Transmission*, 323.

15. *Lidai fabao ji*, T 51:187b14–26; see Adamek, *The Mystique of Transmission*, 351.

16. *Lidai fabao ji*, T 51:187c2–3.

17. See Morten Schlütter, "Transmission and Enlightenment in Chan Buddhism Seen Through the *Platform Sūtra* (*Liuzu tanjing*)," *Chung-Hwa Buddhist Journal* 20 (2007): 379–410.

18. See also John Jorgensen, "The 'Imperial' Lineage of Ch'an Buddhism: The Role of Confucian Ritual and Ancestor Worship in Ch'an's Search for Legitimation in the Mid-T'ang Dynasty," *Papers on Far Eastern History* 35 (1987): 89–133.

6

ORDINATION AND PRECEPTS
IN THE *PLATFORM SŪTRA*

· · · · · · · · · ·

PAUL GRONER

Monastic life has always occupied a central place in Chinese Buddhism and the forms of Buddhism imported into China from India and Central Asia. For more than two millennia Buddhist traditions have been devoted to interpreting and refining the ceremony of initiation (ordination) into the order of monks and nuns and the sets of rules (precepts) regulating the collective life of monastics. At the same time, the tradition has grappled to find ways of meaningfully involving laypeople in a religion that has traditionally been centered around monasteries and their residents. The *Platform Sūtra* occupies an important position in the perennial debate in Buddhism over how to define the special form of purity especially associated with the vows of monastics but also sought after by laypeople. In spite of its monastic setting, the *Platform Sūtra* is very much a text directed at laypeople, and through the special ordination and precept ritual it contains, it seems to play down or even blur the distinction between lay and monastic.

The very title of the *Platform Sūtra* alludes to the theme of ordination, since the term "platform" (*tan*) probably refers to a raised stage on which ordination could be conducted. The title of the early manuscript version of the *Platform Sūtra of the Sixth Patriarch* found at Dunhuang is followed by the explanatory words "including the bestowal of the formless precepts" (cf. Yampolsky, 125, which has a somewhat different translation). Indeed, an ordination ceremony bestowing these "formless precepts" on the audience is embedded in the text, which includes sections on discerning the three bodies of the Buddha within oneself, reciting the four bodhisattva vows, performing the formless repentance, receiving the formless precepts through the recitation of the three refuges, and an explanation of the teachings of the perfection of wisdom (*prajñāpāramitā*) (Yampolsky, 141–46). As I will discuss below, this ordination ceremony is clearly directed toward laypeople as much as, or even more than, monastics. In addition to offering a simplified version of ordination, the *Platform Sūtra* seems to weaken or perhaps collapse the distinction between monk and layman. With its radical attacks on dualistic thinking and the separation of means and end, the text appears to throw into question the traditional basis of monastic life. The first two sections of this chapter offer a focused exploration of the context in which the *Platform Sūtra* was created, including practices related to precepts and ordination, in order to help us gain a better understanding of the text's fundamental claims. Following that, the discussion turns to four areas associated with ordination and precepts in which the *Platform Sūtra* made new or significant contributions.

VINAYA AND PRECEPTS IN CHINESE BUDDHISM

The earliest Chinese Buddhists probably learned about monastic discipline from traveling monks from Central Asia and India. Chinese monks could probably imitate some of the practices they saw these people performing, but the ritual of ordination, the rules governing monasticism, and the complex ceremonies of daily life still required explanation. By the fourth century C.E., Chinese Buddhists had become vitally concerned with the rules or precepts (*jie*) of monastic discipline, a corpus of literature known as *vinaya* in Sanskrit (*lü* in Chinese). The earliest translations concerning monasticism were simple sets of rules without much explanation, and to many Chinese, the texts seemed incomplete. The eminent monk Dao'an (312–385) made one of the first attempts to codify monastic ceremonies in an influential text (no longer extant). Even while compiling it, he called for a good translation of the full *vinaya*.[1] The terse lists of rules that early Chinese monks had been using probably constituted a liturgical text, used in fortnightly assemblies when monks rapidly recited the precepts. In contrast, a full *vinaya* provided lengthy discussions of each rule, including stories about the circumstances behind its formulation, definitions of the terms used, procedures for implementing the rule, and exceptions to its imposition. It also contained details about the rituals followed by monks. However, the *vinaya* was not an easy text to understand. It was filled with technical terms, frequently transliterated rather than translated (using Chinese characters that otherwise do not make sense to approximate the sound of a Sanskrit term).

The major rules in the *vinayas* of the early Indian schools of Buddhism do not differ very much in the various texts that are extant, indicating that early Indian monastics were hesitant to make changes to the *vinaya*. In one story about the so-called "first council" convened after the Buddha died, a monk suggested that because the Buddha had passed into *nirvāṇa* (literally, "extinction"), the saṅgha did not have to observe all of the rules. Other monks objected, however, and the assembly voted not to change any of the rules because the monks feared being criticized. Early Chinese monks must have felt an overwhelming desire to follow the rules set forth by the Buddha. Two of the most famous Chinese pilgrims who wrote travel accounts of their time abroad, Faxian (337–422) and Yijing (635–713), were primarily concerned with obtaining and translating *vinaya*.

Eventually five full *vinayas* from different Indian Buddhist schools (all considered "Hīnayāna"; Indian Mahāyāna movements never produced their own *vinaya*) were translated into Chinese; the first four were completed during a twenty-six-year period early in the fifth century. As Chinese monks discovered the contents of the *vinaya*, they must have felt dismayed at times. After all, how could rules formulated in the fourth century B.C.E. in India be suitable for Chinese disciples living more than eight centuries later? During this same period, a number of Mahāyāna scriptures were also translated into Chinese, many of which contained sections concerning the behavior of bodhisattvas, enlightened beings of compassion whose status sometimes blurred the line between layperson and monastic. In addition, following a long tradition in Buddhism, Chinese authors wrote new apocryphal scriptures that they claimed had been preached by the Buddha in India. The result was the emergence of a number of interpretations of ideal monastic and lay behavior.

As Buddhism evolved and moved into new cultural areas, some of the old rules became inappropriate and irrelevant, yet no mechanism was available to change the *vinaya*. Instead, monastic communities gradually came to ignore some rules and to stress others. At times, they adopted practices not found in the canon. For example, one of the hallmarks of Chinese monastic Buddhism, vegetarianism, is not required in the *vinaya* as long as the animal has not been killed specifically for the recipient. Other rules, such as the prohibitions against eating after noon or handling money, were ignored or circumvented by Chinese monastics. Sometimes rules written for specific temples or schools were used to alter monastic behavior, often by modifying rules from the *vinaya*.[2] This was true of the extensive codes written for Chan monasteries, which, although they relied heavily on the *vinaya*, added or changed many rules.[3] Other practices not included in the *vinaya*, such as the physical labor often associated with Chan, were found at many monasteries. Thus, in many ways actual practice diverged significantly from the prescriptions contained in the *vinaya*.

Another way of expanding and reinterpreting precepts is found in various Mahāyāna texts translated into Chinese that contained what are often called "bodhisattva precepts" bearing a superficial resemblance to the precepts of the *vinaya*. For example, the *Perfection of Wisdom* (*Prajñāpāramitā*) *Sūtra in 8,000 Lines* lists ten good precepts: 1) not killing; 2) not stealing; 3) not engaging in improper sexual relations; 4) not lying; 5) not uttering harsh speech; 6) not uttering words causing enmity between people; 7) not engaging in idle speech; 8) not being covetous; 9) not being angry; and 10) not holding wrong views.[4] The first four closely resemble the most important rules for monks found in the *vinaya*, which if broken would result in permanent expulsion from the saṅgha. However, they are much more vague: no indication is given as to whether the precepts are for lay or monastic practitioners, and they may well have been intended for both. The *vinayas* specifically state that sexual intercourse, stealing, taking the life of a human being, and lying about spiritual attainments should result in expulsion from the monastic order (Skt.: *pārājika*); other types of killing, lying, and sexual behavior are handled with lesser penalties. However, most Mahāyāna scriptures provide little explanation of the bodhisattva precepts, many of which concern mental attitudes rather than the physical or verbal actions that are the focus of the *vinaya*. Infringements of bodhisattva precepts presumably result in karmic punishments rather than adjudication by a religious order.

Another idea complicating Buddhist practice was that proper observance of rules was an internal process rather than a social convention. The *Platform Sūtra* suggests that the bodhisattva precepts originate not in a ceremony of conferral but in the innate potentiality of each person to become enlightened (called "buddha nature" because everyone is understood to have the nature of a buddha). The *Platform Sūtra* prefaces its version of a bodhisattva ordination by quoting a line from the *Brahma's Net Sūtra* (*Fanwang jing*), an apocryphal text composed in China that was one of the most popular sources for the bodhisattva precepts in East Asia. The citation, "From the outset your own nature is pure" (Yampolsky, 141), suggests that observing the precepts is a matter of following one's own nature rather than adhering to rules established by a group. According to the *Sūtra on the Original Action of the Necklace of the Bodhisattva*, an apocryphal text closely associated with the *Brahma's Net Sūtra*, the precepts could be conferred by virtually anyone, including husbands and wives upon each other. Unlike the prohibitions of the *vinaya*, the bodhisattva precepts did not cease upon death but lasted from lifetime to lifetime. One could receive them, but could not discard them. One might violate them, but could never lose them.[5] When bodhisattva precepts were used in this way, they resembled a call to enlightenment more than an initiation into a group of practitioners.

Despite some claims that following the bodhisattva precepts transcended the need to observe traditional rules of the *vinaya*, most monks and nuns in China figured out ways of combining the two systems. After a few centuries of the kind of debate over precepts reflected in the *Platform Sūtra*, a consensus emerged in practice. The bodhisattva precepts were usually combined with rules of the *vinaya* for monks and nuns in a hierarchical system. A person ordaining as a Buddhist monastic might first take refuge (in the "Three Jewels" of Buddha, dharma, and saṅgha), then the five lay precepts,[6] the 10 novice precepts, and the 250 precepts for monks (or 348 for nuns) used in China, before finally receiving the bodhisattva precepts.[7] The *vinaya* precepts were taken only by monastics, but the other parts of this ceremony could all be taken by laypeople (although an abbreviated form of the novice precepts of eight rules were sometimes taken only for a limited time).

DIFFERENT FORMS OF ORDINATION

According to the second edition of the *Encyclopedia of Religion*, the term "ordination" should be restricted to a ritual "publicly designating and setting apart certain persons for special religious service and leadership, granting them religious authority and power to be exercised for the welfare of the community."[8] However, ordination in the Chinese Buddhist tradition could be conferred on either monks and nuns or laypeople. In either case, two closely related homophones were used to refer to the process, "receiving the precepts" or "conferring the precepts" (both pronounced *shoujie*). To develop the definition provided in the *Encyclopedia of Religion*: when the precepts from the *vinaya* were bestowed on a new monastic, the initiate was granted a special status in the group and exercised power for the benefit of the community. A small minority of monastics went even further and lived as recluses, but even then they were considered to have special status as exemplary members of the saṅgha. When laypeople received the five lay precepts or some of the novice precepts, their status as part of a community was more ambiguous. Traditional texts referred to a four-part order or fourfold saṅgha consisting of monks, nuns, laymen, and laywomen. Thus, even if lay believers did not belong to an actual order that enforced the precepts, they belonged to a virtual order in which violations of precepts might result in karmic punishments. The bodhisattva precepts functioned in much the same way. For monastics, receipt of the bodhisattva precepts would emphasize their Mahāyāna beliefs in a way not possible by following the *vinaya* precepts alone. For a lay believer, receiving the bodhisattva precepts might be a way of joining a new (nonmonastic) congregation; it functioned this way in some Pure Land groups during the Song dynasty (960–1279).[9] At other times, receiving the bodhisattva precepts might simply be a way of establishing a karmic connection with a respected teacher, or for laypeople to increase their overall store of good karma or merit. Throughout this chapter, I follow Chinese usage in deploying the word "ordination" to refer to all of these cases, but the reader should be alert to different nuances in meaning.

Several models for ordination existed at the time the *Platform Sūtra* was composed. One was the process for ordaining monks and nuns contained in the different *vinaya* codes. In the *vinaya* most frequently used in the eighth century, the ceremony of full ordination was a long ritual that took place in a sanctified area (or, noncanonically, on a raised platform). In attendance were a minimum of ten fully ordained monks plus a *vinaya* master chosen to perform the role of preceptor. In the course of the ceremony robes were conferred, the candidate was questioned concerning his or her qualifications, reverence was paid to buddhas and monks present, and then a series of injunctions were read, to which the ordinand gave verbal assent.[10]

Other methods of ordination involved bodhisattva precepts, as noted above. The receipt of bodhisattva precepts could be further subdivided into two basic types: conferral by a group and self-ordination. In self-ordinations, the precepts were conferred by buddhas and bodhisattvas as the candidate performed austerities and received a sign from the Buddha. According to the *Brahma's Net Sūtra*:

> If after the Buddha's death, you have a mind to perform good acts and desire to take the bodhisattva precepts, you may confer the precepts upon yourself by taking vows in front of an image of a buddha or bodhisattva. For seven days, you should confess in front of the Buddha [image]; if you see a sign, then you have acquired the precepts. If you do not see a sign, you should [practice] for two weeks, three weeks, or even a year; by that time you should surely receive a sign. After receiving a sign, you acquire the precepts in front of an image of a buddha or bodhisattva. If you have not received a sign, then even if you take the precepts, you have not actually acquired them.
>
> If you acquire the precepts directly from a teacher who has, in turn, [properly] acquired the precepts, then it is not necessary to receive a sign. Why? Because the precepts have already been transmitted through a succession of teachers, a sign is not necessary. . . .
>
> If no teacher capable of granting the precepts can be found within one thousand *li*, you should go before an image of the Buddha or bodhisattva to acquire the precepts. You must receive a sign [from the Buddha in this case].[11]

Self-ordination was clearly an impressive way to receive the precepts because they came directly from the buddhas and bodhisattvas, were accompanied by a special sign from the Buddha that they had been conferred, and frequently involved considerable practice by the recipient. At the same time, such ordinations could weaken the institutional structure of a group. If the precepts were conferred by the buddhas and bodhisattvas, then who would oversee adherence to them? Who could impose penalties? Who could ensure that people receiving them were sincere? Could anyone argue with a practitioner who claimed that he had received instructions to alter the precepts? Issues such as these led most groups to prefer ordinations that involved institutions and lineages of practitioners. However, the allure of self-ordinations could not be easily overcome. Perhaps for reasons like these, the *Necklace Sūtra* listed three types of ordination in descending order, maintaining the primacy of ordinations by groups over self-ordinations: 1) ordinations by the physically present Buddha; 2) ordinations by bodhisattva practitioners who were within a reasonable distance; 3) going before an image of a buddha and receiving the precepts.[12] The bodhisattva ordinations used by some monks and laypeople could be very detailed. The influential ordination manual composed by the Tiantai patriarch Zhanran (711–782) contained twelve separate sections, each involving a number of steps:

1. introduction
2. three refuges (placing faith in the Buddha, his teaching, order of monastics)
3. invitation to Śākyamuni as preceptor, Mañjuśrī as master of ceremonies, Maitreya as teacher, buddhas of the ten directions as witnesses, and various bodhisattvas as fellow students
4. confession
5. aspiration to supreme enlightenment (four bodhisattva vows)
6. questioning about hindrances to being ordained
7. conferral of the precepts through the three collections of pure precepts
8. ascertaining those who have witnessed the ceremony
9. sign from the Buddha confirming the validity of the ceremony
10. explanation of the precepts (ten major precepts of the *Brahma's Net Sūtra*)

11. exhortation to observe the precepts
12. dedication of the merit from the ceremony to all sentient beings[13]

This ordination was composed of elements from a variety of sources, including traditional *vinaya* ordinations, self-ordinations, and bodhisattva ordinations granted by religious orders. The precepts conferred were from the *Brahma's Net Sūtra*, the set of bodhisattva precepts most commonly used in China.

THE SIMPLICITY OF ORDINATION

The image of ordination in the *Platform Sūtra* is considerably shorter and less complex than ordinations prescribed in the *vinaya* and in the Tiantai ritual noted above. It is also simpler than many of the ordination rituals described in other early Chan documents.

The *Platform Sūtra* ceremony is very brief, consisting of five parts (Yampolsky, 141–46):

1. perceiving the three bodies of the Buddha in oneself
2. recitation of the four bodhisattva vows
3. formless confession
4. receiving the precepts in the three refuges
5. a sermon explaining the perfection of wisdom

The precepts are conferred at the very beginning of the ceremony, when the recipient is urged to "receive the precepts of formlessness" by taking refuge in the three bodies of the Buddha that dwell within his own body. The candidate begins the recitation by stating, "I take refuge in the pure *dharmakāya* Buddha in my own body" (Yampolsky, 141). In some respects this step seems to be an abbreviated way of taking refuge in the Three Jewels, since the Buddha is always mentioned first, before the second and third jewels. This interpretation is complicated by the fact that later in the ceremony the candidate takes refuge explicitly in the Three Jewels. Some scholars of the *Platform Sūtra* have tried to resolve this conundrum by suggesting that the first mention of the buddhas within oneself is a substitution for calling on an assembly of buddhas to serve as the recipient's order. The recipient learns that he does not join an external order but rather realizes his own nature, that is, the buddha within him.[14]

The first three elements are simply recited three times each, according to formulae included in the *Platform Sūtra*. Such a ceremony would have been appropriate for a large group like the thousands of lay and monastic believers described at the beginning of the text. However, the same ritual elements could be prolonged and easily turned into a ceremony lasting for weeks. Zongmi (780–841), a patriarch in both the Huayan lineage and the Chan lineage of Huineng's promoter Shenhui (684–758), describes a similar ritual in which the confession can go on for several weeks.[15] A number of sections in the Tiantai ceremony described above are not found in the *Platform Sūtra*, including invitations to Buddha to attend the event, questions to determine whether the candidates for ordination are eligible to receive the precepts, a sign from the buddhas that the ceremony is valid, and explanations of specific precepts. In this sense, the *Platform Sūtra* ordination differs significantly from ceremonies inducting monks into a specific order of religious practitioners, resembling more the kind of self-ordination described in the *Brahmā's Net Sūtra*. However, the ceremony is simpler than a typical self-ordination ceremony; for example, the confession consists of a formula repeated three times rather than a long period of retreat and meditation, and no sign from the Buddha—such as a dream, vision, or feeling of being touched on the head—is required to validate the ordination. Moreover, even though the buddhas mentioned are found within the candidate, nevertheless it is Huineng who confers the precepts.

Other early Chan texts also include descriptions of precepts and ordination rituals. Compared to these, the *Platform Sūtra* appears unconcerned about monastic ordination and less interested in other ordination traditions. For example, a document discovered at Dunhuang attributed to Shenhui entitled *Platform Sermon* (*Tanyu*) seems to be addressed largely to monks, although laypeople also appear to have been included. The text consists of only five parts:

1. four bodhisattva vows (aspiration to enlightenment)
2. obeisance to the Buddhas (three refuges)
3. sincere repentance (confession)
4. exhortation to maintain the precepts
5. sermon on the perfection of wisdom[16]

During the confession, specific sets of precepts are mentioned: the four offenses listed in the *vinaya* that require permanent expulsion of monastics from the Buddhist order (see above), five heinous sins (killing one's father, mother, or an *arhat*; shedding the blood of a buddha; splitting the order), seven heinous sins (the previous five plus killing one's preceptor or teacher), violating the ten good precepts, and any major acts that would block progress on the path. The section on encouragement uses the word *zhaijie* (literally "precepts of purity"), referring to the eight precepts maintained by pious lay believers when they temporarily follow a quasi-monastic lifestyle, perhaps indicating that Shenhui was partly addressing a lay audience. More weighty, however, is the mention of the four offenses requiring expulsion, which shows that the ceremony was intended for monastics as well.

Another ordination ceremony is found in a text produced by the school of Shenxiu (?606–706), Huineng's rival in the *Platform Sūtra*, entitled *The Expedient Means of Realizing Birthlessness in Mahāyāna* (*Dasheng wusheng fangbian men*). This text emphasizes ordination into a group and institutional affiliation, and the ceremony it describes is somewhat more elaborate than that contained in the *Platform Sūtra*. It consists of eight parts:

1. recitation of four bodhisattva vows
2. a request that the Buddhas be preceptors and witnesses

3. three refuges
4. questions about the five capabilities
5. recitation of one's name and performance of repentance
6. encouragement to hold the precepts of the mind
7. meditation
8. a ritualized sermon on the perfection of wisdom[17]

In the first place, in this text, an order or organized group of buddhas and bodhisattvas is mentioned. In addition, the five capabilities described in the fourth section hark back to the treatment of precepts in *vinaya* sources and the literature on bodhisattva precepts, quite distinct from the formless precepts of the *Platform Sūtra*. The five abilities are discussed as follows: "(1) Can you reject all bad associates from now until the time of your enlightenment? (2) Can you become close to spiritual compatriots? (3) Can you maintain the precepts without transgression even in the face of death? (4) Can you read the Mahāyāna scriptures and inquire of their profound meaning? (5) Can you strive to the extent of your own power to save sentient beings?"[18] The five capabilities indicate that recipients were expected to follow the precepts. Shenxiu, the reputed author of the text, had spent time at Yuquansi, a temple noted for its inclusion of precepts, Tiantai traditions, and Chan practices.[19]

The ceremonies described in the *Platform Sūtra* and the two other early Chan texts have much in common. They all include a central portion involving recitation of or exhortations about the precepts. They also consistently preface this with the recitation of vows and the performance of confession, and they follow the precepts with a sermon on the stock topic of the perfection of wisdom. The simplicity of some of these ceremonies, especially the one found in the *Platform Sūtra,* suggests that they may have been intended more as an inclusive ritual creating some sort of karmic tie between a teacher and lay or monastic believers than as a ceremony that admitted people to a specific type of religious organization. Note the opening sentence of the Dunhuang version of the *Platform Sūtra:* "The Master

Huineng . . . transmitted the precepts of formlessness. At that time over ten-thousand monks, nuns, and lay followers sat before him" (Yampolsky, 125). Although hyperbolic, the description may also reflect the excitement that accompanied Shenhui's very successful sale of ordination certificates to finance resistance to the An Lushan rebellion (discussed in John Jorgensen's chapter in this volume) and the subsequent rebuilding of the capitals of the Tang empire. Evidence concerning the use of the *Platform Sūtra* ceremony during the Tang has not survived. In any event, the *Platform Sūtra* clearly propagated a relatively simplified ordination ceremony intended to be used broadly.

THE DISTINCTION BETWEEN MONK AND LAYMAN

The *Platform Sūtra* presents a complicated picture of the differences between monastic and lay practitioners. Later sources in the Chan tradition have, in turn, offered different interpretations of the distinction.

The opening words of the *Platform Sūtra* indicate that the audience for both the sūtra and the ordination ritual includes both lay and monastic followers (Yampolsky, 175). Able lay believers had long been honored in the Chinese Buddhist tradition. Note the lay preacher Vimalakīrti, the protagonist of a scripture that bears his name, who bests all of the monks and bodhisattvas in debate. Depicted frequently in early Chinese art, his example was an inspiration to lay believers, and, as Peter Gregory's chapter in this book shows, the text bearing his name is cited several times in the *Platform Sūtra*.[20] The biography of Huineng included at the beginning of the *Platform Sūtra* is remarkable because it describes the Sixth Patriarch at the time of his enlightenment as a layman who had received no monastic training. In fact, the Dunhuang version of the text does not even mention Huineng's ordination. Even more striking is the fact that Huineng receives Hongren's transmission and Bodhidharma's robe even though he is still a layman. Furthermore, the poetry contest, the central story of the *Platform Sūtra*, stresses Huineng's illiteracy, whereas most monks seem to have been literate, based on the fact that Tang-dynasty governmental regulations for ordination generally required candidates to be able to recite large numbers of scriptures.[21] In fact, there are many indications that high-profile monastics, such as Shenxiu or Shenhui, came from families of the educated elite and had been extensively educated when young.

However, despite the emphasis on lay practice and the claim in the *Platform Sūtra* that Huineng was himself a layman when he received the transmission, other Chan sources emphasize that he did eventually become a monk. Some documents state that he was ordained in 676, when he was either thirty-three or thirty-nine years old. A biography of Huineng that existed by the early ninth century lists all of the monks who participated in his ordination, a degree of detail rarely included in other biographies.[22] In contrast to the Dunhuang version of the *Platform Sūtra*, the Yuan-dynasty version records the ordination.[23] Even the Dunhuang version implicitly recognizes Huineng as a monk by calling him "great master" (*dashi*), a term not used for laypeople. Finally, a later inscription (probably dating from the seventeenth century) claims to mark the site where Huineng's hair—regarded as a holy relic of his premonastic body—was installed after his ordination.[24]

What are we to make of the discrepancy in which texts ignore or stress Huineng's ordination? The imperial government throughout the Tang dynasty displayed a variety of attitudes toward the importance of the precepts and ordinations. Sometimes the state tried to control Buddhism by regulating ordinations; at other times it did not seem to care, or was unable to do so. The extravagant support of Buddhism by rulers such as Empress Wu (624–705, r. 690–705) may have resulted in lax discipline at monasteries, and later government suspicion of monastics (there were no ordinations for several decades following 711).[25] Monasticism was further weakened during the An Lushan rebellion (755–763). The unrestricted sale of ordination certificates (at which Shenhui so famously excelled) meant that anyone, no matter what their qualifications, could acquire the status of a monastic. Many saw this as a simple tax shelter and the whole notion of monkhood was undermined. Furthermore, governmental crackdowns must have forced some devout people to circumvent official ordinations altogether. Documents from Dunhuang reveal that many monks and nuns lived outside of monasteries, frequently with family members.[26] Some scholars have suggested that, given its emphasis on formless precepts, the Dunhuang version of the *Platform Sutra* may have been compiled by monks who were reacting against governmental controls on ordinations.[27] Note the following statement that emphasizes the spirit of practice over outward displays of piety: "If you wish to practice, it is all right to do so as laymen; you don't have to be in a temple. If you are in a temple but do not practice, you are like the evil-minded people of the west [i.e., India, or Amitābha's pure land]" (Yampolsky, 159).

A loosening of the distinction between monastic and lay status is also apparent in other early Chan sources. According to a passage in the *Record of the Dharma Jewel Through the Generations* (*Lidai fabao ji*), Shenhui would lecture every month from an ordination platform to press his arguments about the superiority of his teaching over that of the so-called Northern School of Chan.[28] The format of these lectures is not completely clear, but since they were delivered from an ordination platform, they probably included an ordination ceremony, perhaps like that in the *Platform Sūtra*. We can note too the placement of the ordinations at the beginning of the three Chan texts on ordination discussed above (Shenhui's *Platform Sermon*, *The Expedient Means of Realizing Birthlessness* of Shenxiu's school, and the *Platform Sūtra*). This arrangement suggests that the ordinations may have been used to open meetings that included both lay and monastic practitioners. After conferring the precepts, the lecturer delivered his sermon.

The portrayal of Huineng in the *Platform Sūtra* suggests that his role was not limited to master of ceremonies and lecturer. Huineng himself seems to serve as the Buddha conferring the precepts; hence the text is referred to as a "sūtra." The Buddha is also summoned from within the recipient himself; note how the three bodies of the Buddha are said to be found within the candidate for ordination (Yampolsky, 141–43). The *Platform Sūtra* states that, in later generations, when Huineng is not present, the text is to be transmitted: "If others are able to encounter the *Platform Sūtra* it will be as if they received the teaching personally from me" (Yampolsky, 173). In a sense, the Buddha is still sanctioning the transmission, but through his words in the sūtra rather than by handing down a robe or begging bowl. The authors of the *Platform Sūtra* must have modeled its precept ceremony on a format that probably served as a means to rapidly produce karmic connections with large numbers of people and to collect large sums of money. Such a format might have been used to sell ordination certificates, but in many cases it might simply have been a ceremony to indicate that a person formally took someone as a teacher.[29] Such evidence points to a loose distinction between lay and monastic behavior, a tendency to which the growing practice of bodhisattva ordinations might have contributed.

In other respects, however, early Chan was very much concerned with monastic purity. Many monks associated with the early Chan tradition carefully followed the precepts, in some cases adopting practices more ascetic than those of other monks. Sources that emphasize Huineng's ordination return the monk to a more orthodox position than that found in the Dunhuang version of the *Platform Sūtra*.[30] As critical interpreters of the Chan tradition, we need to remember that the seemingly antinomian rejection of monasticism and meditation by some later Chan groups, particularly by such figures as Mazu Daoyi (706–786) and the Hongzhou School, cannot be taken at face value. The same holds true for the Chan backlash against antinomianism: the claims made by Zongmi about meditation and monastic practices of various Chan groups of his time should not necessarily be taken as accurate.[31] Instead, all such positions can also be seen as criticism of those who would cling to practices in superficial ways that impede spiritual progress. Some of these statements probably refer to the position that a pure mind underlies both purity and defilement and that clinging to either obscures the pure mind.[32]

We have thus uncovered a variety of attitudes from Tang-dynasty and later sources about the distinction between monk and layman in the *Platform Sūtra*. For some, the conferral of precepts may have been a fund-raising device, asking people to make a donation and participate in a ceremony. Or it could have been a way to create a karmic connection with a Buddhist teacher, or simply an attempt to improve one's karma and attract good luck. As the Yuan-dynasty version of the text states: "In coming from afar and gathering together here, you all share in [the same karmic] connection."[33] There is little evidence to support the viewpoint that the *Platform Sūtra* valorizes formal initiation into the monkhood following the traditional ceremony. However, one intriguing piece of evidence has been noted. According to the *Platform Sūtra*, the text itself should be used in a process of transmission that is not unlike ordination. The text states, "Unless a person has received the *Platform Sūtra*, he has not received the sanction. The place, date, and the name of the recipient must be made known, and these are attached to it when it is transmitted" (Yampolsky, 162).[34] A similar understanding of the use of the text as an ordination document comes from ninth-century Japan. The pilgrim Ennin (794–864) wrote a record of his travels in China and a bibliography of the works he brought back. The *Platform Sūtra* is listed with other texts concerning precepts and ordinations. This classification suggests that Ennin might have viewed the text as functioning like precept manuals or ordination documents.[35]

THE CONNECTION AMONG PRECEPTS, MEDITATION, AND WISDOM

Early Indian Buddhism often utilized the tripartite structure of precepts or morality (Skt.: *śīla*), meditation (Skt.: *dhyāna*) or meditative concentration (Skt.: *samādhi*), and wisdom (Skt.: *prajñā*) to chart the path to liberation. Sometimes this conception of practice was sequential. Performing good deeds, avoiding evil, and following precepts were placed first. The cultivation of pure states of mind and the practice of meditation came second. These were followed by the final stage, the achieving of enlightened wisdom. In many texts the three categories do not follow any particular order but are viewed as equally essential for achieving salvation.

The philosophy of the *Platform Sūtra* takes these three categories seriously while criticizing any absolute distinction among them. Buddhist thought has always cast a suspicious eye on the positing of any transcendent goal, such as a final extinction that seems utterly different from or transcendent of the methods used to attain it. This conceptual sensitivity to the relationship between goal and path (the third and fourth, respectively, of the famous Four Noble Truths) also makes sense in psychological terms, since any ultimate goal seems bound to encourage clinging or desire.

The *Platform Sūtra* adopts a number of strategies for talking about these basic categories of Buddhist practice. One approach, in keeping with other early Chan material, is to question the typical order that places observance of the precepts on an elementary level and achievement of enlightenment or buddhahood on a more advanced level. The formless precepts described in the *Platform Sūtra* are similar to "precepts that arise with or accompany meditation (*dinggongjie*)." This concept was based on the view that a person in deep meditative concentration associated with the form realm would not violate any of the precepts associated with the desire realm. However, when the practitioner emerged from the concentration, he might then violate the precepts. A person who had realized *nirvāṇa* in this life would naturally and permanently follow the precepts (*daogongjie*).[36] Thus the Buddha embodied all of the precepts before he enunciated them in response to various problems that arose in the order. This concept was further developed in later works and was adopted by Chan thinkers, who gave it their own particular twist.

The *Platform Sūtra* seems to call into question the sequential understanding of precepts, meditation, and wisdom. The early Northern Chan text on the *The Expedient Means of Realizing Birthlessness*, discussed above, first takes practitioners through the conferral of "the precepts of the mind" (*xinjie*) and ends with the practice of meditation and a sermon on the perfection of wisdom.[37] By contrast, an important section of the *Platform Sūtra* emphasizes the identity of meditative concentration (otherwise seen as merely preparatory) and wisdom (otherwise considered a final goal). The Sixth Patriarch states directly, "Students, be careful not to say that meditation [or meditative concentration] gives rise to wisdom, or that wisdom gives rise to meditation, or that meditation and wisdom are different from each other. To hold this view implies that things have duality" (Yampolsky, 135). Presumably the same analysis can be extended to the pair of terms "precepts" and "meditation."

In a later section of the *Platform Sūtra*, the Sixth Patriarch advances a straightforward negation of the conventional or gradualist understanding of these three entities as sequential steps. Here, Huineng questions a disciple of Shenxiu (who was sent as a spy) concerning the concepts of precepts, meditation, and wisdom. The disciple replies that his teacher "explains them in this way: Not to commit the various evils is the precepts; to practice all the many good things is wisdom; to purify one's mind is meditation" (Yampolsky, 164). In response to this basic Buddhist explanation of the three forms of practice, Huineng counters that he differs, in that he does not set up or establish the three terms of the equation. He justifies his avoidance of these errors by referring to original purity, self-awakening, and sudden enlightenment. Huineng states: "Self-nature is without error, disturbance, and ignorance. Every thought puts forward the radiance of *prajñā* wisdom, and when one is always separated from the form of things, what is there that can be set up? Self-awakening to self-nature, and sudden practice with sudden awakening—there is nothing gradual in them, so that nothing at all is set up" (Yampolsky, 165). Here the Sixth Patriarch suggests that viewing the Buddhist path as a series of steps, moving from precepts to meditation to wisdom, is a form of gradualism. The proper understanding of the path is to collapse beginning and end into one instant of simultaneity. Since enlightenment or complete wisdom already inheres in one's original nature, an external, not-yet-achieved goal cannot be postulated.

THE FORMLESS PRECEPTS

The term *wuxiang* literally means "without marks" or lacking any determinate characteristics. Applied to the precepts, the word refers to rules or prohibitions whose content is not specified. Thus in the *Platform Sūtra* the precepts that accompany ordination are formless in the sense that the practitioner naturally comes to follow them without focusing on their specifics. Rarely found in other Buddhist texts, the term "formless precepts" is included in the title of the Dunhuang version of the *Platform Sūtra* and again at the beginning of the ordination ceremony (Yampolsky, 125, 141). Although the words were dropped from the title of later versions of the text, they are still usually found in the ceremony itself.[38]

The idea of formless precepts is complex. Central to the *Platform Sūtra*, it also bears affinities to other basic ideas of Mahāyāna Buddhism, especially the *prajñāpāramitā* notion of the nonsubstantiality of good and evil. According to the Chinese translation of the *Perfection of Wisdom in 25,000 Lines*, "The bodhisattva should fulfill the perfection of wisdom by basing himself on the non-existence of sin and good action."[39] A similar logic appears in the *Platform Sūtra*'s discussion of the formless precepts, explaining the indwelling dharma body. The basic idea is that one's own original nature transcends the distinction between good and evil, purity and impurity. By cleaving to one's original endowment (buddha nature) and not attaching oneself to forms labeled "good" or "evil," one can maintain the highest— that is, nondual—form of purity. Thus, the Sixth Patriarch explains, "If people think of all the evil things, then they will practice evil; if they think of all the good things, then they will practice good. Thus it is clear that in this way all the dharmas are within your own natures, yet your own natures are always pure" (Yampolsky, 141–42). At the same time—at the end of the same paragraph—the text summarizes the practice of receiving the formless precepts using words drawn from conventional morality: "Taking refuge in oneself is to cast aside all actions that are not good; this is known as taking refuge" (Yampolsky, 142).

Other early Chan teachings take a similar approach to nonclinging. Bernard Faure has investigated the related term "nonintentional precepts" (*wuzuo jie*). Faure quotes Shenhui: "We call morality the fact of not arousing the false mind, concentration the absence of such a mind, and wisdom the realization that the mind cannot lie."[40] In a similar fashion, the *Platform Sūtra* associates observance of the precepts with such concepts as "no-thought" (Yampolsky, 138–39, 153).

In the *Platform Sūtra*, the sermon on the perfection of wisdom at the end of the ceremony is superficially similar to the explanation of the precepts found in other ceremonies, a procedure performed so that the newly ordained person does not unwittingly violate major precepts. However, the explanation in the *Platform Sūtra* is unlike that found in most other manuals insofar as it stresses the nonsubstantiality of good and bad rather than the actual rules. The bestowal of formless precepts is also akin to a confession ceremony, a key part of both bodhisattva precept ordinations and meditation rites in the Tiantai school. When a person confessed specific or general wrongdoing, it was called "repentance of phenomena." In the Tiantai tradition, confession ceremonies would begin in this fashion, but then progress to "repentance in principle," a meditative exercise on the nonsubstantiality of all phenomena, including moral and immoral actions. No specific acts were confessed at that point. In a similar fashion, formless precepts were based on nonsubstantiality and had no specific content, yet were thought to be the basis of all precepts.[41]

The concept of formless precepts presented a challenge to Chan practitioners. The formless precepts could be interpreted as requiring considerable attention and a high degree of proficiency in practice. When the confession in principle mentioned above was conducted, only advanced practitioners were allowed to contemplate the nonsubstantiality of moral categories; it was a dangerous practice for beginning practitioners because it might lead to an antinomian position in which all moral valences were ignored. But in the *Platform Sūtra*, the ordination ritual, rather than marking an early stage in the individual's practice, requires the initiate to master nonsubstantiality, something normally attained only by advanced practitioners. Some modern scholars have suggested that what sets the *Platform Sūtra* apart from earlier texts is precisely that its ordination confers an advanced transmission of Buddhist teachings on beginners.[42] In this way ordination comes to resemble dharma transmission.[43] Zongmi offers one way of understanding this. He suggests that sudden enlightenment provides a glimpse that then has to be cultivated if the practitioner is to maintain enlightenment.[44] Thus, conflating ordination and dharma transmission makes sense if the recipient realizes that this is the beginning of practice, a brief moment of insight that will lead to a more stable form of realization.

Because the formless precepts were not set rules, they also would have been attractive to people who simply wished to be ordained to improve their karma or because it required little commitment to practice while giving them a karmic tie with a teacher. In fact, historical records contain criticisms of such people around the time of Shenhui, though we do not know whether they received the formless precepts.[45]

Ordination in the *Platform Sūtra* is difficult to place in a historical and social context that would enable us to comprehend better what the ceremony might have meant to people around the time the Dunhuang version was compiled. Comparing it with other ordination ceremonies reveals several aspects of the *Platform Sūtra* ceremony. First, it is very simple; it does not refer to any order of practitioner and the original sense of ordination as signifying entry into a group is not apparent. Instead, a ceremony that has its roots in initiation into a group has been revised to call forth the participants' buddha nature, or perhaps their aspiration to enlightenment, with little or no attention to the stages of religious life following ordination. The ceremony was probably performed on a platform in front of large numbers of people in a short period of time. No long periods of confession were required.

Second, the ceremony makes no distinction between lay and monastic recipients. When the historical background of the text is considered along with the presentation of the biography of Huineng, questions arise about the relative value of lay and monastic practice, but more research needs to be done on this issue. If the protagonist of the *Platform Sūtra* was a layman when he received the Chan transmission, what did this signify? The formless precepts could be interpreted in ways that fit both lay and monastic practitioners, a flexibility that may have increased the attraction of the ordination.

Third, one of the most significant innovations of the *Platform Sūtra* is the conferral of the formless precepts, a realization probably more suited to advanced practitioners, on beginners. The distinction between a ceremony inducting one into a group of practitioners and a ceremony indicating that one had mastered certain teachings was thus blurred, much as the distinction among the precepts, meditation, and wisdom was collapsed in the *Platform Sūtra*. When Shenhui's teachings were later interpreted by Zongmi, the *Platform Sūtra* ordination might be seen as leading to an initial sudden experience of enlightenment in the nonsubstantiality of good and evil, an insight that would have to be deepened through subsequent practice. Just as the hierarchy of morality, meditation, and wisdom was collapsed, so was the distinction between beginning and advanced practices blurred.

NOTES

1. Yifa, *The Origins of Buddhist Monastic Codes in China: An Annotated Translation and Study of the "Chanyuan Qinggui,"* Kuroda Institute, Classics of East Asian Buddhism (Honolulu: University of Hawai'i Press, 2002), 8–16.

2. Mario Poceski, "Xuefeng's Code and the Chan School's Participation in the Development of Monastic Regulations," *Asia Major*, third series, 16, no. 2 (2003): 34–35.

3. Yifa, *Origins*, 53–54.

4. The important role of the ten good precepts in early Mahāyāna is discussed in Shizuka Sasaki, "A Study on the Origin of Mahāyāna Buddhism," *Eastern Buddhist* 30, no. 1 (Spring 1997): 94–95.

5. *Pusa yingluo benye jing*, trans. attributed to Buddhasmṛti (Zhu Fonian, ca. 365), *T* no.1485, 24:1021b.

6. Thought to have been instituted by the Buddha, the five lay precepts are used widely in the Buddhist world. They consist of vows not to engage in killing, stealing, sexual misconduct, lying, or taking intoxicants.

7. For a detailed description of this series of ordinations in the twentieth century, see Holmes Welch, *The Practice of Chinese Buddhism 1900-1950* (Cambridge, MA: Harvard University Press, 1967), 285–96. For lay bodhisattva ordinations, see 84, 294.

8. *Encyclopedia of Religion*, 2nd ed., ed. Lindsay Jones (Detroit: Macmillan Reference, 2005), 6851.

9. See Daniel A. Getz, "Popular Religion and Pure Land in Song Dynasty Tiantai Bodhisattva Precept Ordination Ceremonies," in *Going Forth: Visions of Buddhist Vinaya, Essays Presented in Honor of Professor Stanley Weinstein*, ed. William M. Bodiford (Honolulu: University of Hawai'i Press, 2005), 161–84.

10. For ordination following the *Dharmagupta vinaya* and the directions of an influential seventh-century *vinaya* master, see Ann Hiermann, "Some Remarks on the Rise of the Bhikṣuṇīsaṃgha and on the Ordination Ceremony for Bhikṣuṇīs According to the Dharmaguptakavinaya," *Journal of the International Association of Buddhist Studies* 20, no. 2 (1997): 33–85; and Huaiyu Chen, *The Revival of Buddhist Monasticism in Medieval China* (New York: Peter Lang, 2007), 93–131.

11. *Fanwangjing*, trans. attributed to Kumārajīva (Jiumoluoshi, 344–409 or 413), *T* no. 1484, 24:1006c.

12. *Pusa yingluo benye jing*, *T* 24:1020c.

13. *Shou pusajie yi*, Zhanran (711–782), *Z* 59:354b–57a). For an investigation of later Tiantai ordination manuals and how they were used to appeal to lay believers, see Getz, "Popular Religion and Pure Land in Song Dynasty Tiantai Bodhisattva Precept Ordination Ceremonies."

14. Yanagida Seizan, "Daijōkaikyō to shite no Rokuso dangyō," *Indogaku bukkyōgaku kenkyū* 12, no. 1 (1964): 67.

15. Wendi L. Adamek, *The Mystique of Transmission: On an Early Chan History and Its Contexts* (New York: Columbia University Press, 2007), 202–203.

16. Walter Liebenthal, "The Sermon of Shen-hui," *Asia Major*, new series, 3, no. 2 (1953): 139–41.

17. *Dasheng wusheng fangbian men*, *T* no. 2834; the text is also known as *Wu fangbian* (*The Five Expedient Means*). See the translation in John McRae, *The Northern School*

and the Formation of Early Ch'an Buddhism, Kuroda Institute, Studies in East Asian Buddhism, 3 (Honolulu: University of Hawai'i Press, 1987), 171–74; and discussion of the text, 149. See also Adamek, *Mystique of Transmission*, 199; and Bernard Faure, *The Will to Orthodoxy: A Critical Genealogy of Northern Chan Buddhism*, trans. Phyllis Brooks (Stanford: Stanford University Press, 1997), 106–18.

18. McRae, *The Northern School*, 172–73 (with slight changes in format).

19. Mario Poceski, "Lay Models of Engagement with Chan Teachings and Practices Among the Literati in Mid-Tang China," *Journal of Chinese Religions* 35 (2007): 66.

20. See also Poceski, "Lay Models," 91. For an English translation of the sūtra, see Burton Watson, *The Vimalakirti Sutra* (New York: Columbia University Press, 1997).

21. McRae, *The Platform Sūtra*, 22, 54, 72.

22. John Jorgensen, *Inventing Hui-neng, the Sixth Patriarch: Hagiography and Biography in Early Ch'an*, Sinica Leidensia, 68 (Leiden: Brill, 2005), 688–89.

23. McRae, *The Platform Sūtra*, 3, 92, 96, 99.

24. Jorgensen, *Inventing Hui-neng*, 720–21; Furuta Shōkin and Tanaka Ryōshō, *Enō* (Tokyo: Daizō shuppansha, 1982), 127–34; Yanagida Seizan, *Zenshū shisho no kenkyū* (Kyoto: Hōzōkan, 1967), 525–28. The pagoda said to contain Huineng's hair can still be seen at the Guangxiao temple in Guangzhou.

25. Jorgensen, *Inventing Hui-neng*, 162.

26. Hao Chunwen, *Tanghouqi Wudai Songchu Dunhuang sengni de shehui shenghuo* (Beijing: Zhongguo shehui kexueyuan chubanshe, 1998).

27. Jorgensen, *Inventing Hui-neng*, 162–64.

28. Adamek, *Mystique of Transmission*, 340; John McRae, "Shen-hui and the Teaching of Sudden Enlightenment," in *Sudden and Gradual: Approaches to Enlightenment in Chinese Thought*, ed. Peter N. Gregory, Kuroda Institute, Studies in East Asian Buddhism, 5 (Honolulu: University of Hawai'i Press, 1987), 236.

29. McRae, "Shenhui," 254.

30. Jorgensen, *Inventing Hui-neng*, 163.

31. For Zongmi's critique of Chan at his time, see Peter N. Gregory, *Tsung-mi and the Sinification of Buddhism* (Princeton: Princeton University Press, 1991), 224–52.

32. Poceski, "Lay Models." However, much of Poceski's argument rests on a few examples; as he notes, it needs to be expanded to be convincing. A thoughtful discussion of the context of Mazu's critique of monasticism and Zongmi's response can be found in Jinhua Jia, *The Hongzhou School of Buddhism in Eighth- Through Tenth-Century China* (Albany: State University of New York Press, 2006), 67–72.

33. McRae, *The Platform Sūtra*, 46.

34. See also McRae, *The Platform Sūtra*, 86; and for a further exploration of this issue, the chapter by Wendi Adamek in this volume.

35. T. H. Barrett, "Buddhist Precepts in a Lawless World: Some Comments on the Linhuai Ordination Scandal," in *Going Forth*, 116–17.

36. Yanagida, "Daijōkaikyō," 66, 68 (note 20).

37. Faure, *Will to Orthodoxy*, 111–12.

38. *Enō kenkyū*, ed. Komazawa daigaku zenshūshi kenkyūkai (Tokyo: Daishukan sho-
     ten, 1978) 268; McRae, *The Platform Sūtra*, 17.

39. Cited in Étienne Lamotte, *History of Indian Buddhism: From the Origins to the Śaka
     Era*, trans. Sara Webb-Boin, Publications de l'Institut Orientaliste de Louvain, 36
     (Louvain-la-Neuve: Institut Orientaliste, Université de Louvain, 1988), 82.

40. Faure, *The Will to Orthodoxy*, 114.

41. See the statements in the "Encomium" of the Yuan version of the *Platform Sūtra*,
     McRae, 10 and 12. For a discussion of the nonsubstantiality of good and evil,
     see Neal Donner, "Chih-i's Meditation on Evil," in *Buddhist and Taoist Practice in
     Medieval Chinese Society*, ed. David W. Chappell (Honolulu: University of Hawai'i
     Press, 1987), 49–64.

42. Ishii Kōsei, "Musōkai no genryū," *Komazawa daigaku zen kenkyūjo nenpō* 8 (1997):
     132–33.

43. Zongmi notes that in one school of early Chan there was a kind of dharma trans-
     mission ritual that resembled the ritual for full ordination; see Adamek, *Mys-
     tique of Transmission*, 202–203.

44. Gregory, *Tsung-mi and the Sinification of Buddhism*, 196–205.

45. Jacques Gernet, *Buddhism in Chinese Society*, trans. Franciscus Verellen (New
     York: Columbia University Press, 1998), 56–62.

7

THE *PLATFORM SŪTRA* AND CHINESE PHILOSOPHY

. . . .

BROOK ZIPORYN

The Chan movement is sometimes considered one of several attempts to "sinify" Buddhism, making it more accessible and palatable to Chinese audiences. *The Platform Sūtra* may be understood as a watershed in this process. This view is supported not only by the doctrinal ideas put forward in the text, to be discussed at length below, but even by its title and literary form.[1] The first thing that strikes us when we open this text is the vivid depiction of Huineng, the central figure, as an illiterate rustic possessed of an unschooled natural wisdom, confounding the more sophisticated book learning of socially respected figures. Huineng's unrefined hinterland image echoes a long line of valorized fishermen, woodcutters, and mysterious hermits in Daoist and Confucian texts. The earlier Chan movement, unlike some other schools of Buddhism, had already begun to avoid the complex terminology, lists, and categories of scholastic Indian Buddhism, deploying creative, metaphorizing redefinitions of inherited terms and recombining them in novel ways. The *Platform Sūtra* continues this but brings it to a new level, presenting ideas in a more everyday language marked by supposedly impromptu dialogues and compressed formulations heavy with wit, brevity, and poetic paradox, requiring little prior familiarity with technical vocabulary or elaborate exegesis. And then of course there is the title; by calling itself a "sūtra" (*jing*), the text makes an assertion of canonicity normally reserved for texts translated from non-Chinese languages purporting to report the words of the historical Buddha, Śākyamuni. The title of the text implicitly positions the sub-Chinese backwoodsman Huineng on an equal level with the world-honored Indian prince Śākyamuni, hitherto the ultimate authority on all matters of religious truth.

But above and beyond the sinifying thrust of these formal tropes, we can easily identify a number of themes in the teachings attributed to Huineng in this text with deep roots in traditional Chinese thought, both Daoist and Confucian; these radically reconfigure the lineaments of traditional Indic Buddhist thought and practice. The remainder of this chapter briefly examines the themes of this-worldliness, the philosophy of change, the purity of human nature, and the categories of substance and function.

THIS-WORLDLINESS

Traditional Chinese thinking is sometimes characterized as "this-worldly" in orientation, particularly when contrasted to Indic religions and the theoretical structures that accompany them. Though this must not be taken as indicating an absolute black-and-white dichotomy, it is not without some heuristic value, particularly when comparing Indian cosmologies and the ultimate concerns encoded in them—including elaborate speculations about the beginning of the universe, narratives about the adventures of unseen divinities in alternate realms of being, and the postmortem fate of human beings—with the mainstream elite tradition of classical Confucianism. Confucianism seems to evince little interest in accounts of what might have preexisted human life or what might lie beyond it, the nature of realities inaccessible to human sensory apprehension and cosmological speculations. Ultimate value in this tradition is realized not through securing a particular condition in the afterlife, much less through escaping from birth and death in the world, but through a mode of living in the world. The fragmentary but pointed remarks attributed to Kongzi (usually known as Confucius, 551–479 B.C.E.) in the Analects already set the tone for the humanistic disinterest in supernatural and postmortem affairs that distinguishes the tradition. Asked about the spirits of the dead, Confucius advises that his students "respect them, but keep them at a distance."[2] Asked how to serve the spirits of the dead, he answers, "We are not yet able to serve human beings; how can we serve the spirits?" Asked about death, he says, "We do not yet understand life; how can we understand death?"[3] In general, the Analects tells us, Confucius "did not discuss wonders, feats of strength, disorderly behavior, or spiritual beings."[4] All of these were apparently considered irrelevant to the Confucian project of self-cultivation and social harmony.

This agnostic attitude blossoms into full and explicit skepticism in the works of some later Confucian thinkers, such as Xunzi (312–230 B.C.E.). But the rejection of supernaturalism, in Xunzi's case, does not translate into the kind of militant campaign to eradicate superstition and religious rituals waged by similarly skeptical thinkers in the history of European thought. Xunzi says:

> You pray for rain and it rains. Why? For no special reason; it is just like the rain that comes when you have not prayed for it. So when there is an eclipse of sun or moon and we [do the ritual to] rescue them, or when we pray for rain during a drought, or when we decide a great affair only after performing a prognostication, it is not because we think we can actually attain what we seek in this way. It is done just to ornament these events with a cultural form. Thus the gentleman takes these things as cultural forms, while the ordinary people take them as supernatural. To take them as cultural forms is auspicious, while to take them as supernatural is inauspicious.[5]

Xunzi does not say that these rituals should be abandoned or suppressed. Rather, he says that they should continue, but be regarded in a new way—as cultural forms, as social rituals. At the same time, he sets up a hierarchy within the community. The gentlemen are those who understand the religious rituals as aspects of culture, while the ordinary folk are those who believe they are actually communications with spirits or have some kind of genuine supernatural efficacy. We may be able to detect something parallel in the teachings of Huineng. This is most obvious in the depictions of him denigrating the aspiration to be reborn in the western paradise of Amitābha Buddha in favor of notions of Buddhist practice focused intensely on the immanence of ultimate Buddhist realities here and now, available within present human experience and forming an intrinsic and inalienable part of the human world. Huineng, like Xunzi, offers a reinterpretation and also posits a hierarchy: those who seek the Pure Land in the west are "those of inferior capacity," while those who understand it metaphorically as a reference to our own true inherent buddha nature, which is right here and now, are "those of higher wisdom" (cf. Yampolsky, 156). Huineng suggests a similar reinterpretation of many Buddhist terms and rituals, from "repentance" and "taking refuge" to "the three bodies of the Buddha," "the place of enlightenment (*bodhimaṇḍala*)," "the other shore," "*prajñāpāramitā* (the perfection of wisdom)," "Mahāyāna," and "seated meditation" (Yampolsky, 140–48). Indeed, this tendency to read the technical and mythological language of Indian Buddhist texts as metaphors for aspects of the human mind and human virtues is one of the most characteristic features of the early Chan movement in China, including both the so-called "Northern" and "Southern" Schools. Although Huineng reinterprets these rituals, he does not try to eliminate them. Nor even does he assert that all persons must belong to the class of those with higher capacities, any more than Xunzi expects or demands that there be no superstitious common folk. Instead, a secondary, immanentist, nonsupernatural, and humanist interpretation is added for the elite. In Xunzi's case, the traditional forms of the rituals should still be practiced by the educated, albeit with an alternate understanding; they are among the cultural forms that, in Xunzi's Confucianism, it is the specific responsibility of the elite class to promote and preserve. In Huineng's case, however, the lower forms of repentance, meditation, and pure land occupancy are, rhetorically at least, no longer necessarily enjoined for those of higher capacities. Instead, a foreshortened and streamlined version of a ritual is offered, with the emphasis firmly on the reinterpretation and the change of understanding that goes with it, as discussed in the chapter in this book by Paul Groner. But it is clear that the power and appeal of Huineng's move are conditioned by its resonance with similar moves on the part of earlier Chinese thinkers, deploying the two tools of reinterpretation and hierarchy to both preserve existing cultural forms and make space for an elite reappropriation of them that does not depend on doubtful or discredited nonempirical or transcendentalist claims. Parallel to the Confucian recentering of authority and value in the human as opposed to the divine, in present human activity as opposed to another site elsewhere, *The Platform Sūtra* reconfigures true Buddhist authority and value, moving it away from both the India of Śākyamuni and the further, more distant other world of Amitābha, placing it instead squarely in the activity of the self-nature of its Chinese readers.

Huineng says that true purity is not something that need be sought in the western pure land. It is instead already present here, and everywhere, in all people. His way of asserting this further echoes ancient Confucian themes. Huineng identifies three main themes of his dharma gate, his form of Buddhism: no-thought, nonattribute ["nonform" in Yampolsky], and nonabiding (cf. Yampolsky, 137–38). "No-thought" and "nonattribute" in their literal sense can be and had been taken to imply a world-denying and indeed very thoroughly otherworldly orientation: a person living in the world is constantly having thoughts, and all objects in the world have their particular attributes. This points us toward the normal state of experience in both its subjective and its objective aspects. Human experience involves on the one hand a subject, a person constantly immersed in specific thoughts, plans, ideas, memories, fears, hopes, judgments. It also involves, on the other hand, a vast array of things with their own specific characteristics—long, short, black, white, sweet, sour, pleasant, unpleasant—with which this person must interact, perceiving them, understanding them, responding to them. To be free of thought and free of all attributes might then imply embracing a state of mind that ignores and transcends all the attributes of sensory experience of the world. This would be tantamount to a total negation of the most basic features of life in the world as we know it. Huineng, however, reinterprets these phrases so that they do not imply the eradication of sensory experience or life in the world, putting a this-worldly spin on them: nonattribute (or nonform) does not mean literally free of all attributes and characteristics, but rather "right in the attributes *and yet* free of attributes." This is explained as meaning "externally to be separated from all attributes" (cf. Yampolsky, 138). That is, though attributes are present to one—this is green, that is blue, this is long, that is short, this is sweet, that is sour—one is able to separate oneself, free oneself from them. This means to keep from investing, defining oneself in relation to these attributes. The point is that we normally attach ourselves to the specific attributes of things, meaning not only that we desire to possess or to exclude them but also that we come to define ourselves in terms of our relation to them, to invest in them as sources for the confirmation of our true identity. To be free of them means no longer to invest in them this way, since, as we shall see, Huineng suggests that our real self-nature is free of them. But our self-nature is free of them not in the sense of excluding them but in the sense of embracing all of them without prejudice, without partiality, without limit: our self-nature is like space, and these attributes of particular things are like the things appearing in space. Our self-nature allows all but attaches to none—so that it may allow still others to be present, experienced, known, but not attached to. This is precisely what allows us to have attributes more abundantly rather than to evade all attributes. The world of specific characteristics, the basic form of human experience in the world, is emphatically affirmed.

Huineng goes a step further. He does not tell us to allow only the object side of experience to operate while suppressing the subject's activities, to be quiescent like space, passively allowing all objects to appear. For in a similar move, no-thought does not mean literally eradicating the arising of mental events in the human mind—an idea Huineng repeatedly ridicules as being equivalent to death, or as impossible: to cut off thought in one place, he tells us, will only lead to its rebirth somewhere else. Rather, no-thought means to be right there in the thought *and yet* free of the thought. This is explained to mean "to keep the mind from being tainted by any object, keeping one's thoughts free from any and all objects, and not giving rise to thoughts about any objects" (cf. Yampolsky, 138–39). The precise sense of "not giving rise to thoughts about any objects" can be understood by reference to Huineng's reinterpretation of a motionless mind, a desideratum often promoted in earlier Chan writings: "when seeing people, one does not make judgments about whether they are right or wrong, good or bad, in error or correct: this is the motionlessness [or steadfastness] of the original nature" (cf. Yampolsky, 140). In other words, one perceives people and things, subjectively engages them in thought, but makes no value judgments about them. But Huineng tells us explicitly that this does not mean "having a blank mind, eradicating all mental events. To destroy all mental activity is death—which would just mean to be reborn elsewhere" (cf. Yampolsky, 138). In real time, then, thoughts, perceptions, experiences, and attributes are present and constantly occurring. Huineng suggests instead that a particular mental attitude of nonjudgment and nonattachment toward these thoughts makes them as though gone even when fully present. We can view this as an extension of the idea of the self-nature as an all-allowing space: it embraces not only external objects of perception but also internal mental experiences: thoughts, memories, ideas, concepts, responses. These are to be allowed full play, but not to be attached to. Here too we see a kind of reaffirmation of the everyday, of the human, of the contents of the world as we know it, but apprehended in a new mode, recontextualized as appearances within the spacelike self-nature. The extraordinary state of literally eliminating all thoughts is considered impossible and undesirable—in short, another superstitious myth to be exploded.

However, one thing is excluded on the subjective side: judgments of value. This is a feature of the common human experience, perhaps its most central feature. Ordinary human life is a process of constant evaluation. On this point, Huineng asks for a change of an ethical nature, although one well within the realm of the possible in the human world. But why is this one type of human fact to be excluded from the all-allowing space of the self-nature?

THE PHILOSOPHY OF CHANGE

This is answered by the third and most important self-proclaimed theme of Huineng's Buddhism: nonabiding (or "nondwelling"). Huineng makes a surprising statement about this: "Nonabiding is the original nature of human beings" (cf. Yampolsky, 138). The remark connects two of the great themes of classical Chinese thought. The first is attention to and valorization of the process of change and transformation, as opposed to unchanging and eternal verities. The second is human nature as eminently perfectible, here merged with the notion that all sentient beings are endowed with inherently pure buddha nature.

Let us first, in this section, explore the resonances of Huineng's concept of nonabiding with the indigenous Chinese philosophy of change, before moving on to the question of human nature in the following section. The idea of nonabiding puts a further, unexpected twist on the meaning of the motionlessness of the spacelike self-nature and allows us to grasp the deeper meaning of no-thought and nonattribute (or nonform). The term here translated as "abiding" or "dwelling" can in many Buddhist contexts be interpreted to mean simply "attachment." That sense of the term is certainly implied in Huineng's usage; again, like space, all things and all thoughts are to be allowed but not attached to. But Huineng gives this term an important further spin that resonates richly with indigenous Chinese notions of the positive value of change and transformation, quite at odds with the traditional Buddhist emphasis on stillness and quiescence. Far from standing still so that it registers no attributes and gives rise to no activities of its own, the true motionless mind is depicted in a kind of hyperintense *motion*: nonabiding, never staying in the same place.

Huineng explains nonabiding as follows:

Within each moment of experience, not to think of any previous state. For the past experience, the present experience and the subsequent experience to connect up in an unbroken continuity is called bondage. But in relating to all things, to go through each experience without dwelling in it, that is freedom from bondage. This is why nonabiding is the root. (Cf. Yampolsky, 138.)

What is the relation between nonjudgment and nonabiding? Nonabiding means severing the apparent continuity between one moment of experience and another, between the past, the present, and the future. In Huineng's usage, this simple characteristic of nonabiding directly entails "nonduality," "purity," and "the single practice of straightforward mind." All of these meanings derive from the distinctly *temporal* sense Huineng gives to the term, perhaps picking up on its usage in the *Diamond Sūtra*. At least one early Chinese commentary on that scripture, found at Dunhuang and possibly representing a tradition known to the authors of our text, used the same term as an explication of the line in the sūtra that states: "The past mind is unobtainable, the present mind is unobtainable, the future mind is unobtainable." The commentary glosses this to mean: "The past moment is gone, the future moment has not yet come, and the present moment does not dwell."[6] This suggests that the temporality of experience is itself a primary form of nondwelling.

In later versions of the *Platform Sūtra*, dating back to at least 967, Huineng is depicted as having an enlightenment experience when Hongren quotes a passage from the *Diamond Sūtra* that uses the same term to denote the proper state of mind of a creature living in this temporal universe: "Let the mind arise dwelling in nothing whatsoever."[7] Nonabiding, we are told here, is purity, is nondual, and is the practice of straightforward mind, *because* each moment is absolutely separated from previous and past moments. Purity, nonduality, is the *noncoexistence*, the total isolation, of each moment of experience. Nonabiding means the unceasing procession of thoughts, moments of experience, which are discrete and discontinuous. This means that no previous experience is carried over for comparison to the present experience; they are never placed side by side within an embracing framework that bestows on them an overall coherence or places them within a context in terms of which their respective identities can be fixed. At the simplest level, then, nonattachment or nonabiding means not taking an evaluative attitude toward phenomena, not deeming them determinately good or bad, loving or hating them, desiring or rejecting them. This is perhaps why in later editions of the *Platform Sūtra*, just after making this statement about the nonabiding original nature, as if in explanation, Huineng begins his discussion of this term by relating it to the idea of making no value judgments and not attempting to control or requite unpleasant experiences, on the ethical level. He states: "With respect to whatever in the world may be good or evil, beautiful or ugly and so on, up to whoever may be dear to you or whoever may be your enemy, whatever words are said to disturb or wound you, whatever conflict or deceit comes your way, it is all returned to emptiness so that you have no thought of responding with vengeance or harm."[8] For a value judgment requires that we *compare* two things: an ideal or desired state with an actual state. Nonabiding means there are never two states present at the same time. This means there can be no clashing of the way things are and the way they are supposed to be, no disparagement of the actual event taking place by virtue of its failure to be something else—i.e., the way one has imagined or desired it might be in another moment. We can see this as an example of radical world affirmation: what is going on here and now is all there is.

But more importantly, nonabiding, in a temporal, moment-by-moment sense, means no comparison, attitude, deeming, desire, attachment is *possible*, since all of these presuppose a distance, a "twoness," of "me" toward "it," or of one moment toward another, compared to another, held together at the same time. Without this duality or twoness, this very attribute that I am currently experiencing is simultaneously no-attribute; this mark itself is no-mark. For in the very immediacy of its springing up, before it is joined or linked to others to form a coherent story, it is nondual, precisely because of its absolute singularity and particularity. Linkage, consistency, remembering, anticipation are all results of twoness, and hence of a holding over, attachment, demand for resolution or satisfaction from one moment to the next. Where there is no holding over of one experience against another to form a simultaneous twoness, there can be no sense of an agent acting upon a passive object, a doer as opposed to a deed done or an object to which some deed is done. There is nothing but the event itself as it is happening. What is not done by any particular agent, for Huineng as depicted here, is done nondually, by the nature, and such action is always the instantiation of the highest value, a function of buddha nature. The spontaneous action of the buddha nature is thus occurring in every experience and is equivalent to nonabiding, the nondual making present of whatever is occurring. For one entity to act upon another entity, or for a deed to be done with a particular purpose in view, requires that there be a felt presence of a twoness: myself and the object, myself and the world, the end and the means. But all of these depend on dwelling in a moment of time, remembering or anticipating, carrying one moment of experience over to have an impact on another moment. Nonabiding means this is not only undesirable but in a profound sense impossible. Precisely by virtue of impermanence, the inescapable temporality of experience, one has always already been nonabiding, even when dwelling; the present moment is all there is, even when it is filled with contents marked "past" and "future." Hence Huineng can be understood to propose what appears to be a stunning paradox: impermanence itself is the most direct manifestation of buddha nature. (Indeed, in later versions of the *Platform Sūtra*, Huineng is shown, in answer to a question about the *Nirvāṇa*

Sūtra, directly characterizing buddha nature as exemplifying impermanence.[9]) Impermanence, which Buddhism puts forth as the most
fundamental characteristic of the world of *saṃsāra* and precisely
what distinguishes it from *nirvāṇa*, the Buddha's state of liberation,
is itself an expression of buddha nature. This idea pushes world affirmation to its most fundamental level. One may think one is dwelling from moment to moment, but this is actually impossible. Hence
this state of nonabiding is not some ideal state to be attained in the
future; that would contradict the very idea of nonabiding, creating
a putative continuity between this present moment of practice and
some future moment of enlightenment. Rather, nonabiding is the
original state of all living creatures, always already going on. Sudden
enlightenment alone is possible, since any means-end conception of
practice would require a linkage of moments. Instead, there is always
the original nature of man present in and as all events, which can
be noticed at any time, and is operative even if it is not noticed. The
very non-noticing of it is also an instantiation of it, one more nonabiding event. Simply seeing all dwellings as nonabiding in this sense
is to see them as the nature, the sudden apprehension of original
enlightenment.

Thus we find Huineng associating enlightenment with a kind of
flow, with constant change and transformation. He reinterprets the
notion of "the other shore," traditionally a term for the quiescence
of nirvāṇa, saying, "'This shore' means attaching to the emergence of
the arising-and-perishing of objects of perception, like water shaken
by waves. 'The other shore' means ever separating from all objects
so there is no arising-and-perishing, like water constantly flowing everywhere without obstruction [*tongliu*]" (cf. Yampolsky, 147).
Separating from all objects means not dwelling in any moment, constantly letting each one go. Without the twoness derived from holding on to one moment and contrasting it to another, there can be no
determinate entities as such; the determinate deeming of an entity
to have certain characteristics and not others is the result of contrasting it to something other than itself. Hence with nonabiding, no

determinate entities arise and perish. That is why this nonarising-and-perishing is likened not, as one might expect, to the stillness of the water, but rather to its unobstructed flow.

Huineng uses the same image of unobstructed flowing to describe the Dao. This traditional Chinese philosophical term originally means "way" or "course." In its oldest usages, it means a set of practices or activities that lead to the attainment of some skill or value, such as the way of archery or the way of good governance—a course of learning for attaining mastery of a certain valued ability. For Confucius, it meant the way of ritual and benevolence inherited from the sage-kings, which, if practiced, cultivated a person's character and made him an exemplary person capable of exerting a positive influence in his interpersonal relations and thus creating good order in the social world. Hence it was the way both of personal behavior and of governing, a course in both ethics and politics. The term also came to be applied to the way the natural world acts to accomplish its aims: the way of heaven, the natural processes of the sky, which turns through day and night, through the four seasons, through its various weather patterns, and thereby enables all plants and all living things to grow and flourish. Daoist thinkers elaborated on this idea, focusing on the apparently nonpurposive character of the way of heaven and the natural world, thereby elevating the term to a central philosophical category signifying the nondeliberate, invisible, spontaneous process by which the universe generates all things. Early Buddhist translators used the Chinese term to denote both the path of Buddhist practice (Skt.: *mārga*) and the enlightened wisdom that results from it (Skt.: *bodhi*). Huineng uses the term in his critique of the meditative practice of sitting motionless and not giving rise to any thoughts, which he says would make a person no different from an inanimate object and would cause the Dao, the way, to become blocked. He states, "My friends! The Dao must flow unobstructedly [*liutong*]! Why do you instead want to clog and block it? When the mind does not dwell in any phenomenon, the Dao flows unobstructedly" (cf. Yampolsky, 136).

The idea of Dao as unobstructed flow has deep roots in the Chinese tradition. The *Classic of Changes* (*Yijing*), originally a set of prognostication methods and texts, came to be interpreted in the late Warring States period (475–221 B.C.E.) as adumbrating a complete philosophical depiction of the universe as a process of ceaseless change that combined various structural configurations of the forces of *yang* and *yin* (light and dark, male and female, active and responsive, initiatory and completing) to constantly produce new events and situations, thereby bringing life to all creatures. The philosophical commentaries expressing this view draw on both Confucian ideas of the ethical ideal of timeliness, or freely changing ethical situationalism, and Daoist ideas of the constant process of reversion inherent in all things (particularly in the *Daode jing* [*Classic of the Way and Its Power*]) and the unceasing transformation of beings into different forms (particularly in the *Zhuangzi*).[10] The philosophy of change declares that, "Change means constant production and re-production."[11] The same text argues that "the great virtue of heaven and earth is production," that indeed "the Dao is simply the alternate process of now *yin* and now *yang*. To continue it is what is meant by goodness. What brings it to perfect completion is the nature [of man]."[12] Here change itself is identified as the ultimate reality, the most basic fact about the universe, what brings all things into existence, what gives them life. It is also the locus of ultimate value ("to continue it is what is meant by goodness"). "Good" simply means whatever facilitates and enhances this process of change, nonstagnation, constant production of new situations and events. Further, the original nature is defined as the perfect instantiation of the creative process of transformation and change. Ancient commentarial tradition to the *Classic of Changes* asserts that the word translated as "change" in the title actually has three meanings, indicating three aspects of the same reality: "easy," "change," and "unchanging." The easy is the natural, what requires no effort; change is the constant flux of transformation; the unchanging is change itself, the one constant fact and principle of things. In all of these assertions we can see a clear precedent for

Huineng's teachings about the unobstructed flow of the nonabiding original nature of man as the highest good, the unchanging truth, and the original and ultimate fact.

This process of change is conceived, in the philosophy of the *Classic of Changes*, as consisting in an alternation of the contrasted forces of *yin* and *yang*, where an excess of one is met by an effulgence of the other, driven by a tendency to move toward a dynamic balance. Change, in other words, is a dynamic situational process of offsetting one-sidedness. We can detect an echo of this idea in Huineng's teaching of the thirty-six pairs of polarities. Telling his students how to answer questions put in various situations, Huineng gives a long list of contrasting terms that come in pairs: heaven and earth, sun and moon, light and darkness, *yin* and *yang*, water and fire, words and phenomena, being and nonbeing, form and formlessness, pure and muddied, monastic and secular, old and young, large and small, long and short, false and true, deluded and wise, disordered and stable, kind and cruel, and so on. Huineng then tells his students how these are to be applied so as to maintain his teaching of nonattachment and nonabiding: "If someone asks you a question about the doctrine on the basis of being, answer in terms of nonbeing; if he asks on the basis of nonbeing, answer in terms of being; if he asks on the basis of the worldly, answer in terms of the sagely; if he asks in terms of the sagely, answer in terms of the worldly. The two opposed paths follow each other and thus produce the doctrine of the middle way" (cf. Yampolsky, 173, n. 258, from a later version of the *Platform Sūtra*). Whatever attachment is discerned in the question, leading to a sticking point and a dwelling that obstructs the flow of the way, is to be offset by undermining that attachment with a response in terms of the opposite. This stress on flow as produced by the balancing of polarities, bodying forth a center or middle way, is clearly an inheritance of the tradition of the *Classic of Changes*, combining with the Indian Mahāyāna Buddhist notion of *upāya* (Ch.: *fangbian*, "expedient devices"), the nonultimacy of all determinate teachings, to produce a radically new form of Buddhist discourse.

Huineng's radicalization of this idea of change, transforming it into a moment-by-moment impermanence, has important roots in the Indian Buddhist idea, most rigorously explored in the Abhidharma tradition, of momentariness, that every apparently stable entity is in reality an extremely rapid process of arising and perishing. But Huineng's ethical deployment of this idea to the point of undermining the means-end relationship of traditional Buddhist practice—thereby stressing instead the noninterference of one moment in another moment, the nondeliberate nature of true practice, and with it the insistence on sudden enlightenment—echoes another development in indigenous Chinese thought. Guo Xiang (d. 312), whose commentary to the Daoist classic *Zhuangzi* developed a radicalization of classical Daoist and Confucian emphasis on change and transformation, stipulates that the real source of all the world's problems is the carrying over of the traces of one spontaneous ("self-so") event onto another, interfering with the second event's self-so process. "Self-so" for Guo meant 1) not explicable in terms of cause and effect; these terms are themselves the result of holding the traces of one event up for comparison with another event; 2) not motivated by a purpose, which would likewise be the result of holding one moment up to the standard of another moment; 3) self-valorizing—so or right to themselves, fitting themselves perfectly. When the trace of another moment is retained by a subsequent moment, it creates a sense of value, an ideal, and the subsequent process tries to emulate the previous moment, to match it. This is precisely what undermines the subsequent process's true self-so, its match to its own intrinsic standard of rightness. The previous process existed, and functioned attractively, precisely because it was self-so, not because of its emulation of extrinsic ideals. This attractive process, however, becomes an extrinsic ideal for subsequent processes, and this is what gums up, obstructs, interferes with their own spontaneous functioning.[13] Huineng's notion of the unobstructed flowing of nonabiding, which is the perfect instantiation of ultimate value precisely because it breaks any continuity between one moment and

the next, closely echoes Guo Xiang's conception of both change and
ultimate value.

THE PURITY OF HUMAN NATURE

Huineng says that this "nonabiding" is "the original nature of man"
(cf. Yampolsky, 138). The term "human nature" is a highly charged
phrase that played a central part in ancient Confucian philosophical discussions. Most famously, Mengzi (also known in the Latinized
form Mencius, ca. 372–289 B.C.E.) put forth the thesis that human
nature is originally good, meaning that from birth all human beings
had certain spontaneous impulses that, if properly nourished and
cleared of obstructions, could grow into the full-fledged Confucian
virtues. For Mengzi this meant that all human beings equally were
born with the endowments that could make sages of them, under the
right conditions. Moreover, the practice of the ethical virtues was
not a strenuous war against the tendencies of one's own inborn nature, but rather a way of profoundly satisfying them. Xunzi, whom
we have already met, countered this contention with the claim that
human nature was not originally good in any meaningful sense, but
rather decidedly bad—meaning, in the context of Xunzi's thought,
disordered and self-conflicted. The Confucian moral life was thus a
process of fashioning something beautiful against the grain of inborn
impulses, which left to themselves would lead to disorder and vice.[14]
However, Xunzi shared Mengzi's view that all humans are equally endowed with the selfsame human nature, and indeed that all could, in
some sense, become sages. For both Mengzi and Xunzi, the difference
between a sage and an ordinary person was not decided by a difference in endowment at birth, but by the uses to which an identical set
of potentials were put. Mengzi argued for the originally good human
nature as not necessarily the sole trend of innate human psychology,
but nonetheless always present and identifiable in our spontaneous
emotional responses. He pointed to the feeling of commiseration and

alarm that any person will feel—even if only fleetingly, and even if it leads to no concrete action—when seeing a small child about to fall into a well. This is in a person innately, not added from outside through cultural practices or due to threat of punishment or promise of reward, unmotivated by any particular ulterior gain. If this spontaneous tendency is nourished, unobstructed and patiently tended, it will grow into humaneness (*ren*), the cardinal Confucian virtue, just as water will flow downhill if given the opportunity to do so. The other Confucian virtues, such as righteousness (*yi*), ritual propriety (*li*), and wisdom (*zhi*), likewise have their beginnings in spontaneous human tendencies that, if given the opportunity to follow their natural tendencies, will grow into the full-fledged virtues of a sage.[15]

When Huineng asserts in his dialogue with the Fifth Patriarch Hongren that the buddha nature in him, a southern barbarian, is equal to that of any other sentient being, he echoes this tradition within Confucianism. But his use of the term "human nature" in the passage quoted above (as opposed to the term he prefers elsewhere, "self-nature," or the more commonly used "buddha nature") picks up on the Mencian theme of original purity and radicalizes it considerably. As we have seen, Huineng conceives of this original nature as nonabiding, *therefore* nondual, pure, undistractable, and intrinsic. All the traditional Buddhist values, posited as the good results to be obtained through Buddhist practice, are now said to be merely descriptions of this original nature, the nonduality of nonabiding. Original nature is vast like space, for it makes room for the appearance of all possible entities. It is pure, for nothing can ever defile it; whatever occurs fails to dwell in it, to stain it. It is stable and cannot be turned aside. It is in a sense motionless, for there is no transfer of entities from one point to another, no way for anything to be deflected from any one moment to any other moment. It is wisdom, for it reflects each and every possible appearance with precise accuracy, having nothing to stand in its way or distort it. It is liberation, for nothing can bind it fast. And it must be at the beginning of every process rather than the end, for it cannot be reached by stacking entities toward another entity; instead, it is the very basis for making present any entities. In this way, Huineng is able to assert, like Mengzi, that the very highest ideals, the loftiest religious and ethical values, are not things that are added on to human beings from outside but rather the fullest expression of what each human being necessarily always has been since birth. The virtues are found not by adding something to what we are, but by clearing something away. In Huineng's case, this clearing away is of deluded views (which themselves are empty), and it alone is theoretically always adequate for a full revelation of the original nature. For as nonabiding, this original nature is not divisible and cannot be manifested in parts. It must be realized suddenly, when the practitioner in a flash of insight sees that her inherent "buddha nature is always pure," as Huineng states in the verse contest in the *Platform Sūtra*. In the case of Mengzi, the full expression of the original nature is conceived more developmentally, on the model of seeds that may extend and grow, although they are always minimally operative. For Mengzi, however, this original nature cannot fully flourish without a gradual process of cultivation, which involves not just the clearing of obstacles but also the provision of adequate nourishment and a period of time. Mengzi compares the sprouts of the inherent goodness of the nature to sprouts of plants, which must be neither neglected nor obstructed nor starved, nor indeed helped to grow by pulling them up prematurely.[16] From all these points, we can see both the continuity and the innovation in Huineng's conception of the originally pure nature of all human beings.

SUBSTANCE AND FUNCTION

Another of Huineng's tools in reconfiguring Buddhism for Chinese purposes is the pair of categories *ti* and *yong*. *Ti* literally means "body," but in this context it is usually translated "substance," "structure," or even "essence." *Yong* means "use" or "function." These two terms, used as a paired dyad, have no direct analogue in Indic languages.

The dyad gradually emerged as a prominent philosophical tool in the Six Dynasties period (220–589), through a complex development and interaction of indigenous Chinese ideas. The *Daode jing* (chapter 11) had suggested, in a striking trope, that Non-Being (the Dao) gives all things their function, just as the empty space in a room or at the hub of a wheel gives these things their function, their use. It is this Non-Being that we must ourselves, therefore, use in dealing with things.[17] Wang Bi (226–249) picks up this trope and pushes it a step further by combining it with another theme in the *Daode jing*, nondeliberate action (*wuwei*). The Daoist tradition in general sees the deliberate embrace of ideals, and the purposive action that follows from it, as an obstacle to the truly spontaneous and most abundant functioning of those very ideals. A later chapter in the *Daode jing* (38) warns against taking even Daoist virtuosity (*de*) as an object to be consciously followed, of which one might deliberately make use. For as the highest Dao is a Dao that is not known or deliberately embraced as a Dao, the highest use or function of the Dao is not a deliberate making use of the Dao, or Non-Being. Wang thus suggests in his commentary that it is necessary to merge thoroughly with Non-Being, to the point where it is no longer an object of deliberate use. Instead, we must "embody" (*ti*) the Dao, thereby forgetting it as a definite and determinate entity. It is this full embodiment of the Dao that truly allows it to function well; it is the mother of the function of the Dao, and hence of all things. This contrast between embodying (*ti*) and use/function (*yong*) is developed, through some complex turns in Wang's discussion, into the mother/child relation. The manifest usefulness of Non-Being (seen in the space of a room or the hub of a wheel) is *derived from* the more thorough embodiment of Non-Being that does not make of it a something to be used. But for Wang this is not merely a deriving of one thing from another where the offspring can exist separately from its foundation. Rather, in accordance with *Daode jing* (chapter 52), mother and child are here inseparable, like an infant at the mother's breast. Hence Wang pushes the metaphor another step, comparing embodiment/mother to the root of a plant and use/

offspring to its branches. In this way, a kind of root/branch relation is sketched between *ti* (body, substance) and *yong* (use, function). The branches are many and the root is one. The branches depend on, grow out of, and express the root. The branches and root taken together form one whole; they are complementary.[18]

Ti and *yong* are not yet used systematically as technical philosophical terminology by Wang Bi. But later thinkers picked up and developed Wang's hints, drawing additional inspiration from the relation of the structure of the hexagrams of the *Classic of Changes* and their interactions. Wang is traditionally regarded as the authoritative commentator on both the *Daode jing* and the *Classic of Changes*. The latter text uses a system of symbols called "trigrams," three-line figures depicting particular structural configurations of *yin* and *yang*, to be grasped as a qualitative whole. Like other commentators, Wang refers to these complex but static patterns as "trigram-bodies" (*guati*).[19] These bodies enter into relations with one another, delineating various transformations and changes. Each such *ti* thus functions in different ways, depending on the context of relations in which it is situated. Following this line of thinking, we find a static structural whole that also functions in various ways. The structure remains the same, but its effects vary according to context.

Combining this idea with the root/branch idea, we begin to see the outlines of what would finally take shape as the substance/function dyad. The root/branch idea suggests complementary and inseparable parts of a single whole, a fundamental and unified root and diversified and derivative branches. But at the same time, in Wang's original usage, both the root and the branch were the same (non) entity: Non-Being, viewed either as embodied or as deliberately put to a particular use. This jibes well with the further resonances given to the idea by the *Classic of Changes* applications. The terms went through some further modifications while assuming their full stature as technical vocabulary in the works of Chinese Buddhists, as a way to describe both the relation between emptiness (as the ultimate nature of all things) and its manifestations in empirical phenomena and the relation between the underlying single enlightenment of the Buddha and its differing expressions in various teachings. By Huineng's time these two terms denoted well-established categories. The mature applications of the dyad in later Chinese thought include all of these implications. Substance and function not only are complementary parts of a whole but also can be two names for the same thing, as viewed in two different ways. Various thinkers stress one or another aspect of the implications of this terminology.

Philosophically, the *ti/yong* dyad thus has some interesting implications for speculative thinking. Paired categories are characteristic of philosophical thinking in both Chinese and Indo-European traditions; the very project of offering an explanation involves relating a phenomenon of some kind to a more basic reality of which it is an indication. But the structures of these pairs in the different traditions have great consequences for the results of their respective speculations. Some of the pairs of categories common in Indo-European metaphysics, like "reality" and "appearance," "essence" and "manifestation," and "principle" and "instantiation," introduce two apparently distinct entities, between which a relationship must then be established. This relationship presents many metaphysical quandaries, often leading either to tautologies or to infinite regresses. Other pairs present different sorts of problems. Aristotelian terms like "matter" and "form," for example, suggest a raw material and its distinct form or differentiating characteristics, like the bronze of a statue and the statue's shape. These two are so inseparable in any empirical instance that it is impossible to imagine one without the other: every existing thing has both a substance of which it is made and a form or characteristic shape that establishes its particular identity. Yet the two categories, as abstracted by the mind, are mutually exclusive and admit of no overlap. Form is form and matter is matter, so much so that the limit cases of pure form without matter and pure matter without form arise as grounding conceptions underlying this model, and we have again a problem of how these two primal realities are related. Another pair of common categories is "substance" and "attribute," as for example water (substance) and wetness (attribute). The attribute is an inalienable characteristic of the substance, such that the attribute cannot be removed without at the same time removing the substance. Wherever the attribute is found, and only if the attribute is found, is the substance present. Here the problem becomes the redundancy of the two categories, given their absolute inseparability: is there really any substance above and beyond the attributes? If so, what is it, and how can it possibly be characterized or known?

The *ti/yong* dyad, in contrast, although used in a great variety of ways over the course of Chinese history, tends to present not two distinct entities, but two ways of considering the same entity. *Ti* is the entity considered statically and as a single whole; *yong* is the same entity considered dynamically and in its diversified parts, its various expressions, or its various effects on other entities. This means we do not have a question of relating two different things to each other, nor of distinguishing between two strictly coextensive categories. There is no relationship between *ti* and *yong*, because they are really two names for the same thing. However, the categories are not redundant, because they refer to this one thing either with the stability of its encompassing structure and its persistence through time, or with its particular actions and effects at a given time and place. This allows for asserting a strong sense of inseparability while simultaneously making space for continuity within a variety of diverse manifestations, enabling a comprehension of the simultaneity of the continuity and the diversity.

Huineng uses the *ti/yong* dyad in two crucial contexts. First, in explaining the relation between suchness (equivalent to buddha nature, self-nature, or the original nature of human beings) and the arising of thoughts, he tells us, "Suchness is the substance [*ti*] of thoughts; thoughts are the function [*yong*] of suchness" (cf. Yampolsky, 139). This is a further way of stressing that the ideal state of a Buddhist's mind is not blank quiescence, that indeed the flow of mental experience is not only not an obstruction of the full manifestation of buddha nature but rather its very instantiation. The arising of thoughts, the constant flow of experiences, is the direct manifestation of suchness, of original enlightenment, of ultimate reality itself. Experience is the function natural to the substance of suchness. In effect, the flow of experiences and suchness are simply two ways of viewing the same entity, just as substance and function are ways of referring to two aspects of the same whole, viewed either in terms of its structure and presence or in terms of its activity. This provides a strong way of emphasizing the inseparability of the arising of thoughts and buddha nature.

The substance/function pair is used in another of Huineng's most important formulations: his redefinition of the relation between *samādhi* (meditative concentration) and wisdom. Traditionally, Indic Buddhism tends to view these as standing in a relationship of means to ends: a Buddhist cultivates a calm, concentrated, undistracted state of mind through meditation. Once this state of mind is attained, the Buddhist practitioner can apply it to the contemplation of Buddhist truths (e.g., impermanence, suffering, nonself) and perceive them directly in his own experiences. As noted by Peter Gregory and Paul Groner in their chapters in this volume, meditation is traditionally viewed as a tool used to attain wisdom. Wisdom, in turn, is a tool with which to attain liberation from suffering. In sharp contrast, Huineng asserts that "Meditation is the substance of wisdom; wisdom is the function of meditation" (cf. Yampolsky, 135). Here again we have a strong statement of inseparability, meant to caution against considering either meditation or wisdom prior to the other. One cannot first attain meditative concentration and then use it to attain wisdom, nor indeed first attain wisdom and then attain the concentrated state of mind by means of that wisdom. Neither can exist without the other; they occur simultaneously. Indeed, they are two ways of viewing the same event. Huineng compares them to a lit lamp and the lamp's light (Yampolsky, 137). This has enormous implications for the understanding of the content of wisdom: it is no longer to be conceived as a particular set of contents (e.g., the intellectual or even experiential confirmation of Buddhist truths like "all phenomena are impermanent"), much less a body of knowledge that would enable one to explain Buddhism. Rather, it is the active aspect of a particular state of mind—or, more searchingly, the active aspect of the intrinsic character of the mind. The inseparability or simultaneity of meditation and wisdom is actually another aspect of Huineng's stress on original enlightenment and his propensity to give new definitions to old Buddhist terms. In fact, "meditative concentration" really just refers to the inherent calmness and motionlessness of buddha nature, while wisdom refers to the inherent clarity and responsiveness of that same buddha nature, which is the original nature of all humans.

Both the Confucian thinkers and Huineng are able neatly to combine a universalism of identical original endowment for all human beings, as when Huineng asserts his buddha nature in spite of his "barbarian" background and his illiteracy, and an elitism applying to the way that original nature functions in different classes of people, as we saw in Xunzi's division between the gentleman and the common people and Huineng's distinction between those of superior and inferior capacities. Although the *ti/yong* dyad is not explicitly evoked in this context, a similar theoretical assumption may have helped make this perhaps counterintuitive combination coherent to all these thinkers. The same substance (the original nature) might function differently in different contexts, without, for that reason, being a different substance or losing its original qualities, e.g., the pure original nature for Mengzi and Huineng, or the evil original nature for Xunzi. In each case this unchanged original substance is fully present in all people, whether it is functioning as manifest good or evil, delusion or enlightenment.

It should be clear from the above that the teachings presented by Huineng in the *Platform Sūtra* serve as a continuation of established Chinese philosophical themes, building upon the achievements of previous Chinese thinkers while also adding crucial innovations. In this sense it is an exemplary instance of a truly creative synthesis of two systems of thought, which I have here presented as contrasts. One is the Buddhist soteriological and philosophical system with roots in Indo-European categories; the other is the Chinese tradition with very different interests and presuppositions. The creativity of the synthesis resides precisely in its adoption of older themes, its putting new wine in old bottles and old wine in new bottles. By means of this attempt to provide Buddhist commodities with packaging more attractive to a Chinese market, which revives and reinscribes themes long central to Chinese intellectuals, a new product emerges, which is neither the old nor the new, the familiar nor the alien, but somehow works as both—a single substance that has come to function as a classic and indispensable work in both the Buddhist and the Chinese traditions.

NOTES

1. The *Platform Sūtra* exists in different versions and appears to have grown gradually, through accretion, as a literary artifact, with additions being made to a core text over a long period of time. This chapter draws on several editions of the text, regarding Huineng as a literary creation with certain consistent features, a theme on which a number of variations are played. The remarks here refer to some of the literary aspects common to all known editions. See the chapter in this volume by Morten Schlütter for a fuller discussion of this issue.
2. *Analects*, 6:22, my translation; cf. Edward Slingerland, trans., *Confucius: Analects* (Indianapolis: Hackett, 2003), 60.
3. *Analects*, 11:12; cf. Slingerland, *Confucius: Analects*, 115.
4. *Analects*, 7:21; cf. Slingerland, *Confucius: Analects*, 71.
5. My translation; cf. Burton Watson, trans., *Hsün Tzu: Basic Writings* (New York: Columbia University Press, 1963), 85–86.
6. The line from the *Diamond Sūtra* is from *Jingang bore boluomi jing* (*Vajracchedikā*), trans. Kumārajīva (Jiumoluoshi, 344–413), T no. 235, 8:751b. The commentary is *Jingang jing shu*, anon., T no. 2737, 85:126b.
7. See John R. McRae, *The Platform Sūtra of the Sixth Patriarch* (BDK English Tripitaka, Berkeley: Numata Center for Buddhist Translation and Research, 2000), 23, available for free download at http://www.numatacenter.com/default .aspx?MPID=81.

8. McRae, *The Platform Sūtra*, 43.

9. McRae, *The Platform Sūtra*, 76.

10. For the former, also called the Laozi, see Philip J. Ivanhoe, trans., *The Daodejing of Laozi* (New York: Seven Bridges Press, 2002). For the latter, see Brook Ziporyn, trans., *Zhuangzi: The Essential Writings with Selections from Traditional Commentaries* (Indianapolis: Hackett, 2009).

11. See Richard John Lynn, trans., *The Classic of Changes: A New Translation of the I Ching as Interpreted by Wang Bi* (New York: Columbia University Press, 1994), 77.

12. See Lynn, *The Classic of Changes*, 53.

13. See Brook Ziporyn, *The Penumbra Unbound: The Neo-Taoist Philosophy of Guo Xiang* (Albany: State University of New York Press, 2003).

14. See Watson, *Hsün Tzu*, "Man's Nature is Evil," 157–71.

15. See D. C. Lau, trans., *Mencius* (London: Penguin, 1970), esp. 82–83, 160–68 (sections 2A4 and 6A1–15).

16. See Lau, *Mencius*, 78 (2A2).

17. See Ivanhoe, *Daodejing*, 11.

18. See Paul Lin, trans., *A Translation of Lao-tzu's Tao Te Ching and Wang Pi's Commentary* (Ann Arbor: Center for Chinese Studies, 1977), chapter 38.

19. See Lynn, *Classic of Changes*, 25 and passim.

CHARACTER GLOSSARY

. . . .

An Lushan	安禄山	Chengguang	乘廣
An Shigao	安世高	chenlao	塵勞
anxin	安心	chi	遲
Baolin	寶林	chuandeng	傳燈
Baolin Monastery	寶林寺	chuwang	除妄
Baolin zhuan	寶林傳	dagen	大根
Baotang	保唐	Dajian	大鑑
Baotang zong	保唐宗	Dao	道
Bayuexue	八月雪	Dao'an	道安
Beizong	北宗	Daocan	道粲
ben	本	daochang	道場
benjue	本覺	*Daode jing*	道德經
benxin	本心	daogongjie	道共戒
bianxiang	變相	Daoji	道潔
bore sanmei	般若三昧	Daosheng	道生
bujing	不靜	Daoxin	道信
bukong	不空	Daoxuan	道宣
buqixin	不起心	*Dasheng qixin lun*	大乘起信論
Caodong zong	曹洞宗	*Dasheng wusheng*	大乘無生方便門
Caoqi	曹溪	*fangbian men*	
chan	禪	dashi	大師
channa	禪那	dayi	大意
chanxi	禪習	Dayi	大義
Chanzong	禪宗	Dayu Pass	大庾嶺
chen	塵	de	德

deng	等	gong'an (Ja.: kōan)	公案
Deyi	德異	guan	觀
Dezong	德宗	Guanding	灌頂
ding	定	Guangdong	廣東
dinggongjie	定共戒	Guangxi	廣西
Dongshan	東山	Guangzhou	廣州
Dugu Pei	獨孤沛	guanqing	觀清
dun (dull)	鈍	guanxin shi	觀心釋
dun (sudden)	頓	Guifeng Zongmi	圭峰宗密
dunfa	頓法	Hongren	弘忍
dunfamen	頓法門	Hongzheng	宏正
Dunhuang	敦煌	Hongzhou	洪州
dunjian (sudden/ gradual)	頓漸	Huairang	懷讓
		Huang Kan	黃侃
dunjian (sudden seeing)	頓見	Huangmei	黃梅
		Huayan	華嚴
dunjiao	頓教	*Huayan jing*	華嚴經
dunjiaofa	頓教法	hui	慧
dunwu	頓悟	Hui'an	惠安
dunxiu	頓修	Huiguan	慧觀
Emituo fo	阿彌陀佛	Huijian	慧堅
fa	法	Huijiao	慧皎
Fachong	法沖	Huike	慧可
Fahai	法海	Huiming	惠明
Fahua jing	法華經	Huineng	慧能
fangbian	方便	Huishun	惠順
fannao	煩惱	Huisi	慧思
Fanyang	范陽	Huiwen	慧文
Farong	法融	Huixin	惠昕
Faru	法如	Huiyuan	慧遠
Faxian	法顯	Ishii	石井
Faxiang	法相	ji	疾
Fayan zong	法眼宗	jian (gradual)	漸
fayi	法意	jian (seeing)	見
Fazang	法藏	Jiangxi	江西
foxin	佛心	jianxing	見性
foxing	佛性	jie	戒
Fu fazang zhuan	付法藏傳	jing (sūtra)	經
Gao Xingjian	高行健	jing (object, realm)	境
gelao	獦獠	Jingjue	淨覺

Jingtu	浄土	ming	明
Jingzang	淨藏	Mogao Caves	莫高窟
Jiujiang	九江	*Mohe zhiguan*	摩訶止觀
jiyuan wenda	機緣問答	Nanhai	南海
jue	覺	Nanhua Monastery	南華寺
kanjing	看淨	Nanxue	南學
kanxin	看心	*Nanyang Heshang*	南陽和尚問答
kechen fannao	客塵煩惱	*wenda zazhengyi*	雜徵義
kong	空	nian	念
Kongzi	孔子	Niutou zong	牛頭宗
Lao'an	老安	Puji	普寂
Lao-Zhuang	老莊	*Pusajie fa*	菩薩戒法
Laozi/*Laozi*	老子	*Pusajie jing*	菩薩戒經
li (advantage,	利	puti	普提
benefit)		Putidamo	菩提達摩
li (ritual)	禮	*Putidamo Nanzong*	菩提達摩南宗定
Li (surname)	李	*ding shifei lun*	是非論
Li Hua	李華	Qisong	契嵩
Lingnan	嶺南	Qizhou	蘄州
linian	離念	ren	仁
Linji zong	臨濟宗	Ruizong	睿宗
Li Tongxuan	李通玄	rulaizang	如來藏
liumen	六門	Sanlun	三論
liushi	六識	Sengcan	僧璨
liutong	流通	Sengchou	僧稠
liutong fen	流通分	Sengfu	僧副
Liu Yuxi	劉禹錫	shangzuo	上座
Liu Zongyuan	柳宗元	Shaozhou	韶州
Lu (state)	魯	Shengshan	聖善寺
Lu (surname of	盧	Monastery	
Huineng)		Shenhui	神會
lü	律	Shenxiu	神秀
Lunyu	論語	shi	事
Luoyang	洛陽	*Shiji*	史記
Lu Zhen	盧珍	Shitou Xiqian	石頭希遷
Ma Zong	馬總	shou	受
Mazu Daoyi	馬祖道一	shoujie (receive	受戒
menren	門人	precepts)	
mi	迷	shoujie (bestow	授戒
Mijiao	密教	precepts)	

shoujing	守淨	Xianzong	憲宗
shouyi	守一	xiaogen	小根
shouyi cunsan	守一存三	Xie Lingyun	謝靈雲
Shunzong	順宗	xing (nature)	性
Sichuan	四川	xing (practice)	行
Sima Qian	司馬遷	Xingsi	行思
Sŏn	禪	xinjie	心戒
Song gaoseng zhuan	宋高僧傳	Xinzhou	新州
Songshan	嵩山	xu	虛
Suzong	蕭宗	xuanxue	玄學
tai	臺	Xuanzang	玄奘
Taizi ruiying	太子瑞應本起經	Xuanze	玄賾
benqi jing		Xuanzong	玄宗
ti	體	Xu Dai	徐岱
Tanyu	壇語	xufen	序分
Tiantai	天台	Yanagida Seizan	柳田聖山
tongliu	通流	Yan Hui	顏回
wang	妄	Yao Chong	姚崇
Wang Wei	王維	yi	義
Wei Ju	韋據	yifang	一方
Wei Qu	韋璩	Yifu	義福
Weishi	唯識	*Yijing*	易經
weixin	唯心	Yijing	義淨
Weiyang zong	溈陽宗	*Yingluo jing*	瓔珞經
Wenshu shuo jing	文殊說經	yinke	印可
wu	悟	yinyuan	因緣
wuchang	無常	Yinzong	印宗
Wu fangbian	五方便	yixin	一心
wunian	無念	Yixing	一行
wuwei	無為	yixing sanmei	一行三昧
wuxiang	無相	yong	用
wuxiangjie	無想戒	yu	愚
wuxiang xindi jie	無相心地戒	*Yuanming lun*	圓明論
wuxin	無心	yulu	語錄
Wu Zetian	武則天	Yunmen zong	雲門宗
Wuzhen	悟真	Yuquan Monastery	玉泉寺
Wuzhu	無住	Zanning	贊寧
wuzhu	無住	zhaijie	齋戒
wuzhuben	無住本	Zhang Yue	張說
xiang	相	Zhanran	湛然

zhengzong fen	正宗分	Zhou	周
zhenru	真如	Zhuang Zhou	莊周
zhenru sanmei	真如三昧	*Zhuangzi*	莊子
zhi (wisdom)	智	zixu	自序
zhi (direct)	直	zong	宗
Zhicheng	志誠	Zongbao	宗寶
Zhishen	智詵	Zongmi	宗密
Zhiwei	智威	zuo budong	坐不動
zhixin	直心	zuochan	坐禪
Zhiyi	智顗	zushi	祖師
zhizhu	執著	*Zutang ji*	祖堂集
Zhongzong	中宗		

BIBLIOGRAPHY

· · · · · · · · ·

COLLECTIONS AND THEIR ABBREVIATIONS

Dainihon zoku zōkyō 大日本続蔵経. Ed. Maeda Eun 前田慧雲 and Nakano Tatsue 中野達慧. 150 vols. Kyoto: Zōkyō shoin, 1905–12. Abbreviated as Z.

Pelliot Collection of Dunhuang manuscripts, held at the Bibliothèque nationale de France, Paris. Manuscripts designated Pelliot chinois. Abbreviated as P.

Stein Collection of Dunhuang manuscripts, held at the British Library, London. Abbreviated as S.

Taishō shinshū daizōkyō 大正新修大蔵経. 100 vols. Ed. Takakusu Junjirō 高楠順次郎, Watanabe Kaigyoku 渡辺海旭, and Ono Gemmyō 小野玄妙. 1924–34; reprint, Taibei: Xinwenfeng chuban gongsi, 1974. Abbreviated as T.

PRIMARY SOURCES

Bianzonglun 辨宗論. Xie Lingyun 謝靈雲 (385–433). In *Guang hongming ji* 廣弘明集, Daoxuan 道宣 (596–667). T no. 2103.

Caoqi dashi zhuan 曹溪大師傳. Photographic reproduction in Yanagida Seizan, ed., *Rokuso dankyō shohon shūsei*, 405–424. Edited version in Komazawa daigaku zenshūshi kenkyūkai, ed., *Enō kenkyū*, 112–125.

Chuanfa bao ji 傳法寶記. Text in Yanagida Seizan, *Shoki no zenshi*, vol. 1: *Ryōga shiji ki, Den'hōbō ki*, 329–438.

Da Tang xiyu ji 大唐西域記. Xuanzang 玄奘 (602–664). T. no. 2087.

Dunwu wushang bore song 頓悟無生般若頌. Shenhui 神會, ca. 750. S. 468.

Erru sixing lun 二入四行論. Attributed to Bodhidharma. Various Dunhuang manuscripts. Edited text in Yanagida Seizan, ed., *Daruma no goroku: Ninyū shigyōron*.

Fanwang jing 梵網經. Trans. attributed to Kumārajīva (Jiumoluoshi 鳩摩羅什, 344–413). T no. 1484.

Guan wuliang shou fo jing 觀無量壽佛經. Translated by Kālayaśas (Jiangliangyeshe 畺良耶舍, ca. 424–442). *T* no. 365.

Guanxin lun 觀心論. *T* no. 2833.

Jingang bore boluomi jing 金剛般若波羅蜜經 (*Vajracchedikā*). Kumārajīva (Jiumoluoshi 鳩摩羅什, 344–413). *T* no. 235.

Jingang jing shu 金剛經疏. Anon. S. 2047, edited as *T* no. 2737.

Jingang sanmei jing 金剛三昧經. *T* no. 273.

Jingde chuandeng lu 景德傳燈錄. Daoyuan 道原, ca. 1004. *T* no. 2076.

Jueguan lun 絕觀論. Edition in Tokiwa, *A Dialogue on the Contemplation-Extinguished*, 88–102.

Lengqie ren fa zhi 楞伽人法誌. No longer extant. Cited in *Lengqie shizi ji*.

Lengqie shizi ji 楞伽師資記. Jingjue 淨覺 (683–ca. 750). *T* no. 2837. Also edited in Yanagida, *Shoki no zenshi*, vol. 1: *Ryōga shiji ki, Den'hōbō ki*, 49–326.

Lidai fabao ji 歷代法寶記. *T* no. 2075.

Liuzu Dashi fabao tanjing 六祖大師法寶壇經. *T* no. 2008.

Liuzu tanjing 六組壇經. See *Liuzu Dashi fabao tanjing*; and *Nanzong dunjiao zuishang . . . jing*.

Luoyang qielan ji 洛陽伽藍記. Yang Xuanzhi 楊衒之 (ca. 493–547). *T* no. 2092.

Nanzong dunjiao zuishang dasheng mohe bore boluomi jing Liuzu Huineng Dashi yu Shaozhou Dafansi shifa tanjing 南宗頓教最上大乘摩訶般若波羅蜜經六祖惠能大師於韶州大梵寺施法壇經. S. 5475, edited as *T* no. 2007.

Pusa yingluo benye jing 菩薩瓔珞本業經. Trans. attributed to Zhu Fonian 竺佛念 (ca. 365). *T* no. 1485.

(Qinding) Quan Tang wen (欽定)全唐文. Dong Gao 董誥 (1740–1818), et al. 4 vols. Taibei: Dahua shuju, 1987.

"Tang Zhongyue shamen Shi Faru Chanshi xingzhuang" 唐中岳沙門釋法如禪師行狀. In Yanagida, *Shoki zenshū*, 487–96.

Weimojie suoshuo jing 維摩詰所說經 (*Vimalakīrtinirdeśa*). Trans. Kumārajīva (Jiumoluoshi 鳩摩羅什, 344–413) in 406. *T* no. 475.

Xiuxin yao lun 修心要論. P. 3559.

Xu gaoseng zhuan 續高僧傳. Daoxuan 道宣 (596–667). *T* no. 2060.

Zhuyuan zhuquanji duxu 諸源諸詮集都序. Zongmi 宗密 (780–841). *T* no. 2015.

SECONDARY SOURCES

TRANSLATIONS OF THE *PLATFORM SŪTRA* INTO ENGLISH

Buddhist Text Translation Society, trans. *Liu-tsu-ta-shih fa pao t'an ching: The Sixth Patriarch's Dharma Jewel Platform Sutra and Commentary by Tripitaka Master Hsüan Hua*. 2nd ed. San Francisco: Cold Mountain Temple, Sino-American Buddhist Association, 1977. Translation of the later and longer orthodox version of the *Platform Sūtra*, compiled after 1290, based on the modern standard scholarly version in the *Taishō* canon (*T* no. 2008).

Chan, Wing-tsit, trans. *Tan Jing, The Platform Scripture*. New York: St. John's University Press, 1963. Translation of one of the two texts of the *Platform Sūtra* found at Dunhuang, British Library, S. 5475.

Cleary, Thomas, trans. *The Sutra of Hui-neng, Grand Master of Zen, with Hui-neng's Commentary on the "Diamond Sutra."* Boston: Shambhala, 1998. Translation of the later and longer orthodox version of the *Platform Sūtra*, compiled after 1290, based on the modern standard scholarly version in the *Taishō* canon (*T* no. 2008).

Goddard, Dwight, ed. *A Buddhist Bible: The Favorite Scriptures of the Zen Sect; History of Early Zen Buddhism, Self-realisation of Noble Wisdom, the Diamond Sutra, the Prajnaparamita Sutra, the Sutra of the Sixth Patriarch*. Thetford, VT, 1932. 2nd, enlarged ed., 1938. Published numerous times in later editions. Includes a heavily edited and interpreted version of the 1930 translation of the *Platform Sūtra* by Mou-lam Wong.

McRae, John R., trans. *The Platform Sūtra of the Sixth Patriarch*. BDK English Tripitaka. Berkeley: Numata Center for Buddhist Translation and Research, 2000. Also available for free download at http://www.numatacenter.com/default.aspx?MPID=81. Translation of the later and longer orthodox version of the *Platform Sūtra*, compiled after 1290, based on the modern standard scholarly version in the *Taishō* canon (*T* no. 2008).

Red Pine (Bill Porter), trans. *The Platform Sutra: The Zen Teaching of Hui-neng*. Emeryville: Shoemaker & Hoard, 2006. English translation of an early manuscript from Dunhuang (Dunhuang County Museum, no. 77), very close to the text used by Yampolsky (S. 5475). Red Pine also provides a collated edition of the Chinese text; a translation of portions in the longer orthodox version (*T* no. 2008); and a Finding List (p. 297) correlating the early Dunhuang version and the orthodox version.

Wong, Mou-lam, trans. *Sutra Spoken by the Sixth Patriarch Wei Lang on the High Seat of the Gem of Law (Dharmaratha) (Message from the East)*. Shanghai: Yu Ching Press, 1930. Translation of Ding Fubao's edition of the longer orthodox version of the *Platform Sūtra*, very close to the modern standard scholarly version in the *Taishō* canon (*T* no. 2008).

——, trans. *The Sutra of Wei Lang (or Hui Neng) Translated from the Chinese by Wong Mou-lam*. Ed. Christmas Humphreys. London: Luzac, 1944. Published numerous times in later editions. The text of Wong's 1930 translation, edited for readability by Humphreys.

—Revised edition: *The Sutra of Hui Neng*, 4th ed. rev. by Christmas Humphreys. London: Buddhist Society, 1966. In this edition, all Chinese words were changed to their standard Mandarin pronunciation using the Wade-Giles system.

—Reprinted in A. F. Price and Mou-lam Wong, trans., *The Diamond Sūtra and the Sūtra of Hui-Neng*. Berkeley: Shambhala, 1969; Boston: Shambhala, 2005. Uses the 1966 edition.

Yampolsky, Philip B. *The Platform Sutra of the Sixth Patriarch*. New York: Columbia University Press, 1967. 2nd ed., 2012. Translation of one of the two texts of the *Platform Sūtra* found at Dunhuang. British Library, S. 5475. Yampolsky also provides an edition of the Chinese text collated with early Japanese printed editions, building on prior modern Japanese editions by Ui Hakuju and Suzuki Daisetzu and Kōda Rentarō.

OTHER SECONDARY SOURCES

Adamek, Wendi L. *The Mystique of Transmission: On an Early Chan History and Its Contexts.* New York: Columbia University Press, 2007.

Ashiwa, Yoshiko and David L. Wank, eds. *Making Religion, Making the State: The Politics of Religion in Modern China.* Stanford, CA: Stanford University Press, 2009.

Barrett, T. H. "Buddhist Precepts in a Lawless World: Some Comments on the Linhuai Ordination Scandal." In *Going Forth: Visions of Buddhist Vinaya: Essays Presented in Honor of Professor Stanley Weinstein*, ed. William M. Bodiford. Kuroda Institute, Studies in East Asian Buddhism, 18. Honolulu: University of Hawai'i Press, 2005, 101–23.

Bell, Catherine. "Religion and Chinese Culture: Toward an Assessment of 'Popular Religion.'" *History of Religions* 29, no. 2 (1989): 35–57.

Benn, James A. "Written in Flames: Self-Immolation in Sixth-Century Sichuan." *T'oung Pao* 92 (2006): 410–65.

Bielefeldt, Carl. "Ch'ang-lu Tsung-tse's *Tso-ch'an I* and the 'Secret' of Zen Meditation." In *Traditions of Meditation in Chinese Buddhism*, ed. Peter N. Gregory. Kuroda Institute, Studies in East Asian Buddhism, 4. Honolulu: University of Hawai'i Press, 1986, 129–61.

Bielefeldt, Carl and Lewis Lancaster. "*T'an Ching* (Platform Scripture)." *Philosophy East and West* 25, no. 2 (1975): 197–212.

Birnbaum, Raoul. "Buddhist China at the Century's Turn." In *Religion in China Today*, ed. Daniel L. Overmyer. *The China Quarterly* Special Issues, new series, no. 3. Cambridge: Cambridge University Press, 2003, 122–44.

Broughton, Jeffrey Lyle. *Zongmi on Chan.* Translations from the Asian Classics. New York: Columbia University Press, 2009.

Buswell, Robert E., Jr. *The Formation of Ch'an Ideology in China and Korea: The Vajrasamādhi-Sūtra, A Buddhist Apocryphon.* Princeton: Princeton University Press, 1989.

Buswell, Robert E., Jr., ed. *Chinese Buddhist Apocrypha.* Honolulu: University of Hawai'i Press, 1990.

———. *Encyclopedia of Buddhism.* New York: Macmillan Reference USA, 2004.

Chang, Garma C. C., trans. *Treasury of Mahayana Sutras: Selections from the Maharatnakuta Sutra.* University Park: Pennsylvania State University Press, 1983.

Chappell, David W. "From Dispute to Dual Cultivation: Pure Land Responses to Ch'an Critics." In *Traditions of Meditation in Chinese Buddhism*, ed. Peter N. Gregory. Kuroda Institute, Studies in East Asian Buddhism, 4. Honolulu: University of Hawai'i Press, 1986, 163–97.

———. "The Teachings of the Fourth Ch'an Patriarch Tao-hsin (580–651)." In *Early Ch'an in China and Tibet*, ed. Whalen Lai and Lewis R. Lancaster. Berkeley Buddhist Studies Series, 5. Berkeley: Asian Humanities Press, 1983, 89–129.

Chen, Huaiyu. *The Revival of Buddhist Monasticism in Medieval China.* New York: Peter Lang, 2007.

Chen, Jinhua. "An Alternative View of the Meditation Tradition in China: Meditation in the Life and Works of Daoxuan (596–667)." *T'oung Pao* 88, nos. 4–5 (2002): 332–95.

——. *Monks and Monarchs, Kinship and Kingship: Tanqian in Sui Buddhism and Politics.* Italian School of East Asian Studies, Essays, 3. Kyoto: ISEAS, 2002.

——. "The Statues and Monks of Shengshan Monastery: Money and Maitreyan Buddhism in Tang China." *Asia Major*, third series, 19, parts 1–2 (2006): 111–60.

Chen, Jo-shui. *Liu Tsung-yüan and Intellectual Change in T'ang China, 773–819.* Cambridge: Cambridge University Press, 1992.

Ch'en, Kenneth. *Buddhism in China: A Historical Survey.* Princeton: Princeton University Press, 1964.

——. *The Chinese Transformation of Buddhism.* Princeton: Princeton University Press, 1973.

Chau, Adam Y. *Miraculous Response: Doing Popular Religion in Contemporary China.* Stanford: Stanford University Press, 2006.

Chou, I-liang. "Tantrism in China." *Harvard Journal of Asiatic Studies* 8 (1945): 241–332. Reprinted in *Tantric Buddhism in East Asia*, ed. Richard Karl Payne. Somerville, MA: Wisdom, 2006, 33–60.

Cleary, J. C., trans. *Zen Dawn: Early Zen Texts from Tun Huang.* Boston: Shambhala, 1986.

Cleary, Thomas, trans. *The Flower Ornament Scripture.* Boston: Shambhala, 1993.

Cole, Alan. *Fathering Your Father: The Zen of Fabrication in Tang Buddhism.* Berkeley: University of California Press, 2009.

——. *Mothers and Sons in Chinese Buddhism.* Stanford: Stanford University Press, 1998.

Conze, Edward, trans. *The Large Sutra on Perfect Wisdom.* Berkeley: University of California Press, 1975.

——, trans. *The Short Prajñāpāramitā Texts.* London: Luzac, 1973.

Cook, Francis H. *Hua-yen Buddhism: The Jewel Net of Indra.* Institute for Advanced Studies of World Religions. University Park: Pennsylvania State University Press, 1977.

Dalia, Albert A. "Mt. Ox-head, Fa-rong: A Forgotten Exegesis Master in the Rise of Tang Buddhism." *Hualin* 華林 3 (2003): 313–30.

Ding Fubao 丁福保. *Liuzu tanjing zhujie* 六祖壇經註解 (a.k.a. 箋註). N.p.: Ruicheng shuju yinhang, 1922. Other editions include Shanghai, 1919.

Donner, Neal. "Chih-i's Meditation on Evil." In *Buddhist and Taoist Practice in Medieval Chinese Society*, ed. David W. Chappell. Honolulu: University of Hawai'i Press, 1987, 49–64.

——. "The Mahayanization of Chinese Dhyāna." *The Eastern Buddhist* 10, no. 2 (1977): 49–64.

Donner, Neal and Daniel B. Stevenson. *The Great Calming and Contemplation: A Study and Annotated Translation of the First Chapter of Chih-i's "Mo-ho Chih-kuan."* Kuroda Institute, Classics in East Asian Buddhism. Honolulu: University of Hawai'i Press, 1993.

Ebrey, Patricia Buckley. *The Aristocratic Families of Early Imperial China: A Case Study of the Po-ling Ts'ui Family.* Cambridge: Cambridge University Press, 1978.

Eliade, Mircea, et al., eds. *Encyclopedia of Religion.* New York: Macmillan, 1987.

Emmerick, R. E., trans. *The Sūtra of Golden Light: Being a Translation of the Suvarṇaprabhāsottamasūtra.* Sacred Books of the Buddhists, 27. London: Luzac, 1970.

Faure, Bernard. *Le bouddhisme Ch'an en mal d'histoire: Genèse d'une tradition religieuse dans la Chine des T'ang*. Publications de l'École Française d'Extrême-Orient, 158. Paris: École Française d'Extrême-Orient, 1989.

———. "One-Practice Samādhi in Early Chan." In *Traditions of Meditation in Chinese Buddhism*, ed. Peter N. Gregory. Kuroda Institute, Studies in East Asian Buddhism, 4. Honolulu: University of Hawai'i Press, 1986, 99–128.

———. *The Rhetoric of Immediacy: A Cultural Critique of Chan/Zen Buddhism*. Princeton: Princeton University Press, 1991.

———. *La volonté d'orthodoxie dans le bouddhisme chinois*. Paris: Éditions du CNRS, 1988.

———. *The Will to Orthodoxy: A Critical Genealogy of Northern Chan Buddhism*. Trans. Phyllis Brooks. Stanford: Stanford University Press, 1997.

Fontein, Jan and Money L. Hickman. *Zen Painting and Calligraphy*. Boston: Museum of Fine Arts, 1970.

Forte, Antonino. *Political Propaganda and Ideology in China at the End of the Seventh Century*. Napoli: Istituto Universitario Orientale, 1976.

Frodsham, J. D. *The Murmuring Stream: The Life and Works of the Chinese Nature Poet Hsieh Ling-yün (385–433), Duke of K'ang-lo*, 2 vols. Kuala Lumpur: University of Malaya Press, 1967.

Furuta Shokin 古田紹欽 and Tanaka Ryōshō 田中良昭. *Enō* 慧能. Tokyo: Daizō shuppansha, 1982.

Gernet, Jacques. "Biographie du Maître Chen-hoeui du Ho-tsö (668–760): Contribution à l'histoire de l'école du Dhyāna." *Journal Asiatique* 239 (1951): 29–68.

———. *Buddhism in Chinese Society*. Trans. Franciscus Verellen. New York: Columbia University Press, 1998.

Getz, Daniel A. "Popular Religion and Pure Land in Song Dynasty Tiantai Bodhisattva Precept Ordination Ceremonies." In *Going Forth: Visions of Buddhist Vinaya: Essays Presented in Honor of Professor Stanley Weinstein*, ed. William M. Bodiford. Kuroda Institute, Studies in East Asian Buddhism, 18. Honolulu: University of Hawai'i Press, 2005, 161–84.

Gómez, Luis O., trans. *The Land of Bliss: The Paradise of the Buddha of Measureless Light*. Honolulu: University of Hawai'i Press, 1996.

———. "Purifying Gold: The Metaphor of Effort and Intuition in Buddhist Thought and Practice." In *Sudden and Gradual: Approaches to Enlightenment in Chinese Thought*, ed. Peter N. Gregory. Kuroda Institute, Studies in East Asian Buddhism, 5. Honolulu: University of Hawai'i Press, 1987, 67–165.

Gregory, Peter N. *Inquiry Into the Origin of Humanity: An Annotated Translation of Tsungmi's "Yüan jen lun" with a Modern Commentary*. Kuroda Institute, Classics in East Asian Buddhism. Honolulu: University of Hawai'i Press, 1995.

———. *Tsung-mi and the Sinification of Buddhism*. Kuroda Institute, Studies in East Asian Buddhism, 16. Honolulu: University of Hawai'i Press, 2002.

Gregory, Peter N., ed. *Sudden and Gradual Approaches to Enlightenment in Chinese Thought*. Kuroda Institute, Studies in East Asian Buddhism, 5. Honolulu: University of Hawai'i Press, 1987.

——. *Traditions of Meditation in Chinese Buddhism*. Kuroda Institute, Studies in East Asian Buddhism, 4. Honolulu: University of Hawai'i Press, 1986.

Gregory, Peter N. and Daniel Getz, eds. *Buddhism in the Sung*. Kuroda Institute, Studies in East Asian Buddhism, 13. Honolulu: University of Hawai'i Press, 1999.

Groner, Paul. "The *Fan-wang ching* and Monastic Discipline in Japanese Tendai: A Study of Annen's *Futsu jubosatsukai kōshaku*." In *Chinese Buddhist Apocrypha*, ed. Robert E. Buswell Jr. Honolulu: University of Hawai'Press, 1990, 251–90.

——. "The Ordination Ritual in the Platform Sutra Within the Context of the East Asian Buddhist Vinaya Tradition." In *Fo Kuang Shan Report of International Conference on Ch'an Buddhism*. Gaoxiong: Fo Kuang Publishers, 1990.

Guisso, R.W.L. *Wu Tse-t'ien and the Politics of Legitimation in T'ang China*. Western Washington University, Program in East Asian Studies, Occasional Papers, 11. Bellingham: Western Washington University, Program in East Asian Studies, 1978.

Hamar, Imre, ed. *Reflecting Mirrors: Perspectives on Huayan Buddhism*. Asiatische Forschungen. Wiesbaden: Harrassowitz, 2007.

Hao Chunwen 郝春文. *Tanghouqi Wudai Songchu Dunhuang sengni de shehui shenghuo* 唐后期五代宋初敦煌僧尼的社会生活. Beijing: Zhongguo shehui kexueyuan chubanshe, 1998.

Harvey, Peter. *An Introduction to Buddhism: Teachings, History and Practices*. Cambridge: Cambridge University Press, 1990.

Heine, Steven and Dale S. Wright, eds. *The Kōan: Texts and Contexts in Zen Buddhism*. New York: Oxford University Press, 2000.

Herbert, P. A. *Under the Brilliant Emperor: Imperial Authority in T'ang China as Seen in the Writings of Chang Chiu-ling*. Canberra: Australian National University Press, 1978.

Hiermann, Ann. "Some Remarks on the Rise of the Bhikṣunīsaṃgha and on the Ordination Ceremony for Bhikṣunīs according to the Dharmaguptakavinaya." *Journal of the International Association of Buddhist Studies* 20, no. 2 (1997): 33–85.

Hu, Shih (Hu Shi). "Ch'an (Zen) Buddhism in China, Its History and Method." *Philosophy East and West* 3, no. 1 (1953): 3–24.

Hu Shi 胡適. *Shenhui heshang yiji* 神會和尚遺集. Taibei: Hu Shi jinianguan, 1970.

Hurvitz, Leon. *Chih-i (538-597): An Introduction to the Life and Ideas of a Chinese Buddhist Monk*. Mélanges chinois et bouddhiques, 12. Brussels: Institut Belge des Hautes Études Chinoises, 1962.

——. "The First Systematizations of Buddhist Thought in China." *Journal of Chinese Philosophy* 2 (1975): 361–88.

Hurvitz, Leon, trans. *Scripture of the Lotus Blossom of the Fine Dharma: Translated from the Chinese of Kumārajīva*. New York: Columbia University Press, 1976.

In'gyŏng 印鏡. *Mongsan Tŏg'i wa Koryŏ hugi Sŏnsasang yŏn'gu* 蒙山德異와高麗後期禅思想研究. Seoul: Pur'il, 2000.

Ishii Kōsei 石井公成. "Musōkai no genryū 無相戒の源流." *Komazawa daigaku zen kenkyūjo nenpō* 駒澤大學禪研究所年報 8 (1997): 125–34.

Ivanhoe, P. J., trans. *The Daodejing of Laozi*. New York: Seven Bridges Press, 2002.

Jan, Yün-hua. "Patterns of Chinese Assimilation of Buddhist Thought: A Comparative Study of No-Thought (*Wu-nien*) in Indian and Chinese Texts." *Journal of Oriental Studies* 24, no. 1 (1986): 21–36.

———. "Seng-ch'ou's Method of Dhyāna." In *Early Ch'an in China and Tibet*, ed. Whalen Lai and Lewis R. Lancaster. Berkeley Buddhist Studies Series, 5. Berkeley: Asian Humanities Press, 1983, 51–63.

———. "Tsung-mi: His Analysis of Ch'an Buddhism." *T'oung Pao* 58 (1972): 1–54.

Jia, Jinhua. *The Hongzhou School of Chan Buddhism in Eighth- Through Tenth-Century China.* Albany: State University of New York Press, 2006.

Johnson, David G. *The Medieval Chinese Oligarchy.* Boulder: Westview, 1977.

Jones, Lindsay, ed. *Encyclopedia of Religion.* 2nd ed. Detroit: Macmillan Reference, 2005.

Jordan, David K. *Gods, Ghosts, and Ancestors: Folk Religion in a Taiwanese Village.* 3rd ed. San Diego, CA: Department of Anthropology, UCSD, 1999. http://anthro.ucsd.edu/%7Edkjordan/scriptorium/gga/ggamain.html.

Jorgensen, John. "The 'Imperial' Lineage of Ch'an Buddhism: The Role of Confucian Ritual and Ancestor Worship in Ch'an's Search for Legitimation in the Mid-T'ang Dynasty." *Papers on Far Eastern History* 35 (1987): 89–133.

———. *Inventing Hui-neng, the Sixth Patriarch: Hagiography and Biography in Early Ch'an.* Sinica Leidensia, 68. Leiden: Brill, 2005.

———. "The Platform Sūtra and the Corpus of Shenhui: Recent Critical Text Editions and Studies." *Revue Bibliographique de Sinologie* (2002): 399–438.

———. "Ssanggye-sa and Local Buddhist History: Propaganda and Relics in a Struggle for Survival, 1850s–1930s." *Seoul Journal of Korean Studies* 21, no. 1 (2008): 87–127.

Kieschnick, John. *The Eminent Monk: Buddhist Ideals in Medieval Chinese Hagiography.* Kuroda Institute, Studies in East Asian Buddhism, 10. Honolulu: University of Hawai'i Press, 1997.

Kohn, Livia. *Laughing at the Tao: Debates Among Buddhists and Taoists in Medieval China.* Princeton: Princeton University Press, 1995.

Komazawa daigaku zenshūshi kenkyūkai 駒澤大学禅宗史研究会, ed. *Enō kenkyū: Enō no denki to shiryō ni kansuru kisoteki kenkyū* 慧能研究: 慧能の伝記と資料に関する基礎的研究. Tokyo: Daishukan shoten, 1978.

Lai, Whalen and Lewis R. Lancaster, eds. *Early Ch'an in China and Tibet.* Berkeley Buddhist Studies Series, 5. Berkeley: Asian Humanities Press, 1983.

Lamotte, Étienne. *History of Indian Buddhism from the Origins to the Śaka Era.* Trans. Sara Webb-Boin. Publications de l'Institut Orientaliste de Louvain, 36. Louvain-la-Neuve: Institut Orientaliste, Université de Louvain, 1988.

———. *The Teaching of Vimalakīrti (Vimalakīrtinirdeśa).* Trans. Sara Boin. London: The Pali Text Society, 1976.

Lau, D. C., trans. *The Analects of Confucius.* New York: Penguin, 1999.

———. *Mencius.* London: Penguin, 1970.

———. *Tao Te Ching.* New York: Penguin, 1964.

Liebenthal, Walter. "The Sermon of Shen-hui." *Asia Major*, new series, 3, no. 2 (1953): 132–55.

Lin, Paul, trans. *A Translation of Lao-tzu's Tao Te Ching and Wang Pi's Commentary*. Ann Arbor, MI: Center for Chinese Studies, 1977.

Liu, Ming-Wood. *Madhyamaka Thought in China*. Sinica Leidensia, 30. Leiden: Brill, 1994.

Lopez, Donald S., Jr. *Elaborations on Emptiness: Uses of the Heart Sūtra*. Princeton: Princeton University Press, 1996.

———. *The Story of Buddhism: A Concise Guide to Its History and Teachings*. New York: HarperCollins, 2001.

Luk, Charles [Lu, K'uan Yü]. *The Heart Sutra and the Diamond Sutra*. Hong Kong: World Fellowship of Buddhists, 1960.

———. *The Secrets of Chinese Meditation*. London: Rider, 1964.

———. *The Vimalakīrti Nirdeśa Sūtra (Wei Mo Chieh So Shuo Ching)*. Berkeley: Shambhala, 1972.

Lynn, Richard John, trans. *The Classic of Changes: A New Translation of the I Ching as Interpreted by Wang Bi*. New York: Columbia University Press, 1994.

Mair, Victor H. *Painting and Performance: Chinese Picture Recitation and Its Indian Genesis*. Honolulu: University of Hawai'i Press, 1988.

———. *Tun-huang Popular Narratives*. Cambridge: Cambridge University Press, 1983.

Makeham, John. *Transmitters and Creators: Chinese Commentators and Commentaries on the "Analects."* Cambridge, MA: Harvard University Press, 2003.

McMullen, David. *State and Scholars in T'ang China*. Cambridge: Cambridge University Press, 1988.

McRae, John R. "The Antecedents of Encounter Dialogue in Chinese Ch'an Buddhism." In *The Koan: Texts and Contexts in Zen Buddhism*, ed. Steven Heine and Dale S. Wright. New York: Oxford University Press, 2000, 46–74.

———. "Buddhism, Schools of: Chinese Buddhism." In *Encyclopedia of Religion*, 2nd ed., ed. Lindsay Jones. New York: Macmillan, 2005, 2:1235–41.

———. *The Northern School and the Formation of Early Ch'an Buddhism*. Kuroda Institute, Studies in East Asian Buddhism, 3. Honolulu: University of Hawai'i Press, 1986.

———. "The Ox-head School of Chinese Ch'an Buddhism: From Early Ch'an to the Golden Age." In *Studies in Ch'an and Hua-yen*, ed. Robert M. Gimello and Peter N. Gregory. Kuroda Institute, Studies in East Asian Buddhism, 1. Honolulu: University of Hawai'i Press, 1983, 169–252.

———. *Seeing Through Zen: Encounter, Transformation, and Genealogy in Chinese Chan Buddhism*. Berkeley: University of California Press, 2003.

———. "Shen-hui and the Teaching of Sudden Enlightenment in Early Ch'an Buddhism." In *Sudden and Gradual: Approaches to Enlightenment in Chinese Thought*, ed. Peter N. Gregory. Kuroda Institute, Studies in East Asian Buddhism, 5. Honolulu: University of Hawai'i Press, 1987, 227–78.

———. "Shenhui as Evangelist: Re-envisioning the Identity of a Chinese Buddhist Monk." *Journal of Chinese Religions* 30 (2002): 123–48. Also published in *Tanaka Ryōshō Hakushi koki kinen ronshū: Zengaku kenkyū no shosō* 田中良昭博士古希記念論集：禅学研究の諸相. Tokyo: Daitō shuppansha, 2003, 1–26 (reverse).

McRae, John R., trans. *The Vimalakīrti Sūtra*. Berkeley: The Numata Center for Buddhist Translation and Research, 2004.

Nattier, Jan. "The Teaching of Vimalakīrti (*Vimalakīrinirdeśa*): A Review of Four English Translations." *Buddhist Literature* 2 (2000): 234–58.

Nylan, Michael and Thomas Wilson. *Lives of Confucius: Civilization's Greatest Sage Through the Ages*. New York: Doubleday, 2010.

Orzech, Charles D. *Politics and Transcendent Wisdom: The Scripture for Humane Kings in the Creation of Chinese Buddhism*. Hermeneutics: Studies in the History of Religions. University Park: Pennsylvania State University Press, 1998.

Orzech, Charles D., Henrik H. Sørensen, and Richard K. Payne, eds. *Esoteric Buddhism and the Tantras in East Asia*. Handbook of Oriental Studies, Section 4: China, 24. Leiden: Brill, 2010.

Penkower, Linda. "In the Beginning . . . Guanding 灌頂 (561–632) and the Creation of Early Tiantai." *Journal of the International Association of Buddhist Studies* 23, no. 2 (2000): 245–96.

Poceski, Mario. "Lay Models of Engagement with Chan Teachings and Practices Among the Literati in Mid-Tang China." *Journal of Chinese Religions* 35 (2007): 65–99.

———. *Ordinary Mind as the Way: The Hongzhou School and the Growth of Chan Buddhism*. New York: Oxford University Press, 2007.

Robinson, G. W. *Poems of Wang Wei*. Harmondsworth: Penguin, 1973.

Robinson, Richard H. *Early Mādhyamika in India and China*. Madison: University of Wisconsin Press, 1967.

Sasaki, Shizuka. "A Study on the Origin of Mahāyāna Buddhism." *Eastern Buddhist* 30, no.1 (Spring 1997): 79–113.

Schafer, Edward H. *The Vermilion Bird: T'ang Images of the South*. Berkeley: University of California Press, 1967.

Schlütter, Morten. *How Zen Became Zen: The Dispute Over Enlightenment and the Formation of Chan Buddhism in Song-Dynasty China*. Kuroda Institute, Studies in East Asian Buddhism, 22. Honolulu: University of Hawai'i Press, 2008.

———. "A Study in the Genealogy of the Platform Sutra." *Studies in Central and East Asian Religions* 2 (Autumn 1989): 53–115.

———. "Transmission and Enlightenment in Chan Buddhism Seen Through the *Platform Sūtra* (*Liuzu tanjing*)." *Chung-Hwa Buddhist Journal* 20 (2007): 379–410.

Schmidt-Glintzer, Helwig. *Die Identität der buddhistischen Schulen und die Kompilation buddhistischer Universalgeschichten in China*. Münchener Ostasiatische Studien, 26. Wiesbaden: Franz Steiner, 1982.

Shinohara, Koichi. "From Local History to Universal History: The Construction of the Sung T'ien-t'ai Lineage." In *Buddhism in the Sung*, ed. Peter N. Gregory and Daniel A. Getz Jr.. Kuroda Institute, Studies in East Asian Buddhism, 13. Honolulu: University of Hawai'i Press, 1999, 524–76.

Slingerland, Edward, trans. *Confucius: Analects*. Indianapolis: Hackett, 2003.

Stevenson, Daniel B. "The Four Kinds of Samādhi in Early T'ien-t'ai Buddhism." In *Traditions of Meditation in Chinese Buddhism*, ed. Peter N. Gregory. Kuroda Institute,

Studies in East Asian Buddhism, 4. Honolulu: University of Hawai'i Press, 1986, 45–97.

Strong, John S. *The Experience of Buddhism: Sources and Interpretations.* Belmont, CA: Wadsworth/Thompson Learning, 2002.

Suzuki Daisetsu 鈴木大拙, and Kōda Rentarō 公田連太郎, eds. *Tonkō shutsudo Kataku Shin'e Zenji goroku* 燉煌出土荷澤神會禪師語錄, *Tonkō shutsudo Rokuso dangyo* 敦煌出土六祖壇經, *Kōshōji-bon Rokuso dangyō* 興聖寺本六祖壇經. 4 vols. Tokyo: Morie shoten, 1934.

Swanson, Paul L. *Foundations of T'ien-T'ai Philosophy: The Flowering of the Two-truth Theory in Chinese Buddhism.* Nanzan Studies in Religion and Culture. Berkeley: Asian Humanities Press, 1989.

Tagawa, Shun'ei. *Living Yogacara: An Introduction to Consciousness-Only Buddhism.* Somerville, MA: Wisdom, 2009.

Tanaka, Kenneth K. *The Dawn of Chinese Pure Land Buddhist Doctrine: Ching-ying Hui-yüan's Commentary on the Visualization Sutra.* SUNY Series in Buddhist Studies. Albany: State University of New York Press, 1990.

Tanaka Ryōshō 田中良昭. "Recent Developments in the Textual-Critical Study of the Platform Scripture." In *From Benares to Beijing: Essays on Buddhism and Chinese Religion*, ed. Koichi Shinohara and Gregory Schopen. Oakville, ON: Mosaic Press, 1991, 229–60.

———. "Shoki zenshū no dōkyō 初期禪宗の道教." In *Yoshioka Yoshitoyo Hakase kanreki kinen dōkyō kenkyū ronshū: Dōkyō kenkyū no shisō to bunka* 吉岡義豊博士還曆記念: 道教研究論集—道教の思想と文化. Tokyo: Kokusho kankōkai, 1977, 403–28.

Teiser, Stephen F. *The Ghost Festival in Medieval China.* Princeton: Princeton University Press, 1988.

———. *"The Scripture on the Ten Kings" and the Making of Purgatory in Medieval Chinese Buddhism.* Kuroda Institute, Studies in East Asian Buddhism, 9. Honolulu: University of Hawai'i Press, 1994.

Teiser, Stephen F. and Jacqueline I. Stone, eds. *Readings of the Lotus Sūtra.* Columbia Readings of Buddhist Literature. New York: Columbia University Press, 2009.

Thurman, Robert, trans. *The Holy Teaching of Vimalakīrti.* University Park: Pennsylvania State University Press, 1976.

Tokiwa, Gishin. *Laṅkāvatāra ratna sūtram: A Sanskrit Restoration, a Study of the Four-Fascicle English and Japanese Translations with Introduction, and the Collated Guṇabhadra Chinese Version with Japanese Reading.* Osaka: Gishin Tokiwa, 2003.

Tokiwa, Gishin, trans. *A Dialogue on the Contemplation-Extinguished, Translated from the Chüeh-kuan Lun, An Early Chinese Zen Text from Tun Huang.* Kyoto: The Institute for Zen Studies, 1973.

Ui Hakuju 宇井伯壽. *Zenshū shi kenkyu* 禪宗史研究. 3 vols. Tokyo: Iwanami shoten, 1939–1943.

Waley, Arthur and Sarah Allan, trans. *The Analects.* New York: Knopf, 2000.

Watson, Burton, trans. *Hsün Tzu: Basic Writings.* New York: Columbia University Press, 1963.

——, trans. *The Lotus Sutra*. Translations from the Asian Classics. New York: Columbia University Press, 1993.

——, trans. *The Vimalakīrti Sūtra*. New York: Columbia University Press, 1997.

——, trans. *Zhuangzi: Basic Writings*. New York: Columbia University Press, 2003.

Weinstein, Stanley. "Buddhism, Schools of: Chinese Buddhism." In *Encyclopedia of Religion*, ed. Mircea Eliade. New York: Macmillan, 1987, 2:482–87.

——. *Buddhism Under the T'ang*. Cambridge: Cambridge University Press, 1987.

Welch, Holmes. *The Practice of Chinese Buddhism 1900–1950*. Cambridge, MA: Harvard University Press, 1967.

Whitfield, Roderick and Anne Farrer. *Caves of the Thousand Buddhas: Chinese Art from the Silk Route*. London: British Museum, 1990.

Wu, Jiang. *Enlightenment in Dispute: The Reinvention of Chan Buddhism in Seventeenth-Century China*. Oxford and New York: Oxford University Press, 2008.

Wu, Pei-Yi. *The Confucian's Progress: Autobiographical Writings in Traditional China*. Princeton: Princeton University Press, 1990.

Yamamoto, Kosho, trans. *The Mahayana Mahaparinirvana-sūtra*. 3 vols. Karin Buddhological Series, 5. Ube: Karin bunko, 1973.

Yanagida Seizan 柳田聖山. "Daijōkaikyō to shite no Rokuso dangyō 大乗戒経として の六祖壇経." *Indogaku bukkyōgaku kenkyū* 12, no. 1 (1964): 65–72.

——, ed. *Daruma no goroku: Ninyū shigyōron* 達摩の語録: 二入四行論. Zen no goroku 禪の語録, 1. Tokyo: Chikuma Shobō, 1969.

——, ed. "Goroku no rekishi: Zen bunken no seiritsu shiteki kenkyū 語録の歴史: 禅 文献の成立史的研究." *Tōhō gakuhō* 東方学報 57 (1985): 211–663.

——, ed. *Hōrinden: Dento gyōkueishu* 寶林傳: 傳燈玉英集. Zengaku sōsho 禪學叢書, 5. Kyoto: Chūbun shuppansha, 1975.

——, ed. *Rokuso dankyō shohon shūsei* 六祖壇經諸本集成. Kyoto: Chūbun Shuppansha, 1976.

——, ed. *Shoki no zenshi* 初期の禪史, vol. 1: *Ryōga shiji ki, Den'hōbō ki* 楞伽師資記,伝法 宝紀. Zen no goroku 禪の語録, 2. Tokyo: Chikuma shobō, 1971. Vol. 2: *Rekidai hōbō ki* 歴代法寶記. Zen no goroku 禪の語録, 3. Tokyo: Chikuma shobō, 1976.

——, ed. *Shoki zenshū shisho no kenkyū* 初期禪宗史書の研究. Kyoto: Hōzōkan, 1967.

Yang, Mayfair M., ed. *Chinese Religiosities: Afflictions of Modernity and State Formation*. Berkeley: University of California Press, 2008.

Yang Zengwen 楊曽文. *Shenhui Heshang chanhua lu* 神會和尚禪話録. Beijing: Zhonghua shuju, 1996.

Yifa. *The Origins of Buddhist Monastic Codes in China: An Annotated Translation and Study of the "Chanyuan Qinggui."* Kuroda Institute, Classics in East Asian Buddhism. Honolulu: University of Hawai'i Press, 2002.

Yifa and Peter Romaskiewicz, trans. *Yulan Bowl Sutra and Collection of Filial Piety Sutras*. Rosemead, CA: Buddha's Light Publishers, 2008.

Zeuschner, Robert B. "Awakening in Northern Ch'an." In *Buddhist and Taoist Practice in Medieval Chinese Society*, ed. David W. Chappell. Buddhist and Taoist Studies, 2. Honolulu: University of Hawai'i Press, 1987, 85–108.

———. "The Concept of Li-nien ('Being Free from Thinking') in the Northern Line of Ch'an Buddhism." In *Early Ch'an in China and Tibet*, ed. Whalen Lai and Lewis R. Lancaster. Berkeley Buddhist Studies Series, 5. Berkeley: Asian Humanities Press, 1983, 131–48.

Ziporyn, Brook. *The Penumbra Unbound: The Neo-Taoist Philosophy of Guo Xiang*. Albany: State University of New York Press, 2003.

Ziporyn, Brook, trans. *Zhuangzi: The Essential Writings with Selections from Traditional Commentaries*. Indianapolis: Hackett, 2009.

Zürcher, Erik. "Buddhism and Education in T'ang Times." In *Neo-Confucian Education: The Formative Stage*, ed. Wm. Theodore de Bary and John W. Chaffee. Berkeley: University of California Press, 1989, 19–56.

CONTRIBUTORS

. . . .

WENDI L. ADAMEK (Ph.D., Stanford University) teaches East Asian Buddhism at the University of Sydney, and her current research is focused on relationships between Buddhist practices and attitudes toward the environment in China. Her award-winning first book, *The Mystique of Transmission* (Columbia University Press, 2007), is a study of an eighth-century Chan school in Sichuan. Other research interests include Daoism, Buddhist art, network theory, watershed restoration, and environmental literature.

PETER N. GREGORY (Ph.D., Harvard University) is the Jill Ker Conway Professor of Religion and East Asian Studies at Smith College and President and Executive Director of the Kuroda Institute for the Study of Buddhism and Human Values. His research has focused on medieval Chinese Buddhism, especially the Chan and Huayan traditions, on which he has written or edited seven books, including *Tsung-mi and the Sinification of Buddhism* (Princeton University Press, 1991). He is currently working on the historical and doctrinal origins of the Chan tradition.

PAUL GRONER (Ph.D., Yale University) has spent most of his career at the University of Virginia. His research on the Japanese Tendai school resulted in two books: *Saichō: The Establishment of Japanese Tendai* (second ed., University of Hawai'i Press, 2000) and *Ryōgen and Mount Hiei: Japanese Tendai in the Tenth Century* (University of Hawai'i Press, 2002). His other major interest is the precepts and ordinations, which has led to articles on topics such as Japanese nuns and Eison, founder of the Shingon Ritsu tradition.

JOHN JORGENSEN (Ph.D., Australian National University) is Visiting Fellow at Australian National University, researching East Asian Buddhism and Korean new religions. He taught Japanese Studies at Griffith University. His books include *Inventing Hui-neng, the Sixth Patriarch: Hagiography and Biography in Early Ch'an* (Brill, 2005);

and a translation with Eun-su Cho, *The Essential Passages Directly Pointing at the Essence of the Mind: Reverend Baegun (1299-1375)* (Jogye Order Publishing, 2005). He is currently translating Korean Sŏn works and researching Zen scholar Mujaku Dōchū.

MORTEN SCHLÜTTER (Ph.D., Yale University) is an associate professor at the University of Iowa. Most of his work is focused on the relationship between Buddhism and secular society in China, Buddhism in the Song dynasty (960-1279), and the history and doctrinal evolution of Chan. He is the author of *How Zen Became Zen: The Dispute Over Enlightenment and the Formation of Chan Buddhism in Song-Dynasty China* (University of Hawai'i Press, 2008), and a number of book chapters and articles.

HENRIK H. SØRENSEN (Ph.D., University of Copenhagen) is director of the Copenhagen Seminar for Buddhist Studies. He covers East Asian Buddhism, emphasizing the relationship between religious practice and material culture, including religious art. He has focused on Esoteric Buddhism, Chinese Chan, Korean Sŏn, and the Buddhist sculptural art of Sichuan. He coedited and wrote several chapters of *Esoteric Buddhism and the Tantras in East Asia* (Brill, 2010). From 2011 he will begin in-depth research into the relationship between Buddhism and Daoism in medieval China.

STEPHEN F. TEISER (Ph.D., Princeton University) is D. T. Suzuki Professor in Buddhist Studies at Princeton University. He coedited *Readings of the Lotus Sūtra* (Columbia University Press, 2009) and has written books on the intersection between Buddhism and Chinese popular religion. His *Reinventing the Wheel: Paintings of Rebirth in Medieval Buddhist Temples* (University of Washington Press, 2006) won the Prix Stanislas Julien (Académie des Inscriptions et Belles Lettres, Institut de France). He now works on Chinese Buddhist ritual and early manuscripts.

BROOK ZIPORYN (Ph.D., University of Michigan) is a Professor in the Departments of Philosophy and of Religious Studies at Northwestern University, specializing in Chinese Buddhism, Daoism, Confucianism, and comparative philosophy. His most recent publications include *Being and Ambiguity: Philosophical Experiments with Tiantai Buddhism* (Open Court, 2004) and *Zhuangzi: Essential Writings with Selections from Traditional Commentaries* (Hackett, 2009). He has two new books addressing comprehensively some of the key developments in Chinese philosophy (State University of New York Press, forthcoming).

INDEX

. . . .